MW00389866

Franciscan, Catalina, and Other
Gladding, McBean Wares

Ceramic Table and Art Wares: 1873-1942

James F. Elliot-Bishop

Schiffer
Publishing Ltd

4880 Lower Valley Road, Atglen, PA 19310 USA

Library of Congress Cataloging-in-Publication Data

Elliot-Bishop, James F.
Franciscan, Catalina, and other Gladding, Mcbean wares :
ceramic table and art wares, 1873-1942 / James F. Elliot-Bishop.
p. cm.
ISBN 0-7643-1412-2
1. Gladding, McBean and Company--Catalogs. 2. Gladding,
McBean and Company--History. 3. Pottery, American--California--
20th century--Catalogs. I. Title.
NK4210.G515 A4 2001
738.3'7--dc21
2001003204

Copyright © 2001 by James F. Elliot-Bishop

    All rights reserved. No part of this work may be reproduced
or used in any form or by any means—graphic, electronic, or
mechanical, including photocopying or information storage and
retrieval systems—without written permission from the copyright
holder.
    "Schiffer," "Schiffer Publishing Ltd. & Design," and the "Design
of pen and ink well" are registered trademarks of Schiffer Publishing Ltd.

Designed by Bonnie M. Hensley
Cover design by Bruce M. Waters
Type set in Swiss 911 XCm BT/Zurich BT

ISBN: 0-7643-1412-2
Printed in China
1 2 3 4

Published by Schiffer Publishing Ltd.
4880 Lower Valley Road
Atglen, PA 19310
Phone: (610) 593-1777; Fax: (610) 593-2002
E-mail: Schifferbk@aol.com
Please visit our web site catalog at
www.schifferbooks.com
We are always looking for people to write books
on new and related subjects. If you have an idea
for a book please contact us at the above address

This book may be purchased from the publisher.
Include $3.95 for shipping.
Please try your bookstore first.
You may write for a free catalog.

In Europe, Schiffer books are distributed by
Bushwood Books
6 Marksbury Ave.
Kew Gardens
Surrey TW9 4JF England
Phone: 44 (0)20-8392-8585
Fax: 44 (0)20-8392-9876
E-mail: Bushwd@aol.com
Free postage in the UK. Europe: air mail at cost

Contents

Preface

Pottery manufactured in the region of California during the 1930s through the 1960s was referred to as the United States Stoke-on-Trent. As much as Stoke-on-Trent, the famous pottery area in England, California became a location that was a beehive of pottery and porcelain manufacturing activity in the United States.

With the beginning of World War II, Europe, the main source of pottery and porcelain for the United States was cut off. No longer was the mainstay of English or German pottery and porcelains available. England was committed to manufacture products, however the nation was dependant on Atlantic shipping lanes remaining open. Atlantic shipping lanes became the target of the infamous U-Boats that Hitler sent out to curtail all shipping from England and other European nations to the United States. Any boat eventually became a target.

With plentiful supplies of natural gas, large deposits of clay and other materials for use in manufacturing pottery, California rose to the forefront of pottery production. Store buyers from across the nation needed to replenish their stock. From a few potteries, mainly what was known as the big five – Gladding McBean, Pacific, Bauer, Vernon, and Metlox, the industry grew to over 1,600 potteries to fulfill

the demand for gift accessories, which included art ware as well as more utilitarian goods such as kitchenware to tableware.

There wasn't a garage that wasn't brimming with activity, especially in the southern California area. Many of these shops were basically husband and wife teams. One example is Kay Finch. With her husband Braden, she designed and carved the molds, while Braden met with buyers and distributors. Even at Gladding, McBean & Co., Mary K. Grant designed such famous lines as Apple and Desert Rose, while her husband Frederic J. Grant collected the paycheck as vice-president in charge of tableware and art ware. From the big five to the 1,600 potteries, the common goal was to fill the void left by Europe at war.

Many refugees from Europe settled in California, from Hedi Schoop to Susi Singer. These talents all went into creating a ware that eventually became known as that California look. Most wares were colorful, brightening up the dreary years from a decade of economic depression. The housewife wanted something new and exciting. Patio dining became very fashionable, this in effect due to the California potteries. Dinner tables lost their formal Sunday best look only to be set in more colorful and festive dinnerware.

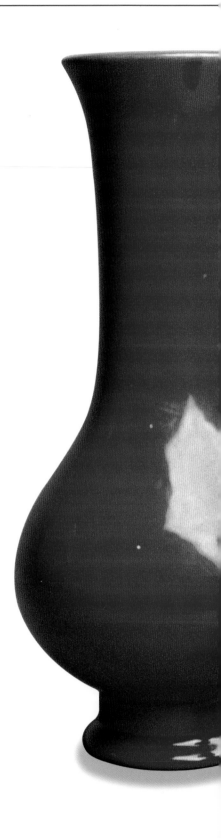

Figurines became very popular with this new fresh California look. Not so serious as their formal and stuffy counterparts from Europe, people all over the nation embraced this new informal California life style. The California potteries very quickly began a sales network, showing at the New York, Chicago, and California gift shows.

In one report that I have read, the East Coast, which was primarily the source of United States manufactured pottery, finally accepted that maybe that quick upstart known as California pottery was going to become the next Stoke-on-Trent for the world.

Unfortunately, the rise of California pottery was very short lived. After the war with both Germany and Japan ceased, the United States Congress saw pottery as a way to rebuild these ravished nations. Favorable import laws were enacted to give an advantage to the import of pottery. In 1951-1952, the import of pottery to the United States increased 200% alone. Low tariffs made the average imported item just 7 cents. The potteries in California could not compete. The Japanese were very quick to copy styles preferred by the American market. Many potteries found almost exact copies of their work being manufactured in Japan. This toll on the potteries was just too much. In 1951, there were 800 companies producing pottery in California, by 1952, there were only 160. The California potteries tried valiantly to remain in business.

They employed a wide variety of tactics, ranging from forming groups to promote Genuine California Pottery to the famous "Buy American" campaign. In the years 1955 to 1960, one by one the potteries closed. In 1962, Gladding, McBean & Co. merged with International Lock Pipe and Joint Co. to form the company Interpace and was able to survive.

It wasn't until the 1970s that the fated doom of the business reached it's final crushing hour. OPEC began their steady increase in oil prices; a business dependent on cheap supplies of fuel found them unable to maintain a bottom line. Almost all of the potteries remaining became money losers. Stock prices declined for these companies and even the mom and pop pottery could not ignore the fuel bill. With imports still with favorable tariffs, and labor unions demanding higher wages, many potteries finally closed. The worker and the owner too had to pay more at the pump and inflation began its all-time highs. Interpace began to sell off the many factories they had purchased during years prior to 1977. The Gladding, McBean & Co. division of Interpace, still manufacturing terra cotta product in Lincoln, California, was sold to Pacific Coast Building Products of Sacramento in 1977. The former Gladding, McBean & Co.'s Franciscan Ware Division was sold to Wedgwood, Inc. of England in 1979.

The extremely few potteries that managed to survive through those trying economic times finally met their fate in the 1980s with mega-mergers and buyouts. The land and business assets became more valuable than the factory. And then came the Environmental Protection Agency. Suddenly many potteries found themselves on the Superfund list of hazardous and environmental disasters. Gladding McBean's property was on the top ten lists for sites to be contained or cleaned up. Most potteries surrendered their property to the state for clean up. Some found ways to keep alive; but, few were able to do so. There are only a hand-full of potteries in California still in business today.

In 1984, Franciscan Ceramics tableware factory in Glendale, California, was finally closed and all operations were moved to, of all places, the Wedgwood Johnson Brother's Division in Stoke-on-Trent in England. As of today, Johnson Brother's is still using the Franciscan trademark manufacturing the most popular of Franciscan's tableware patterns: Desert Rose and Apple. Gladding, McBean & Co., a division of Pacific Building Products, has reproduced the terra garden ware line and continues to manufacture terra cotta sewer tile, roof tiles, and architectural terra cotta.

Today, we collect California pottery including Gladding, McBean terra cotta and Franciscan tableware and art ware, only to remember the once mythical Stoke-on-Trent in the United States – The California Potteries and especially Gladding, McBean's Franciscan Ware and Catalina Art Ware.

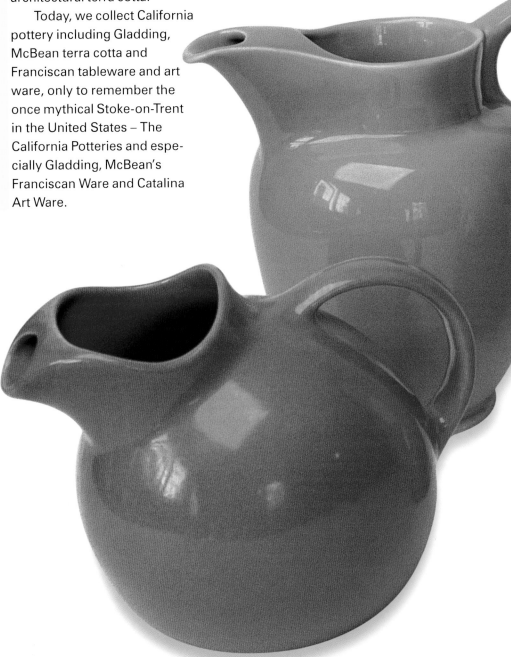

Acknowledgments

Thank you to:

The wonderful people who assisted me in my research at the University of Washington Library and Special Collections, the Seattle Public Library, the King County Library, the California State Library, California State Archives, and the Sacramento Archives and Museum Collection Center. A special thank you to Gary Kurutz and the staff of the California State Library for assisting me and making my weeks researching so productive and fun.

Employees of Gladding McBean, Interpace, and Pacific Coast Building Products. Special thanks to Tony Jaime, George James, Rupert Deese, and Bill Wyatt, and to those who I have met casually over the years who have shared their stories with me.

Delleen Enge, who I met on a very long day ago during a presentation on Franciscan Ware. Her great work on the history of Gladding McBean and Franciscan through the publication of so many books since 1981 has enabled so many people to collect Franciscan Ware.

The people I have met over the years with the same appreciation for Gladding McBean and Franciscan Ware, Marlene, Charlie Liebentritt, Chuck Bove, Paul & Sandy Mattson, Louise Johnson, Karen Gasser, Riley Doty, Dean Six, Patrick Henderson, Mike Nickel, and Mona Potts. And to Ralph Clifford, who is no longer with us but will always be remembered.

The authors who have encouraged me over the years to write this book and have been so generous in their knowledge: Jack Chipman, Harvey Duke, and Carl Gibbs.

A very special thank you to:

Patrick Barry is the person who besides being partners in business is also the wonderful person I share my life with. Without his support, advice, and other things so necessary to an author, I would never have taken the plunge and written this book. It is with his commitment to me that I have been enabled to look beyond normal day-to-day existence and pursue the research of Gladding McBean. From the time that we visited the Gladding McBean plant in Lincoln, we have shared the special love for Franciscan.

The photographic work of Eirik Huset for making this book possible. His assistance and hard work are greatly appreciated. Besides taking most of the photographs, he also lent his own personal collection and is responsible for making available so many Franciscan pieces pictured in this book.

Steven Kormanyos, for lending your fabulous collection for this work. Besides being my very best friend in the world, Steven has been my sounding board and has lent his advice and expertise to me. At the best of times and, of course, the worst, Steven has been there for me. I look back at the time when he would visit Bibelots and Books where I gained my knowledge of books and American pottery and ceramics, and he would sit on the floor for hours handling the Franciscan Ware pattern Autumn. From that moment on, we have had a friendship than only a few really know.

Robin Heath, who has lent his wonderful knowledge of computers. Without him, I would not have had the programs to be able to get this book published. His friendship has been greatly appreciated, though sometimes, I know he wishes Steven and I would talk about something besides just Franciscan.

Reba Schneider, who took me into her business and taught me so very much about Franciscan. She has been a very good friend to me over the years. This friendship started with me rushing to her store to buy Delleen Enge's first book on Franciscan Ware in 1981 and has lasted ever since.

Steve and Carol Berch, for their hospitality on my trips to the Bay Area and for their generous spirit. A special thank you to their son and daughter, Patrick and Sarah.

Without the early support of Sheldon Izen, I would have never discovered collecting. We spent so many wonderful years together and he never once said I could not buy another piece of Franciscan or

Gladding McBean. Without Sheldon, I would not be the person I am today.

If it weren't for my mother, Yvonne Bishop, I would have never even thought about Franciscan. With her great taste, we dined on Franciscan Ivy when I was a child in the 1950s and always reserved Franciscan Ivy for those very special occasions through the 1960s into the 1970s. When I asked her if I could have the Franciscan Ivy, she generously gave the set to me. All the pieces had very special meaning from the time when families had dinner together. And having five brothers and sisters, Janet, Doug, Constance, Susan and, of course Sara, there were quite a few pieces that made it through the years. Which brings me to Sara, my sister, who came to live with me and grew to love Ivy as much as I did. I could always count on Sara to come to my defense when I bought one too many pieces of Franciscan, always making me feel I did the right thing.

The people who brought us Franciscan Ware, the factory workers and office staff. Their hard work and their lives making so very many people happy. They produced a quality product that has endured the test of time. They are what made Franciscan Ware, well, Franciscan Ware.

And to my pets, Jasper, Lucky, Joanie, Alex, and Desi, who have comforted me. Without their unconditional love, life would not have been the same.

A Word About Values

Prices in this book are based on what an item has sold for in the past. Prices noted are for retail price. To determine the price, I have used what I have sold the item for, what I have paid for an item, and what an item has sold for on Internet auctions. Prices change. Usually you sell an item for more to the first people who want one for their collection. After this, price does fall to what is considered to be the going price.

Retail price is the market rate. Expect to pay or sell for less when buying or selling at a flea market or an antique market show. For specialty shows expect to pay more. Dealers that specialize pay more for their goods and have the expensive overhead of doing a high-end show.

The prices in this book are for items that are free of cracks, nicks, dings, fleabites, and wear. If the piece is broken, it usually is not cost effective to have the item repaired. It is almost always cheaper to buy a new one than to repair it.

If you are selling and are not a professional dealer, expect to sell for 30-50% less what the dealer sells the item for. Most dealers cannot afford to be in business if they pay any amount more than 50%. Though when you sell you may sell for less, you will sell the item you no longer use or need. To sell to the retail trade, the time and effort sometimes outweighs the difference in price.

If you are not a professional packer, you may find that selling online can be a burden, if not a disaster. Over the last two years I have heard of more Franciscan arriving broken and lost forever than I have ever heard over 18 years of buying and selling. Everyone agrees that one would rather have the item than a refund.

Though price does reflect rarity, not all items that are rare will sell for more. Demand does play a role, but usually it comes down to how badly someone wants the item and what they are comfortable with paying. What is beautiful to one is ugly to another. Just because you may have not seen one before, does not mean that anyone really wants it or that it is indeed an unusual or desirable item.

It is very rare that you will find an unmarked piece of Gladding McBean or Franciscan. Workers inspected each item before it left the factory and if it was missing the mark, it was sold in the seconds shop.

When in doubt, do your research.

Chapter 1
The Beginning, Lincoln, California, 1873

Gladding, McBean & Company began its journey from a small town in Lincoln, California, and would become one of the world's leaders in the development and manufacturing of clay products and ceramics.

This thriving little city [Lincoln, California] is located on the California and Oregon railroad ten miles northerly from the railroad junction at Roseville and fourteen miles due west from Auburn. It is in the valley part of Placer County and is surrounded by the best of farming country. Toward the east and in the low foothills much fine fruit is raised. It sometimes happens that a town has a productive country on one side of it only while the other side may be cut off by a river or a barren mountain or some other unfavorable circumstance but Lincoln is in the center of a rich producing country in all directions.

Lincoln was named in honor of Colonel Charles Lincoln Wilson, the builder of the first railroad to the Lincoln, California. This railroad, California Central Railroad, was finished to Lincoln on October 31, 1861. The first settlers in what is now Lincoln were John Chapman, G. Gray and John Ziegenbein who came in 1859. Others followed rapidly when the railroad

GLADDING, McBEAN & CO., POTTERY WORKS, LINCOLN, CAL.

reached the place. In 1863 the town was very prosperous there being about 500 inhabitants, six or eight stages running out of Lincoln in different directions. In 1867 the flourmill of Ziegenbein, Heffner & Company burned, with a loss of about $30,000. J. R. Nickerson a fruit farmer nearby was very progressive as a fruit-raiser. Steven D. Burdge was a practical wine-maker having learned the business in Italy. The Burdge Hotel was later named after this active citizen. –W. B. Lardner and M. J. Brook. *History of Placer and Nevada Counties*. Los Angeles, California: Historic Record Company, 1924, 208.

In 1873, coal was found by workmen making a shortcut for a road around the point of a foothill near the town of Lincoln in Placer County, California. The Towle Brothers of Dutch Flat and later of Alta and Towle in 1874-1875 used many yokes of oxen in their lumber business during the summer months. During the winter months these work oxen were sent down to a cousin, Ed Towle, located north of Lincoln for care and pasture. Connected with the home ranch was a rolling ridge of poor-looking, rock-covered ground. It was fenced in and produced early grazing for the work oxen. At the east end of the ridge ran a county road in a northerly and southerly direction. A little over a mile above Lincoln this road, to avoid climbing over this ridge, was made to curve

eastward and pass over neighbor's land and around the point of the ridge. An enterprising road master decided to straighten the county road, so he started a cut through the low ridge. He had proceeded only about ten feet with his new road-cut when he ran into a body of pure white kaolin clay equal to the best Chinese product. This rocky ridge curves around a long distance to the southwest, veined with clay all the way.

Colonel Wilson prospected the locality thoroughly and dug a large shaft down to the coal at a depth of sixty feet, and a mine was started. Hoisting works were erected and samples of the coal were sent to the Sacramento water-works for testing in January 1874. The trial was satisfactory. A test was also made of the coal at Guttenberg's Foundry, an iron works, and castings of iron were reported to be of the best quality.

As they dug through to the coal, layers of clay, sand, and kaolin were found. Professor H. G. Hanks of San Francisco, made an examination of the clay, was impressed with its value, and found its character to be the very best for pottery work of all classes and one quality excellent for firebrick. The layers of the deposit were as follows: four feet of soil, six feet of white clay, sixteen inches of fine white sand with a little water, five feet of coarse cream-colored clay mixed with coarse white sand, twelve feet of

Gladding, McBean & Company Pottery Works.

pure kaolin, twelve feet of clay and coal alternating, eight feet of coal and below this, clay and sand to a depth as yet unknown.

Charles Gladding from Chicago read the account in the *Alta Californian*, a California newspaper. He traveled from Chicago to Lincoln and carried clay samples back to Chicago. From there, to have the clay tested, he sent the samples to Akron, Ohio, to an old friend, who was engaged in the manufacture of vitrified sewer pipe. After burning, he pronounced the quality of the clay fine for making this and other terra cotta wares.

The result was that in May 1, 1875, a new partnership was formed under the name of Gladding McBean & Company, consisting of three Chicago friends,

Charles Gladding, Peter McGill McBean, and George Chambers. Mr. Gladding then returned to Lincoln with a party of expert workmen in the manufacture of vitrified sewer pipe, and arriving there May 12, 1875, immediately erected a suitable building and kiln for the manufacture of this material. The machinery arrived from the East on June 24, 1875, consisting of a boiler engine, pumps, steam press with dies, and a roller crusher. Peter McGill McBean came from Chicago and took charge of the sales department of the business and established an office and yard in San Francisco in August, of which he continued to be in charge up to the time of his death in 1922.

Charles Gladding

A very patriotic as well as enterprising and progressive man, who served his country and flag with devotion during the Civil War and after assisting in building up various large public enterprises in the East came out to the Golden West where waiting opportunities beckoned to the development of its wonderful natural resources was the late Charles Gladding, founder of Gladding McBean & Company manufacturers at Lincoln and the father of Albert J. Gladding the present manager of the plant. Charles Gladding was

born near Buffalo N. Y. on April 28, 1828 and there he grew up afterwards removing to Akron Ohio where he engaged as a general contractor and was interested in the Buckeye Sewer Pipe plant. While living in Akron he was married to Miss Ann Bloomfield who was born at Kidderminster England and came with her parents to Tariffville, Connecticut and later to Akron Ohio where she met Mr. Gladding. Disposing of his holdings in Akron Mr. Gladding moved to Chicago. There he became one of the early contractors who built

Albert J. Gladding

"**ALBERT JAMES GLADDING** - It is interesting to chronicle the career of the successful business man, and especially the career of one who starting out as a youth worked his way upward, and by his perseverance and well-directed energy accomplished his ambitions and became one of the principals in building up a large plant employing hundreds of men, a plant that in turn was the means of building up his town. Such a man is Albert James Gladding vice-president and manager of Gladding, McBean & Company, manufacturers at Lincoln. A native of the great Prairie State he was born at Chicago, Ill. September 8 1858, and a son of the late Charles Gladding the founder of Gladding, McBean & Company . . . Albert J. Gladding is the only one living of the four children born to his parents, his childhood was spent in Chicago and in Riverside and he received a good education in the excellent schools of those cities. He remembers well the stirring times of the Civil War, when his father was at the front and also the sad bereavement of his mother. Then, later the great Chicago fire awed him in 1871, though at that time the family was making their home at Riverside. High school days being over, Mr. Gladding came to Lincoln, Placer County with his father in June, 1875, and took an active part in starting the nucleus of the present business in which he has become such a dominant factor. Thus he took up pottery manufacturing from the bottom working in the different departments and learning the manufacture of architectural terra cotta tile, brick, and pipes, in all of its details gradually assuming the management of the plant and thus relieving his father, who retired and spent considerable time in travel.

Interested in agriculture Mr. Gladding owns a ranch of 1400 acres, the old E. J. Sparks ranch on Coon Creek, which is devoted to raising grain, stock, and fruit. He has also been a builder-up of the city of Lincoln in more ways than one being one of the organizers of the Bank of Lincoln of which he is now the president. He is a member of the California Farm Bureau, the Elevator Corporation and the Farm Bureau Exchange.

The marriage of Mr. Gladding occurred on the old Chandler Ranch near Nicolaus on June 13, 1883, when he was united with Miss Carrie Augusta Chandler a native daughter born on the Chandler place. Her father was the late ex-State Senator Augustus Lemuel Chandler, a Vermonter who became a California pioneer of 1842 and who is represented in another in this history. Mr. and Mrs. Gladding have ten children. Lois Gladding Williams was graduated at the Girls Academy on California Street, San Francisco and she now makes her home in Berkeley. Charles, a graduate of Placer Union High School, is superintendent of Gladding McBean & Company at Lincoln. Augustus Lemuel graduated at Rutgers College where he majored in ceramics. He is in the offices of Gladding McBean & Company in San Francisco. Anita Lucile is a graduate of Mills College and the San Francisco Art School and makes her home in that city. Grace Chandler is a graduate of the College of the Pacific Conservatory of Music and also of the San Jose State Normal School. She is now the wife of Frank Dickey and they make their home in Taft. Albert Chandler was educated at Oakland Polytechnic School and Davis Agricultural College and is serving as assistant superintendent of Gladding McBean & Company at Lincoln. He served in the U. S. N. R. F., in the Officers' Training Camp, Mare Island, during the World War. Doris Bloomfield and Dorothy Noves are twins and both are attending the University of California, while Helen Adeline attends Stanford University and Caroline Jane attends Miss Head's school in Berkeley. The children had completed high school studies before entering upon the higher courses. It was largely through the efforts of Mr. Gladding that the city of Lincoln was incorporated. He was elected a member of the first board of trustees and served more than twenty years being chairman of the board for several terms. With the late John Hoening, he aided in preparing the first city ordinances and he has taken a most active part in the needed improvements, such as the water system sewers and electric lights, the water system; being installed while he was mayor. He was a leader in organizing the Lincoln Union High School and served as a trustee and it was during this time that the new high school was built. Fraternally, Mr. Gladding was made a Mason in Gold Hill Lodge No. 32 F. & A.M. at Lincoln, in which he is a Past Master. He is a member of Delta Chapter No. 27 R. A. M. and Gateway Council No. 13, R. & S. M. both of Auburn; and Marysville Commandery No. 7 K.1. and is a life member of Islam Temple N. M. S. in San Francisco. When Friendship Chapter No. 67, O. E. S. was organized at Lincoln, Albert Gladding and Miss Carrie A. Chandler became charter members and at that time the acquaintance was formed which began the romance of their life and resulted in their marriage. Mr. Gladding, is a Past Patron of the chapter, while Mrs. Gladding is a Past Matron. All of their sons are Masons and the daughters are members of the Eastern Star. Mrs. Gladding is a member and past president of the Woman's Club at Lincoln. Being interested in the cause of education, she has served efficiently as a member and clerk for the board of trustees of the Lincoln grammar schools. For many years, also, she has been active in the great Frances Willard movement for temperance, serving as president of the Woman's Christian Temperance Union for Placer County. Mrs. Gladding holds membership in the Congregational Church and contributes generously to its benevolences and her efforts have wielded a wide influence for good and for a higher moral standard. A firm believer in protection, Mr. Gladding is a stalwart and influential Republican. He is very active in civic affairs and is a member of the various chambers of commerce in the county and in San Francisco as well. During the World War, Mr. and Mrs. Gladding were active in aiding the Liberty Loan and other allied war drives to a successful issue and in forwarding the work of the American Red Cross. Deeply interested in the growth and welfare of his adopted county and city for which he has always been very zealous, Mr. Gladding aids in his liberal and progressive way the various movements that have for their aim the development and up building of the community and the enhancing of the happiness and comfort of the people." -*History of Placer and Nevada Counties*, pages 449-452.

up that city. On the breaking out of the Civil War, he entered the government employ, being placed in charge of transporting supplies to the front with headquarters at Cairo Ill.

When President Lincoln issued his second call for 300,000 men, Charles Gladding resigned his position and leaving his small children in the care of his wife, offered his services in August 1862, by enlisting in Company K 72nd Illinois Volunteer Infantry known as the Board of Trade Regiment. He was commissioned a first lieutenant under Capt. John Reed and served in Ransom's Brigade MacPherson's Division marching under the colors in the various campaigns including the Siege of Vicksburg. He took part in various operations including the battle of Champion Hills, which lead up to the surrender of the stronghold on the Mississippi. During the siege his captain was wounded and Lieutenant Gladding then commanded the company. Afterwards he was stationed at Natchez Miss. While at the front Mr. Gladding had been bereaved of faithful wife who succumbed to an attack of pneumonia in the fall of 1863. His four children needing his care and attention, Lieutenant Gladding then resigned his commission in 1864 and returned to Chicago. There he threw himself into the business whirl of that great city making his residence at

Riverside. Aside from his large business as a contractor he established an extensive trade in the sale of Sanitary Ware and sewer pipe meeting with deserved success in his various operations. However, the Jay Cook failure and the panic of 1872-1873 necessarily made business very slack in his line.

To such an extent he began looking for a change of location. Being desirous of again entering the manufacturing field. His eyes naturally turned to the Pacific Coast where he had a cousin, James Gladding residing in Sacramento. In 1874, he came to California and began the investigation, which led to his favorable consideration of the clay deposits at Lincoln. He was so well impressed that he returned to Chicago and there interested some of his friends and as a result, the formation and incorporation of Gladding McBean & Company followed in May 1875. His energy seem no bounds and it was only a month later when he and his son, Albert J. Gladding were en route on the overland train to California. Arriving in Lincoln in June 1875 they immediately went to work with optimism and enthusiasm and started the potteries which have since grown to such large proportions and have meant so much not only to the town of Lincoln but to the entire Sacramento Valley as well and which have reflected such credit upon the originators.

Paperweight made of terra cotta to promote Gladding, McBean & Co. This was probably given to employees and business associates. On the sides are "Gladding, McBean & Co.," "San Francisco," "Architectural Terra cotta," and "Lincoln CAL."

Side views of paperweight. $250-375.

For many years Mr. Gladding gave his undivided attention to the development of the plant and its business but in time turned the entire manufacturing over to his son and retired from active business devoting his time to reading and research and also to travel of which he was very fond. A prominent Republican he took an active and influential interest in civic affairs He was a member of the Grand Army of the Republic and, of the California Commandery of the Military Order of the Loyal Legion in San Francisco. He was also a Mason and a member of the Eastern Star. The summer of 1893, Mr. Gladding spent in Chicago visiting his friends, as well as the World's Fair and that fall he started on a trip to Europe and Africa during which he visited the British possessions and the Continent and also Egypt and the scenes along the River Nile, returning through the Mediterranean Sea. While stopping at Rome he was suddenly stricken with apoplexy and died on January 17, 1894, his body was cremated and the ashes were placed in the Columbarium in Cypress Lawn San Francisco. –W. B. Lardner and M. J. Brook. *History of Placer and Nevada Counties*. Los Angeles, California: Historic Record Company, 1924, 1031

Peter McGill McBean

A man of enterprise and action was Peter McGill McBean who for many years and until the time of his being taken away, was the president, of Gladding McBean and Company, manufacturers of architectural terra cotta and other Clay products, with headquarters in San Francisco and their plant located in Lincoln, Placer County. Mr. McBean was born in Glengary, Ontario, on January 14, 1844. His father, John McBean a native of Ontario, was of Scotch ancestry his forebear coming from Blair Atholl, Scotland, to Ontario. John McBean was an extensive general contractor, and was one of the builders of the Grand Trunk Railway. He met with success and was a very prominent and influential man throughout the Dominion of Canada.

Peter McGill McBean was named for one of the McGill's, founders of McGill University, a close friend of the family. He was one of a family of nine children, and was reared and educated in Ontario until he was sixteen years of age then he made his way to Chicago, Illinois, to join his brother and thus became familiar with large construction enterprises and gained the experience so valuable to him in after years. He studied finance and upon graduation, large financial interests were left to his judgment; thus, he grew into a wonderful character and a power in the business world of Chicago.

Mr. McBean came out to California in 1875 when they started the plant, and located the headquarters of the offices in San Francisco, where he managed the business of the corporation. Under his masterful business sagacity and acumen it grew to such proportions that additions and new buildings were added from time to time, until today it is the largest plant of its kind west of Chicago and manufacturer of the finest clay product in the United States. Surely it is a splendid record and a great credit to the man at the helm who was striving for the best results obtainable in everything that they manufactured.

Mr. McBean was married in Chicago, October 3, 1873, being united with Miss Agnes Perkins, who was born at Lockport, N.Y., a daughter of Rev. Edger Perkins; the latter was a graduate of Yale and an eminent Presbyterian clergyman in New York State, who was born at Hartland, Conn., and descended from an old New England family. The fortunate union of Mr. McBean and Miss Perkins resulted in the birth of two children: Edith, the Wife of Dr. Henry S. Kiersted, a lieutenant in the United States Army, now retired and, Atholl McBean, who since his father's death is the head of Gladding McBean and Company, and who resides in San Francisco.

Peter McGill McBean was highly appreciated by all who knew him for his truthfulness, integrity, and high sense of honor, believing in justice and fairness in all things and he was known for his kindliness and many charities. All in all, he was a manly man. In stature he was large handsome and very distinguished looking; his was a pleasing personality that attracted people to him and he possessed the magnetism and cordiality that retained friendships once made. Mr. McBean was accounted one of the builders of the West and he was very prominent in the business and financial world of the whole Pacific Coast region. However, the strain of all these years began to tell on him, which resulted in a stroke, at the Fairmont Hotel where he made his residence. After an illness of five months he passed away October 6, 1922, a man greatly missed by a wide circle of friends.

An out and out protectionist, he was an active worker for the success of Republican principles in which he was a true believer. He attended Trinity Episcopal Church but was liberal in his contributions to all denominations and charitable institutions and particularly do the citizens of Lincoln have cause to appreciate the liberality of Gladding McBean and Company in the building up of their city. Mr. McBean was a great home man, so aside from civic

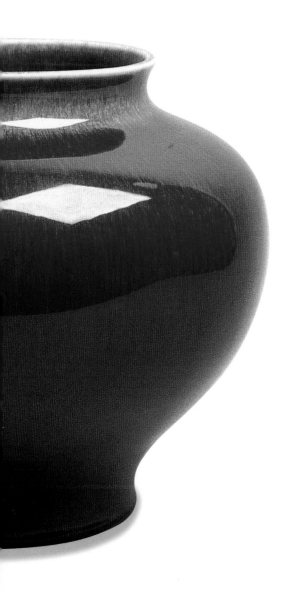

organizations, we find him a member of only the Pacific Union and Burlingame Clubs of San Francisco. –W. B. Lardner and M. J. Brook. *History of Placer and Nevada Counties*. Los Angeles, California: Historic Record Company, 1924, 1056-57

The first carload of vitrified sewer pipes was delivered in San Francisco on August 9, 1875, an event more important in the industrial life of the West than the famous discovery of gold. It was no longer necessary to ship heavy loads of clay products around the Horn some twelve or thirteen thousand miles.

The pottery works began aiding Lincoln in an indirect way by buying thousands of cords of wood for the many kilns in use. This made a sure market for every cord of wood the intending fruit farmers of the nearby foothills could cut and haul to the pottery besides giving employment to several hundreds of men.

The terra cotta manufacture began in 1883. From time to time other classes of clay building products were added.

In 1884, Gladding McBean Company took its first step into manufacturing terra cotta for architectural ornamentation. The first structure built was their two story headquarters in San Francisco, located at 1358-1360 Market Street. This was the first building erected on the West Coast that featured terra cotta ornamentation. The demand for the product increased from this time forward for use in buildings by the West Coast's leading architects.

In 1886, the Gladding McBean Company was incorporated. Its new name was Gladding, McBean & Co.

Joseph Baldwin DeGoyler, a civil engineer with a specialty in chemistry, a son-in-law of Chambers, came to Lincoln in 1888 to assist the young corporation. DeGoyler oversaw every operation in the fledgling architectural department. Careful records were kept on every building, including photographs that were taken on glass plates. DeGoyler oversaw the production of terra cotta for over 1800 buildings. The Lincoln plant alone shipped from 250 to 300 train carloads of finished product per month. The manufactured product was shipped all over the United States, Canada, Mexico, and on into different portions of the world including Hawaii, the Philippines, Japan, Australia, and New Zealand.

The Lincoln plant had an enviable record for safety in the first fifty-five years of operation. There were but four fatal accidents. More injuries of course, but these were reduced by a safety campaign involving competitive features. Cash prizes for the best suggestions were paid each month.

The first garden pottery line, including vases, flowerpots, benches, tables, fountains, and birdbaths, was made in Lincoln in 1893 and sold in San Francisco. Later, around 1903, it was carried in stock in the warehouses in San Francisco and Oakland.

Charles Gladding died in 1894, and was succeeded by his son, A. J. Gladding. George Chambers died in 1896.

In October 1903, as reported in *The Clay Worker*, "Gladding, McBean & Co., brick manufacturers and contractors with headquarters in the Rialto Building on Mission Street, report business is unusually good for the season. Then in November, *The Clay Worker* reported: "Gladding, McBean & Co., brick contractors of this city have secured a contract for work in the new James L. Flood Building on Market Street."

The management and staff of Gladding, McBean and Co. were proud of the architectural terra cotta they produced, and also the use of their hollow tile for floors, partitions, arches, and columns. Hollow tile is a product that is made of terra cotta and is used in the construction of building walls and floors. Shaped much like bricks, only larger and hollow, hollow tile was a substitute for using brick in construction. The hollow tiles were sold as fireproof building products for use in either commercial or home building. The 1906 earthquake and fire that destroyed San Francisco would put these products to their test. Unfortunately, these products did not pass the test. The hollow tile collapsed due to the intense heat produced from the fire and the ironwork buckled.

After the great earthquake and fire, the demand for building products soared. However, instead of using hollow tile, builders used concrete and iron mesh. To cover the concrete, Gladding, McBean & Co. developed polychrome or varicolored finishes for their architectural terra cotta. In this area, DeGoyler, as an expert chemist, led the way. A whole new palette of finishes was introduced.

Having lost their own headquarters on Market Street, Gladding, McBean & Co. relocated to the southwest corner of Eddy and Hyde Streets. After the city was rebuilt, they moved to the Crocker Building, where the headquarters remained until the 1920s.

At about this time, Peter McBean recruited to his staff a head modeler of great talent, Pio Oscar Tognelli. Pio was born in Italy in 1880 and trained at the Academia delle Bellearti in Florence. It was here that he was influence by the Beaux Arts style. In the 1920s he moved into the main office in San Francisco as head of the art department.

In 1913, Gladding, McBean & Co. secured the contract for terra cotta for the Hobart Building on Market Street near Montgomery. Willis Polk designed the building. Willis Polk went on afterwards in a relationship with Gladding, McBean & Co. He traveled to Spain, where he was greatly influenced by the roof tile and encouraged Gladding, McBean & Co. to enter into production to replicate these "Latin" tiles

"AUGUSTUS LEMUEL GLADDING - young man of much enterprise who is a native son of Placer County Cal., is Augustus Lemuel Gladding born at Lincoln, January 12 1889 a son of A. J. and Carrie (Chandler) Gladding. After completing the grammar school, Gus Gladding, as his many friends know him, continued his studies at the Placer County High School, graduating in the class of 1908. He then entered Rutgers College in New Brunswick N. J. where he was graduated in 1912 receiving the degree of Bachelor of Science in Ceramic Engineering. During these years he had experience during the vacations in the Gladding McBean and Company's manufacturing plant at Lincoln and became familiar with the manufacture of clay products. After his graduation he took a position in the plant under his father as ceramic engineer continuing actively until 1918 when he volunteered his services to the War Industries Board and spent a year in Washington in charge of the clay products section of the building material division of the War Industries Board. About two months after the signing of the armistice he returned to Lincoln, where he continued his position with Gladding McBean and Company. In 1921 he was elected secretary of the company and transferred his field of operation with his headquarters in the company's offices in San Francisco at the same time taking up his residence in Berkeley. On the formation of the Gladding McBean Corporation in 1924, Mr. Gladding was elected its vice-president in charge of manufacturing. Mr. Gladding was married in New Brunswick N. J. November 19, 1913, being united with Miss. Ruth Clarke Viehmann, who was born in Concord, New Hampshire. She is a graduate of Miss. Gardner's School in New York and Miss Ely's School in Greenwich, Conn. Their marriage has been blessed with three children Mary Abbott, Janice Chandler and Augustus Lemuel Jr. Mr. Gladding served acceptably as a member of the board of trustees in Lincoln resigning during his second term when he removed to Berkeley. Fraternally, he was made a Mason in Gold Hill Lodge No. 32 F. & A. M. at Lincoln and is a Scottish Rite Mason belonging to Sacramento Consistory, and with his wife is a member of Friendship Chapter No. 69 O. E. S. at Lincoln in which Mrs. Gladding is a Past Matron. She is also a member of the Woman's Club of Lincoln. At college, Mr. Gladding was a member of Delta Kappa Epsilon Fraternity. He is a member of the University Club in San Francisco and both he and his wife are members of the Hillside Club in Berkeley. Mr. Gladding is also a member of the Ceramic Society of Columbus Ohio." – *History of Placer and Nevada Counties*, page 1029.

in a modern medium. Tile was a very profitable business for Gladding, McBean & Co. Gladding, McBean & Co. produced two books on Latin Tiles to encourage architects to use its new line of tile.

A big fire in July 1918 wiped out the greater portion of the plant in Lincoln. The factory was lost; but, the heroic effort of the volunteer fire department was credited for saving the architectural terra cotta department, kilns, and towering smokestacks. Even though the company was experiencing a slow down in orders due to World War I, the firm rebuilt immediately, erecting fireproof structures built of concrete and clay building blocks of their own manufacture—even the stairs throughout the building were made of concrete.

In Lincoln, when the Public Library and the city Auditorium were built, Gladding, McBean & Co. gave the clay product building materials for their construction and they also gave a great portion of the same kind of material for the construction of the New Union High School.

During the boom period of the 1920s, Gladding, McBean & Co. continued to meet the demand of its market. In 1921, Gladding, McBean & Co. was awarded the contract for the new Standard Oil Building, which was said to be the largest building west of Chicago at this time.

When Peter McGill McBean died in 1922, his son Atholl McBean succeeded him as president of the company. In 1923, A. J. Gladding served as vice-president of the company.

Tile, given away as a promotional to business associates and employees. The tile reads "Gladding McBean & Co" "San Francisco and Lincoln." $450-550.

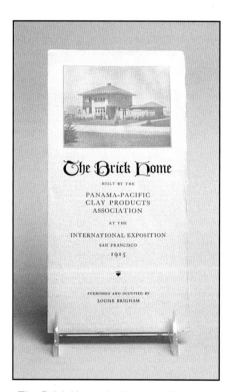

The Brick Home built by the Panama-Pacific Products Association. 1915. $25-35.

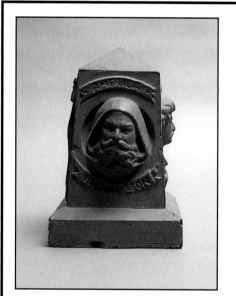

Terra cotta promotional piece dated 1890. This obelisk has great architects from America – Richardson, France – Carnier, and England – Barry. The side panel reads "Compliments of" "Gladding McBean & Co Manufacturers of Architectural Terra cotta Etc" "Lincoln Placer Co San Francisco Office 1358 & 1360 Market St 1890." $1,200-1,400.

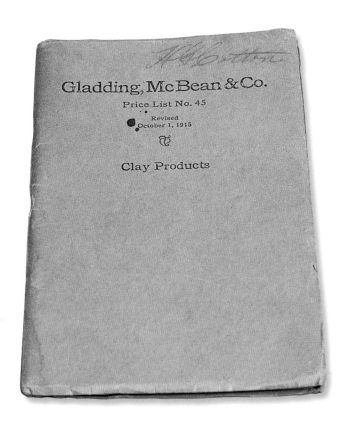

Gladding, McBean & Co. Price List No. 45, Revised October 1, 1915, Clay Products. $175-225.

South Elevation of buildings 1 and 22, Gladding, McBean & Co., June 1st 1921.

South Elevation Building 1 and 3A, Gladding, McBean & Co., March 15, 1922.

"One of the most enlightening and attractive displays in the Industrial Exposition [In SF during the month of October from the 7th -28th, California Industrial Exposition] was that of Gladding McBean & Co. Installed under the supervision of W.O. Raiguel. Their presentation of garden pottery in a large and convenient alcove was a work of art in arrangement, workmanship, and conception. A beautifully shaped fountain, perfectly enameled flanked on either side by corner pyramids of vases and jars filled with ornamental shrubbery formed a wonderful background that was a display in itself. The table in the center presented a top of beautiful natural variegated color with a matt finish; supported at either end by pedestals of highly ornamental design of the same terra cotta material. Against the wall on either side were harmonizing garden seats and pedestals. Flower boxes, pots and vases, big and little were there in tasteful arrangement as to size and color. There was displayed a wide range of colors in unglazed, dull glass and high luster enamels. Some shapes were adapted to polychrome; others to natural unglazed colors and the huge oil jars were beautiful in either. Warm gray and buff enamels showed up against the green and the shrubbery. And a sprinkling of Chinese Blue and splashes of color like a Jacob's coat or an artist's pallet gave variety and touch to the whole. A neat fireplace on either side Plant Images and well placed Madonna's and Bambini in old ivory and Della Robbia blue gave the final touch.

But the most brilliant and perfect products of workmanship and art, a challenge to the uninitiated, to the artist and the workman alike, were the large polychrome fruit baskets. Not only were the baskets perfect in themselves; but the perfection of imitation of various fruits both as to color an as to form was simply marvelous. One could ask, "How can it be done in clay?" There were lemons and oranges, grapes and figs, apples and pears, peaches and plums, persimmons and pomegranates, bananas and pineapples, all mellow and ripe enough to eat. On the whole, this exhibit was one to suggest the uses of terra cotta for permanent ornamentation as well as for structural work in a manner and in ways that most people had much considered." - *The Clay Worker*, November 1,1922

23

Improved Flower Pots and Saucers.

No. 218.

Our improved Flower Pots and Saucers far excel the old style in strength, uniformity of shape, etc. These pots are of a light yellow color, made of a clay much superior to that which is usually put into such goods. As will be seen in the cut, they are made so that the shoulder of one rests on the edge of the other, thus preventing the wedging of one into the other, which is the main cause of breakage in transit.

Price List.

POTS.		SAUCERS.	
2 inch Pots	$1.50 per 100		
3 inch Pots	2.00 per 100	3 inch Saucers	$1.50 per 100
4 inch Pots	3.00 per 100	4 inch Saucers	2.00 per 100
5 inch Pots	4.00 per 100	5 inch Saucers	2.50 per 100
6 inch Pots	5.00 per 100	6 inch Saucers	3.50 per 100
7 inch Pots	7.00 per 100	7 inch Saucers	5.00 per 100
8 inch Pots	10.00 per 100	8 inch Saucers	6.50 per 100
9 inch Pots	15.00 per 100	9 inch Saucers	8.00 per 100
10 inch Pots	25.00 per 100	10 inch Saucers	10.00 per 100
12 inch Pots	35.00 per 100	12 inch Saucers	15.00 per 100

☞ When ordering our Improved Pots, if you also require the Saucers, be particular to state it in your order.

Packing of Flower Pots and Saucers, extra.

Shingled Pot and Saucer.   .   Palm Tree Pot.

No. 222.

No. 219.

No. 222, 4 inch, per dozen	$1.00	No. 219, 14 inch, each	$ .75
No. 222, 6 inch, per dozen	1.50	No. 219, 16 inch, each	1.50
No. 222, 8 inch, per dozen	2.50	No. 219, 18 inch, each	2.00
		No. 219, 22 inch, each	3.00

A catalog page from the *Gladding, McBean & Co. Catalog No. 22*, circa late 1890s, showing flowerpots and saucers made of terra cotta that were in stock items and could be ordered. Catalog 22 included sewer pipe, stock terra cotta for building surfaces, tiles, garden ware, roof tile, sewer tile, and other items manufactured of terra cotta.

LAWN VASES.

No. 28.   No. 26.

No. 26.	Width, 27 inches.	Height, 38 inches.	Price, $20.00
No. 28.	Width, 26 inches.	Height, 42 inches.	Price, 25.00

No. 28, an EGYPTIAN VASE.—Copy of a Vase found in the ruins of Thebes. Though broken in many pieces, on placing the fragments together it was found to be entire, and is now in the British Museum. Antiquarians think it more than 3,000 years old.

A catalog page from the *Gladding, McBean & Co. Catalog No. 22*, circa late 1890s, showing lawn vases made of terra cotta. No. 28, an Egyptian vase, was a copy of one found in the ruins of Thebes and in the collection of the British Museum.

Terra Cotta Garden Vases.

The beauty and attraction of yards and lawns are much enhanced by the tasty disposal of a few Vases. We can furnish them in numerous designs, at half the cost of iron, while the material of which they are made is much better adapted to the healthy growth of plants.

For safe shipment, we make our Vases in two parts; the upper part is known as the *Bowl*, and the lower part as the *Stand*.

When the bowl and stand are placed together, the open space marked B should be filled with cement, so that the water will be forced to pass down and out through the hole in the stand, marked A.

If you paint the Vases, they should be oiled inside and out with boiled linseed oil, before painting.

TERRA COTTA VASES.

Nos. 1 to 5.   Nos. 12 and 13.   No. 10.

No. 24.   No. 15.

Prices and Dimensions.

No. 1	Width, 13 inches.	Height, 12 inches.	Price, $1.25
No. 2	Width, 15 inches.	Height, 13 inches.	Price, 1.50
No. 3	Width, 17 inches.	Height, 15 inches.	Price, 2.00
No. 4	Width, 20 inches.	Height, 18 inches.	Price, 2.50
No. 5	Width, 23 inches.	Height, 20 inches.	Price, 3.00
No. 10	Width, 15 inches.	Height, 14 inches.	Price, 1.75
No. 12	Width, 13 inches.	Height, 18 inches.	Price, 2.50
No. 13	Width, 17 inches.	Height, 21 inches.	Price, 3.50
No. 15	Width, 14 inches.	Height, 21 inches.	Price, 3.00
No. 24	Width, 18 inches.	Height, 22 inches.	Price, 4.50

TERRA COTTA VASES.

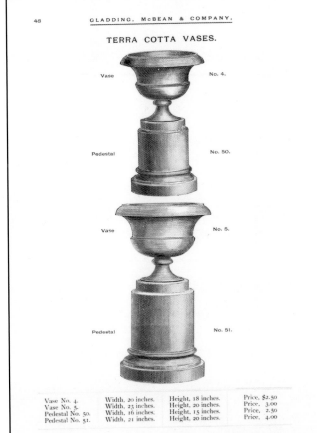

Vase   No. 4.

Pedestal   No. 50.

Vase   No. 5.

Pedestal   No. 51.

Vase No. 4.	Width, 20 inches.	Height, 18 inches.	Price, $2.50
Vase No. 5.	Width, 23 inches.	Height, 20 inches.	Price, 3.00
Pedestal No. 50.	Width, 16 inches.	Height, 15 inches.	Price, 2.50
Pedestal No. 51.	Width, 21 inches.	Height, 20 inches.	Price, 4.00

TERRA COTTA VASES.

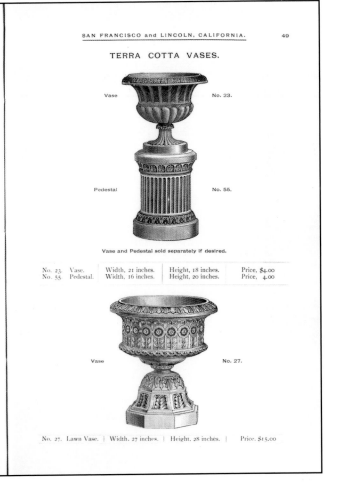

Vase   No. 23.

Pedestal   No. 55.

Vase and Pedestal sold separately if desired.

No. 23.	Vase.	Width, 21 inches.	Height, 18 inches.	Price, $4.00
No. 55.	Pedestal.	Width, 16 inches.	Height, 20 inches.	Price, 4.00

Vase   No. 27.

No. 27.	Lawn Vase.	Width, 27 inches.	Height, 28 inches.	Price, $15.00

Catalog page from the *Gladding, McBean & Co. Catalog No. 22*, circa late 1890s, showing terra cotta garden vases.

Catalog page from the *Gladding, McBean & Co. Catalog No. 22*, circa late 1890s, showing terra cotta garden vases.

Terra cotta building medallion made for Sperry Products.

Proctor Gamble company emblem for installation in a building. This picture may be from as late as the 1950s.

Ernest Kadel's Office,
Lincoln, 1911.

Gladding, McBean & Co., through the
talent of sculptor Ernest Kadel, created
building ornamentation known
throughout the world for its excellence.

Worker wetting down molded terra cotta pieces.

Pieces being hauled up to the kiln. The kiln is in the background.

Capital sculpted for the Northwestern Bank Building, Portland, Oregon, and c. 1913.

Portrait of the sculptors and modelers in front of a large urn for the Biltmore Hotel in Los Angeles, 1922.

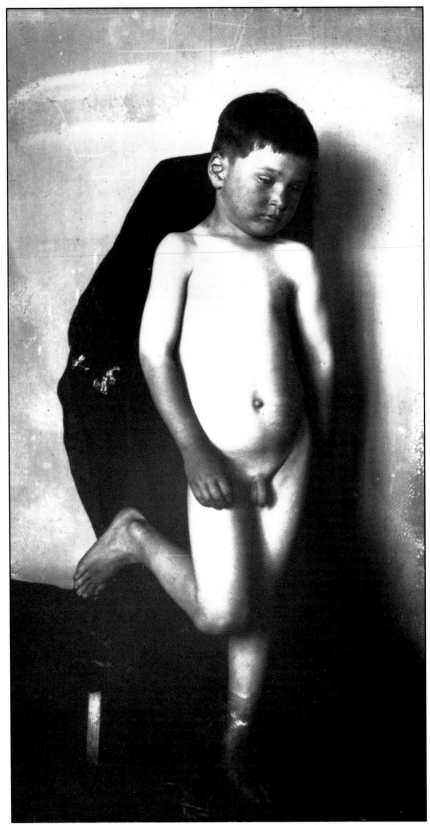

This little boy is the model for the terra cotta garden ware — from the child wrapped with cloth wall plaques to the boy with dolphin water fountain head. It is said that this child belonged to one of the workers, who would bring him in to model. The wall plaque was No. 8, Bambino, height 11", $225-275.

This was a decorative panel to go on the Sacramento Weinstocks-Lubin Store which opened its new flagship store on K and 12th Streets on June 2, 1924. Studio portrait. Left to right: F. Alamand, unknown, Ernest Kadel, Fred Finney, unknown. Bottom: Ernest Molinario.

Studio portrait. Back row, left to right: F. Alamand, Squalla, unknown, Ernest Kadel. Bottom row, left to right: Ernest Molinario, P.O. Tognelli, and Vittorio Russo.

In the drafting room, shields for the Claus Spreckels Building in Los Angeles. Sitting near the right shield is Ernest Kadel. This image is dated 1925.

Group portrait. Back row, left to right: Ernesto Molinario. Middle row, left to right: Ernest A. Kadel, Fred Finney, unknown, F. Alamand. Bottom row, left to right: P.O. Tognelli, Vittorio Russo.

Men in modeling room. Note the terra cotta samples on the wall to the right.

Workers in the molding room. They would hand pack the clay into the molds. They then removed the molded clay after drying and used special tools to shape the items. There was a particular set of tools for each mold, which would be kept in a box for use only with that mold. All tools were hand fashioned and made specifically for finishing a particular shape.

Ernest Kadel standing in front of the Fort Moore Pioneer Memorial clay model, 1957.

Chapter 2

Acquisition of Tropico Potteries & Other West Coast Potteries, 1923

In June of 1923, Gladding, McBean & Co. acquired the controlling stock of Tropico Potteries, Incorporated, adding new products, mining sites, properties, assets, and holdings to the company. Tropico Potteries, Incorporated first began production in 1920 on Los Feliz Boulevard in Glendale, California. This was the site of the Tropico Pottery, which was founded in 1904 and known earlier as the Pacific Art Tile Works. Tropico specialized in small faience and floor tile. With the acquisition of Tropico Potteries, Incorporated, Gladding, McBean & Co. officially had a holding in Southern California. Though they marketed heavily in Southern California, having additional factory space and equipment would expand their capacity for production of architectural terra cotta and tile. F. B. Ortman, who would later be President of Gladding, McBean & Co. in the 1940s, was instrumental in this merger. F.B. Ortman was President of Tropico Potteries, Incorporated. Gladding, McBean &Co. and Tropico Potteries, Incorporated would be operated as separate corporations. Soon after acquiring the controlling stock of Tropico Potteries, Incorpo-

rated, Gladding, McBean & Co. opened a pottery sales yard on Los Feliz Boulevard, at what would be now known as the Glendale Plant.

With demand for pottery products, and especially architectural terra cotta and ornamental faience tile, out stepping the production in Southern California, the firm of Gladding, McBean & Co. of San Francisco, largest and oldest pottery concern west of Chicago, has established a firm foothold in Los Angeles. Control by that company of Tropico Potteries Incorporated one of the foremost clay products firms in this section of the country has just been secured. B. M. Wotkyns, President of Tropico Potteries, Incorporated and vice-president of Stephens & Company investment bankers of Los Angeles, made announcement of the consummation of the deal. And while no figures were made public, experts in clay products business believe that $500,000 was invested in the transaction by the Bay City concern. The value of the property is estimated to be in excess of $1,000,000.

Tropico Potteries, Incorporated was incorpo-

Charles Gladding

"**CHARLES GLADDING** - A native son of Placer County and the mayor of Lincoln the city where he was born, Charles Gladding first saw light on June 26, 1887 when he entered the family circle of Albert J. and Carrie (Chandler) Gladding . . . Charles was reared in Lincoln receiving his education in public schools after which he finished at the Placer County High School. From a boy of twelve years he put in his vacation time working at the plant Gladding McBean and Company, thus becoming familiar with the manufacture of clay products in which they specialize. In 1906, his school days being over he entered the company's offices in Lincoln and thus became closely associated with his father in the management of the plant and grew up with the business. The plant was destroyed by fire and he saw it rebuilt in a more extensive and elaborate scale. In 1924, he became superintendent of the plant for the Gladding McBean Corporation, a position for which his experience well qualifies him and he is giving it all of his time energy and best efforts.

The marriage of Charles Gladding occurred in his native place, when he was united with Miss. Hattie Nelson, who was born in Lincoln a daughter of N. T. Nelson a pioneer and successful rancher of Lincoln and their union has resulted in the birth of one child Jean Gladding. Mr. Gladding is active in civic matters and is now serving his second term as a member of the board of trustees for Lincoln. In 1924 he was elected chairman of the board or mayor and he is serving the municipality efficiently. He is progressive and desires the best of improvements for the city and the highest standard of civics. He was made a Mason in Gold Hill Lodge No. 32 F. & A. M. at Lincoln and is also a Scottish Rite Mason his membership being in the Sacramento consistory while he and his estimable wife are members of Friendship Chapter No. 69 O. E. S. at Lincoln. Mrs. Gladding is also a member of the Woman's Club of Lincoln. Mr. Gladding is a member and Past President of Silver Star Parlor N. S. G. W. in Lincoln and is greatly interested in preserving pioneer history and landmarks for the benefit of the archives of the State and for future generations. Politically, he is a stalwart Republican and in a modest but effective way works for the success of his party." – *History of Placer and Nevada Counties*, page 1031.

rated in 1920 by Mr. Wotkyns and his associates in Stephens & Company, after which the new corporation purchased the properties and assets of the Pacific Minerals and Chemical Company, located largely near Tropico Station. F. B. Ortman, clay products expert, at that time chief ceramic engineer for the Northwestern Terra cotta Company of Chicago, was brought to Los Angeles to manage the new plant. Immediately its business forged ahead. Its success was considered phenomenal, and its products were in such demand that in spite of expansion of its works, the company was constantly behind in filling orders.

And today the demand for pottery products in Los Angeles and Southern California is not only continuing strong but is steadily increasing. Architectural terra cotta has been one of the principal features of the Tropico concern, and this product is being used extensively in the large office buildings springing up in many parts of the city. Among the notable of these buildings is the new Bank of Italy structure for which the American Institute of Architects awarded Tropico Potteries, Incorporated, the prize for turning out the highest type of material. In addition to its plant at Tropico Station and the industrial site it occupies, Tropico Potteries, Incorporated, owns mineral deposits in San Bernardino County

and conducts extensive clay mines near Corona and Elsinore. –"Clay Working News of LA & Southern CA," *The Clay Worker*, July 7, 1923.

Later in August of 1923, *The Architect and Engineer* reported the following news about the acquisition with greater detail of Tropico Potteries, Inc. and the transaction.

Gladding McBean & Company one of the oldest and best known pottery and terra cotta manufacturer on the Pacific Coast, have taken over the Tropico Potteries, Inc. in Glendale which will give them increased facilities for handling their growing Southern California business.

For some time Gladding McBean & Company have been interested in acquiring a plant in Southern California and I finally came to the conclusion that their interests would best be served by purchasing the controlling stock in Tropico Potteries Inc., the deal being consummated about a month ago.

In addition to buying all of the holdings of Stephens & Co., they also purchased all of the other outstanding stock; with the exception of that held by parties directly connected with the acting management of the company and other friendly Los Angeles interests.

The company in no sense loses its corporate identity, but will continue to be operated as a separate and distinct corporation with

35

the same active management as heretofore it will of course be the policy of both companies to work in close cooperation under standardized methods and policies, and it is confidentially believed that the merger will make it possible to render better service to the clients and customers of both companies in Southern California than was heretofore possible by either concern.

Tropico Potteries, Inc., was incorporated the latter part of 1920, and on January 1, 1921, purchased all of the assets of the Pacific Minerals & Chemical Company chief of which were the plant and plant site located at Glendale and extensive clay properties located in the Temeseal Canyon near Corona. The common Stock control of Tropico Potteries, Inc. rested with Stephens & Company investment bankers of San Francisco, Los Angeles and San Diego. The active management of the plant was entrusted to Mr. F. B. Ortman who came to California from the Northwestern Terra cotta Company of Chicago and whose indefatigable energy more than any other one thing has contributed to the success of the enterprise.

The company's business since the late above mentioned has been regarded as successful, and practically all of the earnings have been put back into the plant in additions and betterment's, so that the capacity at the present time is about double

that of the former Pacific Minerals & Chemical Company. The company manufactures terra cotta, faience tile, sewer pipe and kindred products. The following are some of the buildings upon which Tropico Potteries, Inc., has furnished terra cotta: Bank of Italy building, Los Angeles, Morgan, Wells & Morgan, Architects, First Methodist Episcopal Church, Los Angeles, John C. Austin, Architect, Pacific Southwest Bank Branch, Long Beach, W. Horace Austin, Architect, Security Trust & Savings Bank, Glendale Alfred F. Priest, Architect, Stephens & Company Building, San Diego, John and Donald Parkinson Architects, Robinson Store, Los Angeles, Dodd & Richards, Architects, Commodore Hotel, Los Angeles Leonard L. Jones, Architect, City Hall, Long Beach, W. Horace Austin, Architect, City National Bank, El Paso, Texas, Trost & Trost, Architects, and the Arnold Automotive Building, Los Angeles, T. Beverly Keim, Architect" - Gladding, McBean & Co. Take Over Tropico Potteries, Inc.," *The Architect and Engineer*, August 1, 1923

With the acquisition of Tropico Potteries, Inc., Gladding, McBean & Co. expanded its tile production to include ornamental tiles for commercial and residential buildings.

Shortly after this takeover, ornamental tile enjoyed a renaissance in the United States and the parent

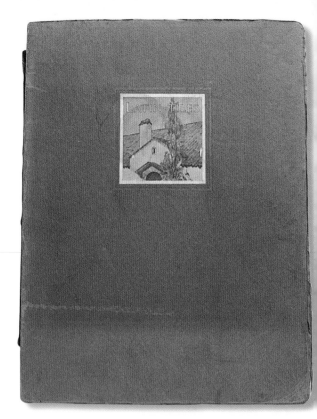

Latin Tiles – Gladding, McBean & Co., 1923. This book consists of images of terra cotta roof tile installations manufactured by Gladding, McBean & Co. Included are details of construction and specifications. $75-125.

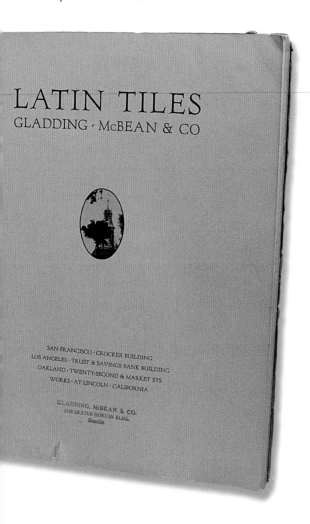

LATIN TILES
GLADDING · McBEAN & CO

SAN FRANCISCO · CROCKER BUILDING
LOS ANGELES · TRUST & SAVINGS BANK BUILDING
OAKLAND · TWENTY-SECOND & MARKET STS
WORKS · AT LINCOLN · CALIFORNIA

GLADDING, McBEAN & CO.
1100 DEXTER HORTON BLDG.
Seattle

company anticipating a heavy demand by the building industry, quickly moved to enter the tile market. The firm sent one of its principal artists, J.E. Stanton, to Europe and the Near East to study the use of tile in architecture. In an enthusiastic response to his findings, the Tropico Potteries proceeded to hire a talented staff of artists, and their kilns began producing a wide array of colorful tile. Soon the Tropico works achieved a national reputation for their ingenious use of the products. Their success was due in large measure to the keen interest of architects and the general public in Persian, Spanish-Moorish, Mexican-Aztec, and Pueblo design styles. [. . .] Gladding, McBean, of course, touted their work in the architectural magazines of the 1920s. The use of Tropico products for the Los Angeles City Hall was an especially proud accomplishment and was widely promoted. The Tropico works also advertised that its art and research department could create tile murals depicting literary and historical scenes or any other subject a client desired. Company advertisements suggested using this art form instead of paintings or stained glass in churches, banks, schools, and public libraries. -Gary Kurutz, "Murals in Tile-The Decorative Tile of Gladding, McBean & Company" California State Library Foundation Bulletin, Number

26, January 1989.

Gladding, McBean & Co. incorporated on April 26, 1924 as the Gladding McBean Corporation. However, on August 4, 1925 the corporation changed its name officially back to Gladding, McBean & Co. As will be seen in the quote that follows, in one of the most unusual of circumstances, the families of Gladding, McBean, and Chambers, who owned the company prior to the incorporation, no longer had a controlling interest in the firm. However, Atholl McBean was instrumental in the merger and would remain on as the company's President and Board Director. Other members of the Gladding, McBean, and Chambers family would continue to work in various capacities within the company.

And the past year they purchased the Tropico plant in the south part of the state for $700,000 and have besides put over $300,000 into improvements and enlargements at the Lincoln Plant. To accommodate these new expansions, articles of incorporation have been filed with the Secretary of State. Much of the stock of Gladding, McBean & Co., which has been owned by members of the Gladding, McBean and Chambers families for nearly half a century, has been acquired by businessmen of San Francisco and Los Angeles. The new corporation will be named "Gladding McBean Corporation." The new corporation will take over the business of the old, including the Tropico organization and new capital will be admitted. It is announced that it was merely a matter of business convenience as there will be no change in the plans or in the policies and personnel of the management. -"Pacific Coast News," *The Clay Worker*, July 1, 1924 and December 1, 1924.

In 1924, Charles Gladding, the son of A. J. Gladding, became manager of the clay pits and of the pipe, brick, and tile departments. Joseph Baldwin DeGoyler managed the terra cotta and art departments. They added the manufacture of garden pottery, as there was a growing demand for this beautiful ware for lawns, porticoes and interior decoration. A.L. "Gus" Gladding was in charge of the Los Angeles offices. M. F. Johansen was plant manager. Max D. Compton was in charge of the terra cotta department; T. C. Walker managed the main factory including the pipe and tile departments. Atholl McBean remained president of the company.

Gladding, McBean & Co. acquired additional property and equipment from the bankruptcy sale of Calco Tile in 1924 for their own production of tile. This equipment was moved to the Glendale Plant; however, the company declined to take over the Huntington Park property for the production of tile.

The plant and other physical assets of Calco Tile Manufacturing Corp., Huntington Park, CA have been taken over and are being liquidated jointly by Gladding, McBean Co. and the Pomona Tile Manufacturing Co., both of LA, at the request of a banking organization which has had charge of the defunct plant. The Calco concern was organized in 1923 to engage in the manufacture of floor and wall tile and has operated at only a small part of its capacity during the last several years. Present assets have an estimated book value of some $160,000. The plant is now being dismantled and the equipment is being sold. Pomona Tile Company has also purchased for itself in a separate deal the stock and equipment of the West Coast Tile Manufacturing Co. of LA. — "Dismantle Calco Tile Plant, Pomona Buys West Coast Tile," *The Clay Worker*, January 1, 1924.

In 1925, Gladding, McBean & Co. became owner of the Northern Clay Company including the Auburn Plant in Auburn, Washington. The name and personnel of the Northern Clay Company was continued after the purchase. Mr. MacMichael remained with the company and became a Vice-President of Gladding McBean. A. Lee Bennett also remained with the company as chief chemist. Later in 1936 he would become Vice-President, Southern Division of Gladding, McBean & Co. Willis E. Clark, widely known in the brick and terra cotta industry in the Northwest, was added to the sales force. Sales offices were opened in Seattle in the Dexter Horton Building and in Portland

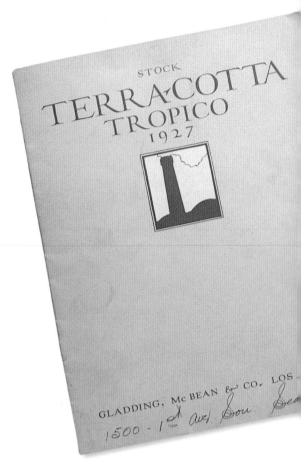

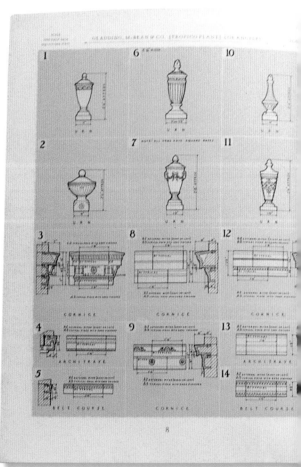

in the United States National Bank Building to handle the product from both the Northern Clay Company and Gladding, McBean & Co.

The plant in Auburn grew to ten times its original size, employing from 75 to 100 men and acquiring nearly five acres of land. A payroll of $15,000 was paid out monthly at the plant. Equipment and fixtures were valued at $100,000 and the plant produced an average of 250 tons of clay products a month. Such buildings as the Dexter Horton, Olympic Hotel, Northern Life Securities, and the Federal building were supplied with architectural terra cotta.

Tile production was increased due to the acquisition of Tropico Potteries, Incorporated. With the equipment and the workmen for the production of tile, Gladding, McBean & Co. was now a major producer of decorated tiles.

The GMcB [Gladding, McBean & Co.] plant at Glendale is now turning out more than 50,000 sq feet of hand-painted tile each month. An average of 85 men are employed in the department. The plant covers 37 acres. Other products are being produced; garden ware, sewer tile etc. — "Pacific Coast News," *The Clay Worker*, June 1, 1926 In February of 1927, Gladding, McBean & Co. took over the Denny-Renton Clay & Coal Co. of Seattle. The purchase included all properties of the Denny Renton Clay & Coal Company, which were the Taylor, Washington, mines

and plant and the Mica, Washington, plant near Spokane, Washington. Raymond R. Smith, who was the manager of the company's brick and tile department in San Francisco, came to Auburn to superintend the Denny operations. Smith was with the Denny plant from 1909 to 1925. Beyond this, there were no changes to the Denny organization.

In 1927, the Northern Clay Company, the Auburn Plant, and the Denny Renton Clay & Coal Company's names were changed to Gladding, McBean & Co. Also in 1927, Gladding, McBean & Co. closed their Van Asselt, Washington, plant acquired from the purchase of the Northern Clay Company, only finishing up some local contracts. The work previously done there was moved to the Auburn plant to which most of the workmen were transferred. The company also had clay pits at Sumas and Cummer, Washington

From an article that was the weekly motor log appearing in the *Seattle Star*, March 21, 1929, staff writer Harry B. Mills visited the Auburn plant.

The parking strip has been planted to grass and holly trees, the latter having achieved a growth of about 12 feet above the ground. While many of the samples are shown through photographs of the finished product as actually used in buildings, still another important exhibit has been set up in a little garden back of the office, with three walled sides, grass and

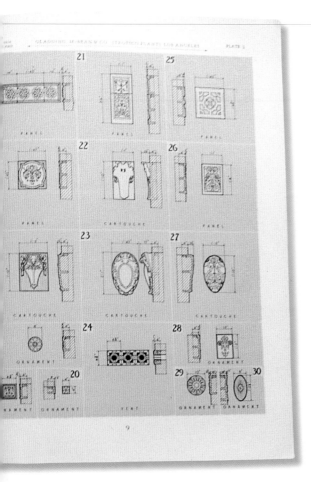

Stock Terra cotta Tropico 1927. Gladding, McBean & Co. catalog 1927. $75-85.

shrubbery. Here panels along the walls allow for showing many colorful samples and the pillars and garden pieces are seen, as they would appear in attractive home surroundings.

Three clays secured from Green river deposits, one type that is shipped here from California and ground and pulverized firebrick are the main components of terra cotta. These are fed from automatic hoppers on to a moving belt, which takes the whole combination into mixing tumblers where water and a small percentage of barium carbonate are added.

When this whole has been thoroughly mixed it is ready for pressing into molds with color added or not as the particular job may call for. These colors are ground right in the plant and the whole world is drawn on for these various glazes. They are ground uniformly on an upper floor, go into tanks and are drawn off on the floor below (the pressing room) as needed.

The pressed product is then fired for 96 hours at an even temperature when it is ready to step out and assume its place in the structures, which house our modern business laboratories.

The very first step is the passing along to the drafting room of the architect's drawings or the artist's plans. Oftentimes these creative minds have failed to allow for the peculiarities of terra cotta, and whole plans must be drawn up on the scale of one foot and seven inches to every foot desired in the finished product. This allows for the shrinkage, which comes in the firing of the pressing units. These plans then go into the modeling room. Here under the watchful eye of Louis Shubert, head modeler, a force of four artists work out in actual clay the designs, which have been prepared by the drafting room. This oftentimes is very delicate work requiring the use of a human model. The clay model then goes into the plaster of Paris room where it is coaxed by another group of highly skilled workmen to a uniform thickness. From this the cast is made which is used in the pressing room.

On the day of our visit, a set of models for decorative friezes for the Medical and Dental building being erected in Vancouver [Washington] were drying. The New Orpheum, Medical and Dental building, American Automobile Co., Marlborough Arms apartments and many other of Seattle newer structures also used these terra cotta decorations. — "Paper Tells Interesting Story of Local Industry," *Auburn Globe-Republican*, March 21, 1929.

Of interesting note, in 1927, The Emporium Department Store in San Francisco began to market the terra cotta garden ware from Gladding, McBean & Co. Besides selling

Factory Employee Pin, date unknown. $125-155.

to architects and pottery yards, Gladding, McBean & Co. now had a foothold in marketing their ware to leading Department Stores, which later would enable the company to market other wares for the home such as dinnerware and art ware.

The Emporium Department Store, at San Francisco, CA., has set up an attractive outdoor garden in which there is placed a complete line of garden furniture made of burned clay. In an area of 7,000 feet there are benches, bird-baths, plaques, stepping stones, ferneries, window boxes, jars, fountains, and other pieces of clayware. The garden faces a busy thoroughfare and is an excellent advertisement for molded clay products. — "The Emporium Department Store," *Ceramic Industry*, December 1, 1927

Gladding, McBean & Co. in 1927 took over the Los Angeles Pressed Brick Company. The takeover of this Los Angeles, California, plant solidified the primacy of Gladding, McBean & Co. as the largest terra cotta manufacturer west of the Mississippi.

Charles H. Frost established Los Angeles Brick Company in 1887. Los Angeles Pressed Brick Company was the principal producer of face brick in the region and also produced terra cotta for buildings throughout the west. Frost's business owned and operated four plants equipped with 31 kilns in Los Angeles at 922 Date Street, Santa Monica (the former Sunset Brick and Tile Company), Point Rich-

mond in Northern California, and Alberhill in Riverside County. It was from the Alberhill site that a rich deposit supplied Frost's company with white and gray clay. The former Los Angeles Pressed Brick Company plant would now be known as Gladding, McBean & Co.'s Los Angeles plant.

The most startling event in the clay world of the Pacific Coast is the gigantic merger of the organizations of Gladding McBean & Co. SF [San Francisco] and the LA [Los Angeles] Pressed Brick Company.

LA [Los Angeles] Pressed Brick Company enjoyed rapid growth. In 1923 completely overhauled and practically rebuilt their plant into perhaps the most up to date plant in the world. They acquired large deposits at Aberhill. In addition, they have a plant in Santa Monica, CA.

The merger was effected by a group of stockholders who had acquired stock in the companies; the members of the group have been placed in control of the new organization. General management will be consolidated. The consolidation of the two companies was signalized by the election of Atholl McBean as President of the LA [Los Angeles] Pressed Brick Co. F. Ortman who has been vice president of the GMCB [Gladding, McBean & Co.] organization and general manager for its southern interests has been named Vice-president of the LA Pressed Brick Company

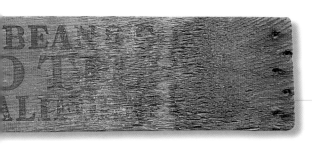

Crate board from Gladding, McBean & Co. Tropico Tile, Los Angeles, California. No price determined.

and will act as general manager of the combined interests. Howard Frost, ex-president of LA [Los Angeles] Pressed Brick remains as a director with intensive stock holdings. All other personnel will remain the same. The managing offices of the two organizations in Los Angeles will be consolidated, an entire floor in the new Finance Building taken for that purpose. *The Clay Worker,* date unknown.

Tropico Potteries, Incorporated filed for dissolution of the corporation December 17th, 1928. It was at this time that Gladding, McBean and Tropico Potteries, Incorporated completed the merger into one corporation and henceforth would be known only as Gladding, McBean & Co.

TO ACQUAINT YOU BETTER WITH
MAX D. COMPTON
READ NORRIS LEAP'S ARTICLE ON PAGE 15

Max D. Compton. "The Fates seem to have their own way of managing things. That is the only sensible explanation why Max Compton today is a Californian and unquestionably the world's top authority on the chemistry and the techniques of glaze manufacture. Compton should have become a forester, by now probably chief forester for the State of New York. Instead, the Fates dealt themselves into his life. They introduced a university professor who was afraid of bees. And so Max Compton today, a writer for Popular Ceramics, is chief glaze ceramic engineer for GMcB, world's largest producers of diversified ceramics products. The company's main plant in LA occupies 40 acres.

The story is only slightly wacky. It has a strong flavor of Horatio Alger, Jr., except that Compton never married the boss's daughter. It starts just before the turn of the century when Max was born on a farm near Clarksville, NY, a crossroads village about 80 miles south of Buffalo. His father died when Max was seven and his mother when he was thirteen. "I suppose, in a way," he says now, "it was good for me. It taught me to work."
It might have taught another youngster to whine. But it taught Max to work. And work he did. He had gone to grade school in Friendship about five miles from Clarksville. Now he wanted to go to high school. And he went. He must have been fired by some inner blaze about as hot as the inside of the kilns he now uses. That was pre-World War I and a buck was hard to get. He worked before school and after school, at night and on Saturdays and Sundays. He did everything a kid could do to earn a dime or a dollar. It's hard to pry anything out of him about that period. About all he will say is "Well, I didn't have time to go to any parties."

It must have been a rough go. He must have been on the skinny side and small for Max today is only of medium height and dripping he wouldn't weigh 140. But he made it and the next thing was college. He doesn't quite remember why, now but his ambition then was to become a forester. Possibly it was because he seems always to have an affinity for things beautiful, and most youngsters instinctively seek beauty in the things that grow in the field and forest. At any rate, he determined to go to Alfred University, a State university at Alfred, NY. It was about 40 miles from home. His principal reason for choosing Alfred was that the tuition was free. He intended to take two years there and then go on to Syracuse. He started at the university and found a job slinging hash from 6 pm to midnight with a side order of work Saturdays in a machine shop. However, that left his Sundays entirely free — free not only of work but also of revenue. To him that was time wasted. He heard about a professor who kept bees but needed help. It seems the professor was afraid to go near the bees. Max went after the job of keeping bees, a job he could do Sundays. He got it. And that's the way he became acquainted with Professor Charles F. Binns.

Alfred University was one of only four in the whole nation that gave courses in ceramics engineering. (The other three were Ohio State, Washington State and Rutgers.) And Binns was a professor of ceramics. He was author of "Potter's Craft," a textbook that still has a wide sale. Furthermore, he was a warming, intriguing personality. He not only talked about ceramics, but he could perform. Max watched him turn out a piece of stoneware on a potter's wheel, and he had to take a try at it himself. His try was a flop, but Max wasn't the kind to accept the first verdict. He was a try, try again fellow. And if that weren't enough, he'd keep right on trying. It seems he tried until he had changed courses. He took everything in ceramics he could get — clays, forming, drying, burning, glazing, cements, glass, porcelains and kindred subjects of mechanics and physics. He says his biggest course was chemistry. That was the course he gave the key to the whole subject. He had the curious experience of being graduated in 1922 but not getting his diploma as a ceramics engineer until he had been working as a ceramics engineer for many months. All of his jobs in college had left him short of time in which to do his thesis. He sent it in from California, and here in LA he received his diploma.

When that commencement June came around, Max wrote to ceramics manufacturers, job-hunting. He got replies from four. One of them was the Los Angeles Pressed Brick Co. And Max had a sister and several friends in LA. A classmate friend had got a job the year before with the Los Angeles Pressed Brick Co., and, of course, as ceramics engineer.

Max came to LA. The company had had two ceramics engineers, one an Englishman and one a Chinese. It was a day when compositions of ceramic bodies and of the glazes were secrets, often handed down from father to son. Max's classmate had succeeded to the job of the Englishman; Max was successor to the Chinese. Both the Chinese and the Englishman had destroyed their notes or left only material that could not be deciphered. The Englishman had been in charge of tile and brickwork, the Chinese of terra cotta. Max's classmate the year before had solved the easy way the puzzle left by the Englishman. He had gone to the purchasing agent and found the supplies the Englishman had bought over a period of time. It was not difficult to figure out the proportions. It worked until he got dug in. Max had a tougher time. His classmate's methods wouldn't work. Max had to apply the lessons he had learned in college.

He did the job successfully. He did so well that a year later when Gladding, McBean & Co. bought the company he was kept on. He worked on wall tile until 1929. It was during that period he learned how necessary research is in the manufacture of ceramics. "The body of any given ceramics," he says "changes constantly, because the materials of which it is made are never quite the same for long." He cited talc. "Talc," he said, "Will be different in different parts of the same vein. You may have a vein ten feet thick, but that at the top and the middle and the bottom will have different densities."

For that reason, he says, it is impossible to make a formula for a body, and then a formula for a glaze to fit it and have it invariably a success. He said the company management once years ago decided to make set formulas so that the same formula could be used in each of its several large plants. That way a single glaze formula could be used in all of the plants for the same product. It was a good idea in every respect but one. It wouldn't work.

In 1929 he was sent to the company's Lincoln plant outside Sacramento. There he worked on terra cotta glazes until he was made superintendent of the terra cotta department. That kept him too busy for much experimental and research work. It wasn't until he came back to LA in 1937 that he got back into the laboratory. He worked on pottery glazes at first. In 1939 he took over all of the company's glazes, and in 1940 started developing a glaze for china that went into production in 1942. He produced glazes for art ware that possibly never could have been equaled by either moderns or ancients. On shelves and in odd corners of his office are sample of most of the ware the factory has produced in all his long years with it. The war forced the factory to abandon art ware and it never returned to production of it. It seems too bad, for there on his shelves are samples gathering dust. And when the dust is wiped off, there comes alive such colors as seldom are seen on anything made by man.

One of them is an oxblood red used on large decorative bowls and vases. He experimented with that glaze in odd moments over a period of a dozen or fifteen years. The color comes out in the kiln. By control of heat he controlled the behavior of the coloring. He obtained wood-grain effects. The standard result was to have an overall oxblood color with a beige lip to the vessel. Another unique glaze he produced was a Persian blue — a turquoise blue with pebble effect. [Author's note: This glaze was used on the Montebello Art Ware line.] Those were just two glazes of thousands he produced. He made a glaze for china translucently pure, with astonishing properties. He picked a china plate at random from some samples and showed how he could using the edge of the plate as a cutting bit, chip a groove in the concrete floor, and without harm to the plate. While rummaging through his samples, a pottery tumbler fell to the concrete floor and went bouncing off into a corner. "You can bounce that one on concrete like a ball," he said, and grinned. He still likes research work but says he doesn't do much of it. I may not write a formula for a week or two at a time these days," he said. "Then again I may get busy and jot down a hundred in one day." He is glad, now, that he got the job keeping bees so long ago. Wherever he goes he sees his handiwork. His pottery ware and his china are world famous. His tiles and bricks and terra cottas are everywhere. "I think," he said "I probably did better than I would have done as a forester." –"To Acquaint You Better with Max Compton, Ceramist." E. Norris Leap, *Popular Ceramics*, 10/01/51

Top left: Pacific Gas and Electric Building, San Francisco, California, 1925.

Top center: Detail of column work for the U.S. National Bank, Portland, Oregon, 1926.

Top right: U.S. National Bank, Portland, Oregon, 1926.

Bottom: Entrance to the Ramboz Residence, Pasadena, California, 1928.

San Diego Trust & Savings Bank, San Diego,
California, 1929.

Bullock's Wilshire Store, Los Angeles,
California, 1929.

Northern Life Tower, Seattle,
Washington, 1929.

FLOWER POTS & VASES

No. 112
OIL JAR
Height, 52 in.; top width, 12 in.;
base, 10½ in.
Price, each, $30.00

No. 88
OIL JAR
Height, 33 in.; top width, 14½ in.
Price, each, $35.00

No. 87
OIL JAR
Height, 33 in.; top width, 12 in.
Price, each, $30.00

No. 81
Height, 18 in.; width, 20 in.
Price, each, $15.00

No. 111
OIL JAR
Height, 27 in.; top width, 12 in.;
base, 9 in.
Price, each, $35.00

No. 35
Height, 21 in.; top width, 21 in.
Price, each, $15.00

No. 79
Height, 15 in.; top width, 20 in.
Price, each, $10.00

No. 83
Height, 17 in.; top width, 18 in.
Price, each, $15.00

No. 110
Height, 17½ in.; top width, 22 in.;
base, 12 in.
Price, each, $15.00

Garden Pottery is made in a wide range of colors and in unglazed, dull glaze and high luster enamels

FLOWER POTS & VASES

No. 44
Height, 22 in.; top width, 30 in.
Price, each, $22.50

No. 14
Height, 30 in.; top width, 17½ in.
Price, each, $17.50

No. 46
Height, 22 in.; top width, 34 in.
Price, each, $30.00

No. 42
Height, 19 in.; top width, 26 in.
Price, each, $17.50

No. 11
Height, 20 in.; top width, 13¼ in.
Price, each, $12.50

No. 236
Height, 16 in.; top width, 18¼ in.;
base, 10¼ in.
Price, each, $12.50

No. 71
Height, 26 in.; top width, 26 in.
Price, each, $25.00

No. 90
Height, 24 in.; top width, 21 in.
Price, each, $30.00

No. 69
Height, 27 in.; top width, 27 in.
Price, each, $30.00

Some shapes lend themselves particularly well to the use of polychrome (two or more colors), others to unglazed natural clay colors. Some, like the Oil Jars, are equally beautiful in either

CALIFORNIA STATE LIBRARY

FLOWER POTS & VASES

No. 40
Height, 21 in.; top width, 24 in.
Price, each, $20.00

No. 32
Height, 20 in.; top width, 34 in.
Price, each, $40.00

No. 115
Height, 19 in.; width, 20 in.;
base, 14½ in.
Price, each, $25.00

No. 85
Height, 24 in.; top width, 26 in.
Price, each, $22.50

No. 95
Height, 25½ in.; top width, 18¼ in.
Price, each, $25.00

No. 86
Height, 24 in.; top width, 26 in.
Price, each, $22.50

No. 113
Height, 20½ in.; top width, 24½
in.; base, 11¼ in.
Price, each, $30.00

No. 63
Height, 20 in.; top width, 23 in.
Price, each, $20.00

No. 65
Height, 21 in.; top width, 26 in.
Price, each, $25.00

These pots in the warm gray and buff enamels bring a glint of light in the garden when seen against the green background of lawn or shrubbery

FLOWER POTS & VASES

No. 89
Height, 18 in.; width, 19 in.
Price, each, $10.00

No. 100
PAINT POT
Height, 15½ in.; width, 13½ in.;
Base, 11½ in.
Price, each, $10.00

No. 114
Height, 16½ in.; top width, 20 in.;
base, 10½ in.
Price, each, $20.00

Shape 225

12 in. inside diameter, top; height 11½ in.
Price, each, unglazed, $3.00; glazed, $5.00
14 in. inside diameter, top; height 13½ in.
Price, each, unglazed, $4.00; glazed, $6.00
16 in. inside diameter, top; height 15½ in.
Price, each, unglazed, $5.00; glazed, $7.00
18 in. inside diameter, top; height 17 in.
Price, each, unglazed, $6.00; glazed, $8.00

Shape 230

12 in. inside diameter, top; height 11 in.
Price, each, unglazed, $5.00; glazed, $6.00
14 in. inside diameter, top; height 16 in.
Price, each, unglazed, $5.00; glazed, $7.00
16 in. inside diameter, top; height 18½ in.
Price, each, unglazed, $6.00; glazed, $8.00
18 in. inside diameter, top; height 20½ in.
Price, each, unglazed, $7.00; glazed, $9.00

No. 60
Height, 11 in.; width, 16 in.
Price, each, $7.50

No. 227
Height, 10¼ in.; width, 14½ in.;
base, 8¾ in.
Price, each, $5.00

No. 96
Height, 14½ in.; width, 13½ in.
Price, each, $8.00

No. 245
Height, 4½ in.; top width, 10 in.
Price, each, $2.50

Shape 240
SAUCERS
12 in. inside dia. bottom. Price, each, $1.50
14 in. inside dia. bottom. Price, each, $1.75
16 in. inside dia. bottom. Price, each, $2.00
18 in. inside dia. bottom. Price, each, $2.25
20 in. inside dia. bottom. Price, each, $2.50

No. 246
Height, 5½ in.; top width, 9½ in.
Price, each, $2.50

Pot No. 227, with its simple graceful curves, shows to advantage in lustrous Chinese blue. Pot No. 100 is made in a Jacob's Coat of running glazes and has the charm of a discarded palette

FOUNTAINS

No. 1050
WALL BIRD BATH
Height, 8¼ in.; width, 20 in.;
depth, 16⅝ in.;
Price, each, in one color, $15.00
Price, each, in polychrome,   20.00

No. 1103
DRINKING FOUNTAIN
Height, 32¼ in.; top width, 18½
in.; base, 13½ in.
Price, each, in one color $40.00
Price, each, in polychrome,   45.00

No. 1100
BIRD BATH
Height, 36 in.; top width, 26 in.;
Price, each, $50.00

No. 1104
DRINKING FOUNTAIN
Height, 35½ in.; top width, 14½
in.
Price, each, $35.00

No. 2
PEDESTAL
Height, 36 in.; top width,
14 in.
Price, each, $20.00

No. 1101
PEDESTAL BASE
Height, 10 in.; top width, 40 in.
Price, each, $20.00

No. 247
SAUCER BASE
Diameter, 30 in.; rim, 6 in. high
Price, each, $25.00

No. 3
PEDESTAL
Height, 36 in.; top width,
10 in.
Price, each, $17.50

No. 501
WALL FOUNTAIN
Height, 13½ in.; bottom width,
12½ in.
Price, each, $20.00

No. 1008
BIRD BATH
Diameter, 25¼ in.; depth, 4¾ in.
Price, each, $20.00

No. 500
WALL FOUNTAIN
Height, 13½ in.; top width,
12½ in.
Price, each, $17.50

*In the Bird Baths and Fountains the sparkle of water and the flutter of birds against the brilliant enamels
add a final touch of beauty to the garden*

FLOWER BOXES, SEATS, TABLES & PEDESTALS

No. 1010
FLOWER BOX
Height, 36 in.; top, 14 in. x 51 in.
Price, with legs as shown, $75.00

No. 1059
Height, 17 in.; top, 14 in. x 46½ in.
Price, per set, $75.00

No. 1001
Height, 19¼ in.; top, 60¼ in. x 26 in.
Price, per set, $90.00

No. 1060
Height, 13¼ in.; top, 14 in. x 46½ in.
Price, each, $75.00

No. 1005
Height, 18 in.; top, 54 in. x 18 in.
Price, per set, $70.00

No. 4
Height, 27 in.; top width
9 in.
Price, each, $15.00

No. 1000
Height, 28 in.; top, 60 in. x 30 in.
Price, per set, $125.00

*These seats and pedestals make excellent accents at the end of garden vistas. When used against walls the
darker enamels are usually to be preferred*

ORNAMENTAL PIECES

No. 7
SMALL BAMBINO
Size, 9 in. x 11 in.
Price, each, $7.50

No. 9
Height, 22½ in.; bottom width,
16½ in.
Price, each, $50.00

No. 8
SMALL BAMBINO
Size, 9 in. x 11 in.
Price, each, $7.50

No. 10
Height, 15½ in.; top width,
12½ in.
Price, each, $30.00

No. 6
BAMBINO
Diameter, 24 in.
Price, each, $15.00

No. 5
Diameter, 14½ in.
Price, each, $50.00

No. 1102
POND LILY LEAF
Diameter, 36 in.
Price, with 2 turtles, $50.00

No. 12
Height, 16 in.; top width, 21 in.
Price, each, $30.00

No. 1101
FROG
Height, 8 in.; width, 15 in.
Price, each, $12.50

*The Madonnas and Bambini in their old ivory and Della Robbia blue often lend to a wall the spot of color
and touch of sentiment which endears the place forever*

Gladding, McBean & Co. Garden Pottery, c. 1908-24.

From the Gladding, McBean & Co., this ruler was used for tile and terra cotta. It is a shrinkage ruler. The marks indicating the inches are for measuring an item before it is fired. After the item is fired, then the item will be the correct size.

Garden Pottery, Glendale, California. "Part of an outdoor exhibit at the Tropico plant of Gladding, McBean & Co. A wall fountain on a terra cotta pier, a brick-enclosed pool with a fountain figure, a variety of pots, and flagstones of 12-by-12-inch tile are shown. These are but a few of the great variety of garden pieces produced by this Company." – *Shapes of Clay*, August 1928.

Early terra cotta tiles, the one on the left is for the base of terra cotta roof tile and is an end cap. $45-95. The one on the right is an octagonal tile. $45-75.

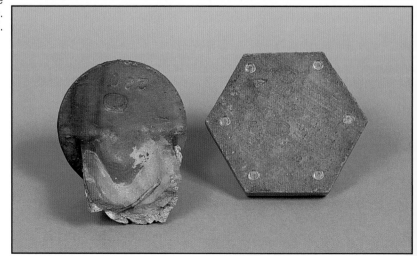

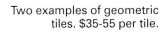

This is later production tile based on an earlier pattern. The four tiles are from the 1960s-70s. It is marked "Franciscan." $95-125 set.

Two examples of geometric tiles. $35-55 per tile.

Early Tropico tiles in stylized floral shapes. $25-38 per tile.

Bathroom tile installation for the Buster Keaton residence, Hartford Drive & Cove Way, Beverly Hills, California. As noted on the back of the photograph, "Plain Faience Tile floor and wainscots; Decorative Tile borders and inserts. Architect: Gene Verge. Tile Contractor: Calhoun Tile & Mantel."

Early Gladding, McBean & Co. tile in a geometric style. $45-65 per tile.

This tile installation was completed for the Mr. Newman residence in Bronxville, New York. Date unknown, this is from the Glendale Plant company files which were destroyed in 1984.

Decorative tile panels for the Dufwin Theatre, Oakland, California. These murals are on 17th Street between Telegraph & San Pablo in downtown Oakland. The theatre was renovated into offices in 1984 and these were rediscovered under layers of paint. These tiles were featured in an article in *California Arts & Architecture*, January 1929.

The decorative tiles are the most desirable. This is a floral basket. $75-125.

Chapter 3

The Stock Market Crash of 1929 and the Acquisition of the West Coas

From a small corporation with one factory and one office in San Francisco, Gladding, McBean & Co. became one of the foremost and leading companies on the West Coast for architectural terra cotta, ceramic tile, terra cotta garden ware, and brick products. From homes to commercial buildings, the products of Gladding, McBean & Co. flourished. Gladding, McBean & Co. now had plants and mines from Los Angeles to Seattle and was a major distributor of wares from the West Coast to the East Coast.

From January 1st to December 31st 1928, Gladding, McBean & Co. saw their stock value and profits increase.

In These Days of sky-rocket finance, an industry is generally rated according to its estimate on the stock market. According to that measure, the brick and clay industry must be listed as one of the best in the West. Gladding, McBean & Co. are easily the outstanding representatives of the clay products industry on the Pacific coast. Their stock on the market has registered as high as 98 since the first of the year as against a range of 60-71 for 1928. This is largely the result of their last

annual statement, which shows them to be conservative in their valuations and exceptionally firm in position as well as conservative in operation. This report places 1928 as one of the most satisfactory in their history. After paying $3 per share dividends, $421,360 was added to surplus, giving a total earning of at least $4.97 per share. Book value increased from $43.57 at the beginning of the year to $45.59 at the close. Although property valuation shows a decrease due to a large writing off to cover depreciation the current position still shows a ratio of better than seven to one. Liberal writing off for depreciation, and strong current position are the two factors that have strengthened the stocks materially. An established 2 per cent stock dividend payable semiannually provides a conservative growth in capital to correspond to the natural growth. A quarterly dividend of $1 per share now provided for yields 3.4 per cent on the present stock valuation. The company owns clay properties at Lincoln, and Glendale, CA and Auburn, WA besides the Tropico Potteries and

Opposite page:
United Shopping Tower,
Seattle, Washington, 1930.

Opposite page:
Shapes of Clay. Gladding, McBean
& Co. publication, various years,
$35-45 each.

real estate in San Francisco,
Los Angeles, Santa Monica
and Vallejo, California. –
"Pacific Coast News," *The
Clay Worker*, February 28,
1929

In October 1929, came
Black Monday, the crash of the
Stock Market. However, trade
reports portrayed a better year
for Gladding, McBean & Co. in
1930.

Since taking over the
Renton plant in Washington,
the Gladding, McBean & Co.
have built it into a plant
employing about 130 men.
Storage sheds have been
added. All the dryers have
been repaired and put in
excellent condition, and
$40,000 worth of new
machinery has been added.
They have perfected quarry
tile for interior work, which
is being shipped to California and other points. They
have increased the special
firebrick shapes for refractory purposes. Among
others they have sold runner
tile and refractory products
to the Pacific Coast Steel
Company. A new brick has
also been made for pulp
digesters in paper mills.
Acid brick has been added
in a variety of shapes, and
shipped as far as Chili. Many
new shades of face brick

have also been developed
and marketed. The bricks for
the Northern Life Tower in
Seattle were produced in the
Renton plant. For 1930
officials of the company
have planned the addition of
Spanish and Tudor roof tile.
They will also be prepared
to furnish glazed brick in
many different shades like
which has been used in the
County/City building in
Seattle. There are also other
developments in the offing,
which will necessitate more
new equipment and remod-
eling.

George W. Fackt of Los
Angeles has been made
assistant general manager of
the Gladding, McBean & Co.,
with offices in the
company's headquarters in
Los Angeles. Fackt is a
recognized authority on
terra cotta and a graduate
ceramic engineer. He was
formerly vice-president and
general manager of the
Northwestern Terra cotta
Company of Chicago the
largest manufacturer of terra
cotta in the Middle West and
was later organizer of the
Denver Terra cotta Com-
pany, which was merged
with the Northwestern.

The Gladding, McBean &
Co. are anticipating a bigger

year in 1930 with the re-sumption of more active building operations. 1929 was not bad. Net profits were $4.99 per share as against $4.97 the previous year. Total assets of the company also figured $10,647,080 as against $10,198,568 for 1928. Total current assets stood at $3,557,923 as against $3,156,022 for the year before. Surplus increased from $3,584,255 to $3,786,527.

Real Gold Brick Yes, gold brick, all right, and used to trim the Charles F. Berg storefront in Portland. Real 18 carat gold is used, designs inlaid on a striking black and gold terra cotta, in which the facade is finished. Perry G. Lindgren, manager for Gladding, McBean & Co., who supplied the terra cotta work, calls attention to the fact that this is the third building of its kind in the United States, the other two being the American Radiator skyscraper in New York and the 12 story Richfield Oil building in Los Angeles. Lindgren's description of the process of preparing the tile is instructive.

Summarizing, he tells how the architect prepares the drawings showing how the terra cotta will be used, with full details as to mea-surement and ornamenta-tion. These drawings go to the terra cotta factory, where they are enlarged to actual size, and plaster Paris models are made for each individual piece. These molds are sent to the

pressing department where the prepared clay is pressed into them. The pieces being removed are placed in dryers in which humidity is maintained that they may dry from the center out. Thoroughly dried, they are sent on to the spraying department. An expert chemist supervises this work and prepares the glazes. The body of the terra cotta has been made of pure clay with an intermixture of china and ball clays from England, to which are added chemicals and various oxides to produce the desired colors. It is not a mere matter of gauging color by the eye. The colors are brought out by high temperatures, and the right temperature must be used or the color is destroyed. Burning is done in muffled kilns by indirect heat, temperatures varying from 2,200 to 2,400 degrees. Temperatures are gradually raised to the desired point. Eleven or twelve days are required, four or five for burning and the remainder for cooling. In case of the gold trim as in the Berg building, the gold, colloidal gold is applied before the tile is entirely cooled, and a second burning follows. Then each piece is trimmed to exact size, and numbered in accordance with the architect's drawing so that the builder knows exactly where it goes. –"Pacific Coast News," *The Clay Worker*, April 1, 1930.

However optimistic the following article was on July 1, 1930, it could not foresee that

54

the company was living off of its contracts that were negotiated and signed prior to the crash of the stock market.

Gladding, McBean & Co. is looking forward to a prosperous close of 1930, the first half of the year having up very well. The financial position of the company is exceptionally good. The semi-annual stock dividend of 2 cent allowed in March transferred $128,332 from surplus to capital account. The stock dividend of 4 per cent year, together with the $3 cash dividend per share, amounts to $5.32 or 9.2 per cent on the stock at its present level of 58. Two years ago the company increased its capitalization to 500,000 shares and split the stock on a four to one About 227,000 shares are now outstanding.

The Gladding, McBean & Co. was founded a capital of $12,000. Its assets now are near $11,000,000. It was incorporated in 1886. The parent plant is at Lincoln, California to which were added branches in Los Angeles, Glendale, and Alberhill, in Southern Calif. and Auburn in Washington. In 1923 they acquired the Tropico Potteries, Incorporated, the Los Angeles Pressed Brick Tropico in the South, and the Denny, Renton Clay & Coal and the Northern Clay Company in the North. In was added the Simons Brick Company of Los Angles and the Ameri-

can Fire Brick Company of Spokane. This makes them the largest clay products manufacturers on the west coast with twelve plants and nine sales offices. The purchase of the American Fire Brick Company passed to them the plants at Spokane and at Mica, Wash.

Reports that they had merged with the American Encaustic Tiling Company have been denied. Also, reports that Goldman, Sachs Trading Company had acquired substantial blocks of their stocks, the latter reports growing out of the fact that capitalists associated with the management are interested also in the Western Branch of' the Goldman, Sachs company. Gladding, McBean & Co. has had an unbroken dividend record for over fifty years. The surplus in 1926 amounted to $2,697,000 and has since mounted to over $2,700,000. Some large orders are responsible for their strong position in the dull year of 1930. A 3,000-ton order for terra cotta in Los Angeles and a 1,200-ton order for vitrified Clay lining, for use in it sewer lines in Honolulu are samples. President Atholl McBean reports the first half of 1930 somewhat above the previous year, with prospects for the latter half being considerably above. This is also requiring considerable plant improvement and addition. – "Pacific Coast News," *The Clay Worker,* July 1, 1930.

By 1931, the companies profits were down, so much so

that a new venture had to be made to bring the company back from the brink of bankruptcy. By October, the depression had deepened. Millions of people were out of work.

Atholl McBean, the San Francisco clay products manufacturer and capitalist, has been appointed by President Hoover as the CA state representative of the general advisory board on the matter of employment relief organization. For this, McBean is eminently fitted. He was president of the San Francisco Chamber of Commerce for 1919, 1920, and 1922 and was also president of the Industrial Association. Atholl McBean is head of the Gladding, McBean & Co. clay products organization. He is also director of the Associated Oil Company, in the Crocker First National Bank, in the Pacific Telephone & Telegraph Company, the North American Investment Corporation, the Atlas-Diesel Engine Company, and in several insurance companies. All this gives in access to inside information of what it is possible to do. — "Clay Products Manufacturer Honored by President Hoover," *The Clay Worker*, October 1, 1931.

Company job orders no longer recorded tons of terra cotta, but square feet of tile, and advertisements in architectural and design magazines emphasized pottery, roofing, floor tile, and multi-colored machine-made ceramic veneer. A 1932 advertisement clearly stated the reality of a new era:

"Modernizing old buildings means new work for architects; greater values for real estate. Replacing with terra cotta or tile means a modern and up-to-date exterior. Let us help you with suggestions."

After gradually laying off their employees because of the lack of work and overhead at the Auburn plant of Gladding, McBean & Co., the Auburn plant was closed in December 1932. This was due to the many floors of empty space in the buildings throughout the country during the crisis of the Great Depression. The only building built with terra cotta in Seattle from 1930 through the 1940s was the Woolworth building in downtown Seattle. All operations were consolidated with the Renton plant turning out brick, the Taylor plant producing sewer pipe, and the Mica, Washington, plant specializing in the output of common and face brick. All Washington plants operated on a limited schedule. The Taylor coal and clay mines and the town were condemned by the Seattle Water Department in order to include the area inside an expanded watershed.

In July of 1932, the pipe unit at the plant in Lincoln, California, was destroyed by fire. By March 1933, in rebuilding, they made many changes and improvements in the machinery that was destroyed.

As the demand for building materials dwindled, Gladding, McBean & Co. began to look for new products. In 1932, experimental dinnerware was made at the Lincoln plant using a semi-porcelain clay body that was used for smaller Lincoln

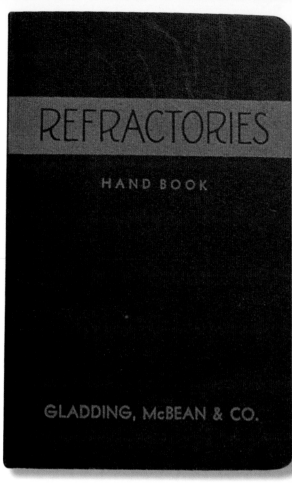

Refractories Handbook, Gladding, McBean & Co., 1930. $35-45.

garden pottery shapes. The ware was shipped to Glendale for testing but crazed badly in autoclave tests. The ware was never put on the market.

Experimental work started in December 1932 at the Glendale plant aimed at producing a pottery line using the "Malinite" body. Dr. Andrew Malinovsky, in 1928, developed for Gladding, McBean & Co. a high talc one-fire tile, but it was not used for this purpose due to the later purchase of the Prouty patents for the manufacture of a high talc tile clay body from the American Encaustic Tiling Co. On November 19, 1928, U.S. Patent #320539 was issued to Gladding, McBean & Co. for Dr. Malinovsky's one-fire talc body and the name of the clay body as registered as "Malinite." In 1929, British and general European patents were issued for "Malinite."

Dinnerware and art ware were to be made in solid color glazes. Three California firms had already introduced solid color dinnerware two years earlier. They were the J.A. Bauer Pottery Co., Pacific Clay Products Co., and Catalina Clay Products Division of Santa Catalina Island Co. Gladding, McBean & Co. did lab testing on all three companies' products in an autoclave and found that they all crazed badly.

Preparatory for further expansion to the Lincoln plant on January 1st, 1933, Gladding, McBean & Co., together with the Central Pacific Railway Company—their service line, filed suit to clear title to some city blocks and adjoining lands in Lincoln, California.

In an interoffice memorandum from A. Lee Bennett, Chief Ceramist, Glendale plant to J. E. Stanton, who was the head of Sales Promotion Department at the Glendale plant, on January 17, 1933: "Our conclusions are that our proposed dinnerware may be expected to be superior, in almost every respect, to the three competitive dinnerware lines with which we have made comparative tests." The patented "Malinite" one-fire clay body did not craze as the glaze and the clay body was fired together, bonding the glaze to the clay body. This one-fire glazed clay body has proven the test of time, as it is very rare to find Gladding, McBean & Co. dinnerware or art ware crazed today.

The decision was made to use the patented "Malinite" body for the production of dinnerware and art ware and to use "Prouty" tunnel kilns for pottery firing.

The "Prouty" tunnel kilns maintained a continuous flow of ware; having two tunnels with a rather small cross-section, very accurate temperature control within the kilns was achieved. The kilns were about 75 feet long; natural gas was used as the fuel and the kiln temperature was checked every 20 seconds by electric "pyrometers."

The first "Prouty" tunnel kilns were acquired from the purchase of the West Coast properties of the American Encaustic Tiling Co. Ltd. in 1933.

Gladding, McBean & Co., LA [Los Angeles] & SF [San Francisco], has concluded

Gladding, McBean & Co. *Pottery* 1932 catalog. $350-450.

arrangements for the purchase of all the Pacific Coast properties of the American Encaustic Tiling Co., Ltd, Zanesville, Ohio, including plants at Hermosa Beach and Vernon, near LA [Los Angeles], clay mines and other holdings. The purchasing company will continue operations at the plants and mines and proposes to increase production facilities. Production will be in charge of Frank A. Philo, heretofore acting in like capacity for the selling company and who will become a vice-president of the Gladding, McBean & Co. – *The Clay Worker*, August 1st 1933.

American Encaustic Tiling Company, Ltd. had purchased the plant of the Proutyline Products Company at Hermosa Beach in 1926. The new plant was enlarged three to five times its capacity by American Encaustic Tiling Company, Ltd. prior to the purchase by Gladding, McBean & Co. The Hermosa Beach plant manufactured a complete line of colored wall tile and trim using a talc body. This was the first plant to ever use a successfully manufactured talc body tile. Gladding, McBean & Co. in this purchase acquired from American Encaustic Tiling Company, Ltd. the Proutyline trademark "Hermosa Tile." All tile produced by Gladding, McBean & Co. would now be marketed as "Hermosa Tile." Gladding, McBean & Co. continued manufacturing tile at the Hermosa Beach plant until operations were moved to the Glendale plant in 1937.

POTTERY

GLADDING, McBEAN & CO.
1932

Gladding, McBean & Co. catalog *Pottery,* 1932.

On February 17, 1933, J. E. Stanton approved nine colors for the proposed dinnerware line. They are as follows:

A. Pigeon Blood Red – Gloss
B. Ming Red – Gloss
C. Celestial Ivory – Matt
D. Naples Yellow – Gloss
E. Apple Green – Gloss
F. Verde Green – Semi-matt
G. Turquoise Blue – Gloss
H. Mexican Blue – Gloss
I. Autumn Brown – Gloss

In November of that year, Frederic J. Grant called on Atholl McBean in San Francisco and suggested that Gladding, McBean & Co. start making dinnerware in a small way, if plant room were available. Mr. Grant, a chemical engineer, had been President of the Weller Pottery in Zanesville, Ohio, but had resigned.

COLORS OBTAINABLE IN POTTERY

Pieces shown in this catalogue on pages 4 to 34 inclusive are obtainable
in any of the above colors. All the above glaze colors are subject to a certain amount of variation under the fire, particularly the high glazes. Average colors are shown. The unglazed ware has a wide variation, often on
the same piece. This is one of its most charming characteristics.

· 2 ·

POTTERY

This book shows the wide range of pottery pieces designed in our ceramic studios and burned in our kilns. These pieces are not only for the
garden, but also for general uses of decoration and utility indoors and out.

Gladding, McBean & Co. has been producing this pottery for fifty
years. Its manufacture began in the earliest years of the company's existence at a time when no other terra-cotta plant on the Pacific Coast was
attempting anything of the sort. Gladding, McBean & Co., therefore,
has pioneered in pottery-making. And the company feels that it has carried the art to an impressive height of excellence.

In every detail but color the following illustrations speak for themselves. The range of color is shown on the chart on the opposite page,
for all pottery pieces shown on pages 4 to 34 inclusive. On page 35 is
a chart showing the range of color for the Semi-Porcelain Pottery illustrated on pages 36 to 39 inclusive.

The pottery shown on pages 4 to 34 inclusive is suitable for outdoor
and porch use. This type of ware is not guaranteed to be water-tight.

The prices quoted throughout are for glazed pieces. By deducting
ten per cent from the quoted price the price for any unglazed piece
will be arrived at.

The prices do not include crating and transportation charges. In this
connection it will be noted that the crated weight of every piece is
given.

This pottery is on display at, and may be ordered from, any of the
retail salesrooms listed on page 40.

In photographing the pieces, and in reproducing the photographs for
the book, the strictest care was taken to make the pictures as faithful
as possible to the objects themselves. We are confident that in every
instance the pottery will be found lovelier than its picture. The poet
might well have had this pottery in mind when he wrote:

"A thing of beauty is a joy forever."

· 3 ·

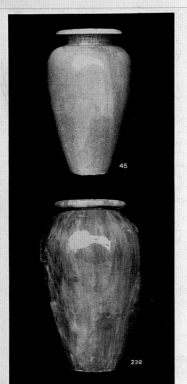

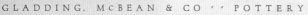

GLADDING, McBEAN & CO ·· POTTERY

· 4 ·

GLADDING, McBEAN & CO ·· POTTERY

· 5 ·

Gladding, McBean & Co. catalog *Pottery,* 1932.

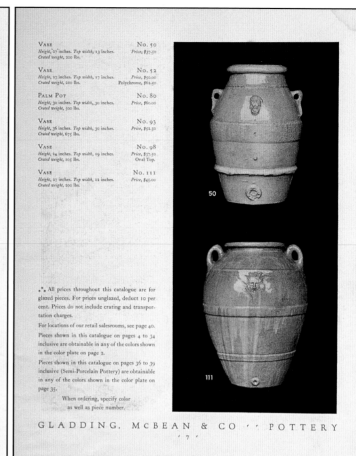

VASE	No. 50
Height, 27 inches. Top width, 13 inches.	Price, $37.50
Crated weight, 200 lbs.	
VASE	No. 52
Height, 27 inches. Top width, 17 inches.	Price, $50.00
Crated weight, 210 lbs.	Polychrome, $62.50
PALM POT	No. 80
Height, 30 inches. Top width, 30 inches.	Price, $60.00
Crated weight, 500 lbs.	
VASE	No. 93
Height, 36 inches. Top width, 30 inches.	Price, $52.50
Crated weight, 675 lbs.	
VASE	No. 98
Height, 14 inches. Top width, 19 inches.	Price, $37.50
Crated weight, 105 lbs.	Oval Top.
VASE	No. 111
Height, 27 inches. Top width, 12 inches.	Price, $45.00
Crated weight, 200 lbs.	

⁂ All prices throughout this catalogue are for glazed pieces. For prices unglazed, deduct 10 per cent. Prices do not include crating and transportation charges.

For locations of our retail salesrooms, see page 40.

Pieces shown in this catalogue on pages 4 to 34 inclusive are obtainable in any of the colors shown in the color plate on page 2.

Pieces shown in this catalogue on pages 36 to 39 inclusive (Semi-Porcelain Pottery) are obtainable in any of the colors shown in the color plate on page 35.

When ordering, specify color as well as piece number.

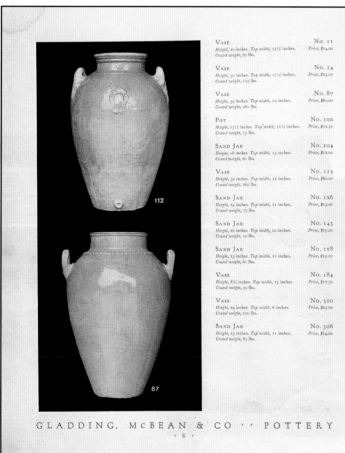

VASE	No. 11
Height, 20 inches. Top width, 12½ inches.	Price, $14.00
Crated weight, 60 lbs.	
VASE	No. 14
Height, 30 inches. Top width, 17½ inches.	Price, $25.00
Crated weight, 125 lbs.	
VASE	No. 87
Height, 34 inches. Top width, 12 inches.	Price, $60.00
Crated weight, 260 lbs.	
POT	No. 100
Height, 12½ inches. Top width, 12½ inches.	Price, $12.50
Crated weight, 75 lbs.	
SAND JAR	No. 104
Height, 16 inches. Top width, 13 inches.	Price, $12.00
Crated weight, 60 lbs.	
VASE	No. 112
Height, 32 inches. Top width, 12 inches.	Price, $60.00
Crated weight, 261 lbs.	
SAND JAR	No. 126
Height, 24 inches. Top width, 11 inches.	Price, $15.00
Crated weight, 75 lbs.	
SAND JAR	No. 143
Height, 22 inches. Top width, 10 inches.	Price, $15.00
Crated weight, 70 lbs.	
SAND JAR	No. 158
Height, 23 inches. Top width, 11 inches.	Price, $15.00
Crated weight, 60 lbs.	
VASE	No. 184
Height, 8½ inches. Top width, 15 inches.	Price, $17.50
Crated weight, 50 lbs.	
VASE	No. 300
Height, 29 inches. Top width, 8 inches.	Price, $25.00
Crated weight, 100 lbs.	
SAND JAR	No. 306
Height, 23 inches. Top width, 11 inches.	Price, $14.00
Crated weight, 85 lbs.	

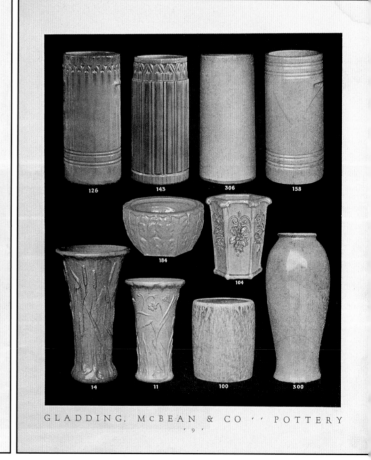

Gladding, McBean & Co. catalog *Pottery,* 1932.

60

FRUIT BASKET (Polychrome) — No. 12
Height, 16 inches. Width, 21 inches.
Crated weight, 140 lbs. — Price, $50.00

SEAT — No. 16
Height, 18½ inches. Top width, 12½ inches.
Crated weight, 85 lbs. — Price, $25.00

FRUIT BASKET (Polychrome) — No. 68
Height, 22 inches. Width, 18 inches.
Crated weight, 165 lbs. — Price, $60.00

VASE — No. 81
Height, 18 inches. Top width, 12 inches.
Crated weight, 125 lbs. — Price, $22.50

VASE — No. 88
Height, 33 inches. Top width, 14½ inches.
Crated weight, 250 lbs. — Price, $52.50

VASE — No. 90
Height, 24 inches. Top width, 21 inches.
Crated weight, 190 lbs. — Price, $35.00

VASE — No. 95
Height, 25¾ inches. Top width, 18½ inches.
Crated weight, 165 lbs. — Price, $37.50

VASE — No. 102
Height, 32 inches. Top width, 12½ inches.
Crated weight, 265 lbs. — Price, $56.50

VASE — No. 132
Height, 16 inches. Top width, 10 inches.
Crated weight, 90 lbs. — Price, $17.50

SAUCER — No. 240
In seven diameters. 10 inches, $1.75. 12 inches, $2.00. 14 inches, $2.50. 16 inches, $3.25. 18 inches, $4.00. 20 inches, $5.00. 22 inches, $10.00.

∗∗∗ All prices throughout this catalogue are for glazed pieces. For prices unglazed, deduct 10 per cent. Prices do not include crating and transportation charges.

For locations of our retail salesrooms, see page 40.

Pieces shown in this catalogue on pages 4 to 34 inclusive are obtainable in any of the colors shown in the color plate on page 2.

Pieces shown in this catalogue on pages 36 to 39 inclusive (Semi-Porcelain Pottery) are obtainable in any of the colors shown in the color plate on page 35.

When ordering, specify color as well as piece number.

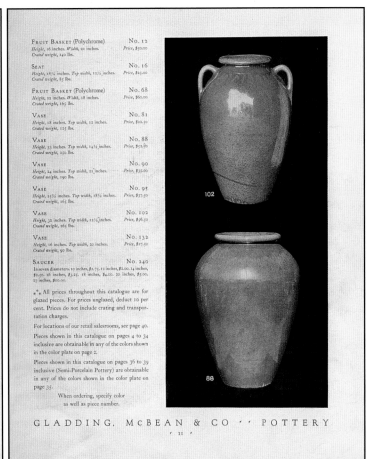

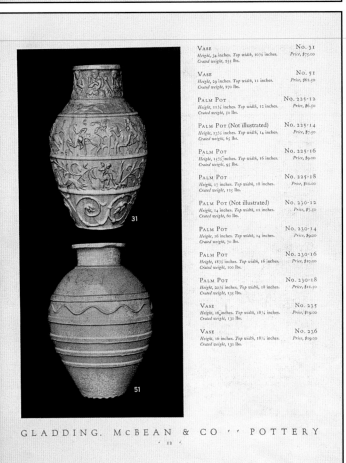

VASE — No. 31
Height, 34 inches. Top width, 10½ inches.
Crated weight, 255 lbs. — Price, $75.00

VASE — No. 51
Height, 29 inches. Top width, 11 inches.
Crated weight, 270 lbs. — Price, $62.50

PALM POT — No. 225-12
Height, 11½ inches. Top width, 12 inches.
Crated weight, 50 lbs. — Price, $6.50

PALM POT (Not illustrated) — No. 225-14
Height, 13½ inches. Top width, 14 inches.
Crated weight, 65 lbs. — Price, $7.50

PALM POT — No. 225-16
Height, 15½ inches. Top width, 16 inches.
Crated weight, 95 lbs. — Price, $9.00

PALM POT — No. 225-18
Height, 17 inches. Top width, 18 inches.
Crated weight, 125 lbs. — Price, $10.00

PALM POT (Not illustrated) — No. 230-12
Height, 14 inches. Top width, 12 inches.
Crated weight, 60 lbs. — Price, $7.50

PALM POT — No. 230-14
Height, 16 inches. Top width, 14 inches.
Crated weight, 70 lbs. — Price, $9.00

PALM POT — No. 230-16
Height, 18½ inches. Top width, 16 inches.
Crated weight, 100 lbs. — Price, $10.00

PALM POT — No. 230-18
Height, 20½ inches. Top width, 18 inches.
Crated weight, 135 lbs. — Price, $11.50

VASE — No. 235
Height, 16 inches. Top width, 18¼ inches.
Crated weight, 130 lbs. — Price, $19.00

VASE — No. 236
Height, 16 inches. Top width, 18¼ inches.
Crated weight, 130 lbs. — Price, $19.00

Gladding, McBean & Co. catalog *Pottery,* 1932.

· 14 ·

VASE .... No. 25
Height, 11 inches. Top width, 12½ inches.   Price, $10.00
Crated weight, 55 lbs.

VASE .... No. 35
Height, 21 inches. Top width, 21 inches.   Price, $25.00
Crated weight, 130 lbs.

VASE .... No. 60
Height, 11 inches. Top width, 16 inches.   Price, $10.00
Crated weight, 65 lbs.

VASE .... No. 96
Height, 14½ inches. Top width, 13½ inches.   Price, $10.00
Crated weight, 55 lbs.

VASE .... No. 106
Height, 29 inches. Top width, 18 inches.   Price, $40.00
Crated weight, 145 lbs.

VASE .... No. 116
Height, 16 inches. Top width, 16½ inches.   Price, $16.00
Crated weight, 95 lbs.

VASE .... No. 117
Height, 17½ inches. Top width, 17½ inches.   Price, $16.00
Crated weight, 95 lbs.

VASE .... No. 118
Height, 17 inches. Top width, 14½ inches.   Price, $16.00
Crated weight, 95 lbs.

VASE .... No. 130
Height, 14 inches. Top width, 18 inches.   Price, $16.00
Crated weight, 90 lbs.

VASE .... No. 131
Height, 20 inches. Top width, 15 inches.   Price, $15.00
Crated weight, 70 lbs.

.*. All prices throughout this catalogue are for glazed pieces. For prices unglazed, deduct 10 per cent. Prices do not include crating and transportation charges.

For locations of our retail salesrooms, see page 40.

Pieces shown in this catalogue on pages 4 to 34 inclusive are obtainable in any of the colors shown in the color plate on page 2.

Pieces shown in this catalogue on pages 36 to 39 inclusive (Semi-Porcelain Pottery) are obtainable in any of the colors shown in the color plate on page 35.

When ordering, specify color as well as piece number.

· 15 ·

FOUNTAIN FIGURE .... No. 47
Height, 20 inches. At base, 21 x 13 inches.   Price, $62.50
Crated weight, 120 lbs.

GARDEN FIGURE .... No. 48
Height, 27 inches. At base, 16 inches.   Price, $75.00
Crated weight, 240 lbs.

GARDEN FIGURE .... No. 49
Height, 31 inches. At base, 24 inches.   Price, $125.00
Crated weight, 300 lbs.

FOUNTAIN FIGURE .... No. 94
Height, 11½ inches. At base, 9½ x 7 inches.   Price, $20.00
Crated weight, 25 lbs.

DOLPHIN FOUNTAIN HEAD .... No. 144
Height, 12 inches. Width, 6 inches.   Price, $6.00
Crated weight, 10 lbs.

BOY & TURTLE GARDEN FIGURE No. 145
Height, 15 inches. Bottom width, 14 inches.   Price, $32.50
Crated weight, 50 lbs.

TURTLE GARDEN FIGURE .... No. 151
Height, 6 inches. Length, 15 inches.   Price, $15.00
Crated weight, 20 lbs.

BOY .... No. 185
Height, 13 inches. Width, 7½ inches.   Price, $22.50
Crated weight, 22 lbs.

GARDEN ORNAMENT (Fawn) .... No. 186
Height, 20 inches. Top length, 15 inches.   Price, $25.00
Crated weight, 45 lbs.

GARDEN ORNAMENT (Deer) .... No. 187
Height, 20 inches. Length, 15 inches.   Price, $25.00
Crated weight, 45 lbs.

FOUNTAIN FIGURE .... No. 1106
Height, 37 inches. At base, 30 inches.   Price, $100.00
Crated weight, 370 lbs.

STATUETTE .... No. 1107
Height, 15½ inches. At base, 8 inches.   Price, $27.50
Crated weight, 40 lbs.

STATUETTE .... No. 1108
Height, 19 inches. At base, 9 inches.   Price, $27.50
Crated weight, 40 lbs.

STATUETTE .... No. 1109
Height, 27½ inches. At base, 7 inches.   Price, $34.00
Crated weight, 55 lbs.

· 16 ·

· 17 ·

Gladding, McBean & Co. catalog *Pottery,* 1932.

GLADDING, McBEAN & CO ·· POTTERY

· 18 ·

WALL FOUNTAIN HEAD	No. S-12	
Height, 4½ inches. Width, 4½ inches. Crated weight, 10 lbs.		Price, $1.75
WALL FOUNTAIN HEAD	No. S-13	
Height, 6 inches. Top width, 6 inches. Crated weight, 15 lbs.		Price, $3.00
FROG	No. 59	
Height, 5 inches. Width at base, 7½ inches. Crated weight, 12 lbs.		Price, $5.00
BIRD BATH SHELL	No. 76	
Height, 6½ inches. Top width, 14 inches. Crated weight, 42 lbs.		Price, $15.00
FOUNTAIN FIGURE (Lizard)	No. 107	
Height, 7½ inches. At base, 7 inches. Crated weight, 15 lbs.		Price, $6.00
SMALL FROG	No. 180	
Height, 2¼ inches. Top width, 3½ inches. Crated weight, 2 lbs.		Price, $1.50
MEDIUM FROG	No. 181	
Height, 3 inches. Top width, 4½ inches. Crated weight, 2 lbs.		Price, $1.75
GAZING GLOBE PEDESTAL	No. 188	
Height, 26 inches. Top width, 7 inches. Crated weight, 90 lbs.		Price, $16.50
GAZING GLOBE (Mirrored Glass)	No. 188-A	
Diameter, 10 inches. Crated weight, 10 lbs.		Price, $10.00
FAWN FOUNTAIN HEAD	No. 500	
Height, 13½ inches. Top width, 11½ inches. Crated weight, 55 lbs.		Price, $15.00
LION FOUNTAIN HEAD	No. 501	
Height, 13½ inches. Top width, 11½ inches. Crated weight, 55 lbs.		Price, $15.00
LION FOUNTAIN HEAD	No. 502	
Height, 8 inches. Width, 11 inches. Crated weight, 20 lbs.		Price, $10.00
WALL FOUNTAIN BOWL	No. 504	
Height, 8 inches. Top width, 11 inches. Crated weight, 35 lbs.		Price, $10.00
WALL FOUNTAIN BOWL	No. 507	
Height, 9 inches. Width, 18 inches. Crated weight, 110 lbs.		Price, $20.00
BIRD BATH	No. 1008	
Height, 4½ inches. Outside diameter, 26 inches.		Price, $20.00
WALL FOUNTAIN BOWL	No. 1050	
Height, 8¼ inches. Width, 20 inches. Crated weight, 110 lbs.		Price, $20.00
LILY PAD (with two turtles)	No. 1102	
Width, 30 inches. Crated weight, 110 lbs.		Price, $50.00
DRINKING FOUNTAIN	No. 1103	
Height, 33 inches. Top width, 19 inches. Crated weight, 200 lbs.	Polychrome,	Price, $45.00 $50.00
DRINKING FOUNTAIN	No. 1105	
Height, 63 inches. Top width, 18 inches. Crated weight, 400 lbs.		Price, $50.00
FROG	No. 1110	
Height, 8 inches. Width, 15 inches.		Price, $12.50

GLADDING, McBEAN & CO ·· POTTERY

· 19 ·

VASE	No. 42	
Height, 19 inches. Top width, 26 inches. Crated weight, 200 lbs.		Price, $26.50
BIRD BATH	No. 67	
Height, 43 inches. Diameter at top, 30 inches. Crated weight, 250 lbs.		Price, $85.00
VASE	No. 69	
Height, 27 inches. Top width, 27 inches. Crated weight, 250 lbs.		Price, $40.00
VASE	No. 71	
Height, 26 inches. Top width, 26 inches. Crated weight, 250 lbs.		Price, $37.50
BIRD BATH	No. 75	
Height, 34 inches. Diameter at top, 30 inches. Crated weight, 250 lbs.		Price, $80.00
SAUCER BASE	No. 247	
Height, 6 inches. Diameter, 36 inches. Crated weight, 200 lbs.		Price, $37.50
BIRD BATH	No. 1098	
Height, 25 inches. Diameter at top, 18 inches. Crated weight, 110 lbs.		Price, $25.00
BIRD BATH	No. 1099	
Height, 25 inches. Diameter at top, 15¾ inches. Crated weight, 110 lbs.		Price, $25.00
BIRD BATH	No. 1100	
Height, 36 inches. Diameter at top, 26 inches. Crated weight, 190 lbs.		Price, $75.00
STATUETTE	No. 1107	
Height, 13¾ inches. At base, 8 inches. Crated weight, 45 lbs.		Price, $27.50

** All prices throughout this catalogue are for glazed pieces. For prices unglazed, deduct 10 per cent. Prices do not include crating and transportation charges.

For locations of our retail salesrooms, see page 40.

Pieces shown in this catalogue on pages 4 to 34 inclusive are obtainable in any of the colors shown in the color plate on page 2.

Pieces shown in this catalogue on pages 36 to 39 inclusive (Semi-Porcelain Pottery) are obtainable in any of the colors shown in the color plate on page 35.

When ordering, specify color as well as piece number.

GLADDING, McBEAN & CO ·· POTTERY

· 20 ·

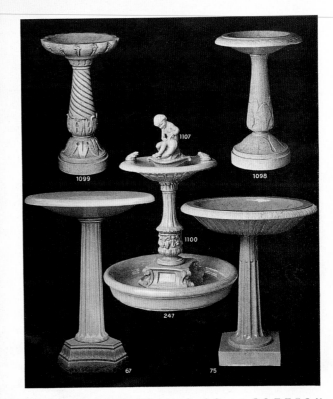

GLADDING, McBEAN & CO ·· POTTERY

· 21 ·

Gladding, McBean & Co. catalog *Pottery,* 1932.

63

Page 22 (left):

189 78 74

508

1101

GLADDING, McBEAN & CO ·· POTTERY

' 22 '

Page 23 (right):

VASE   No. 40
Height, 24 inches. Top width, 24 inches.   Price, $31.00
Crated weight, 235 lbs.

VASE   No. 65
Height, 21 inches. Top width, 26 inches.   Price, $35.00
Crated weight, 180 lbs.

DRINKING FOUNTAIN   No. 74
Height, 34 inches. Top width, 19 inches.   Price, $55.00
Width of bowl, 23¾ inches.
Crated weight, 220 lbs.

WALL FOUNTAIN   No. 78
Height, 36 inches. Top width, 17½ inches.   Price, $55.00
Width of bowl, 26½ inches.
Crated weight, 210 lbs.

VASE   No. 85
Height, 24 inches. Top width, 26 inches.   Price, $30.00
Crated weight, 180 lbs.

WALL FOUNTAIN   No. 189
(Same design as No. 78)
Height, 24 inches. Top width, 11½ inches.   Price, $35.00
Crated weight, 150 lbs.

WALL FOUNTAIN   No. 508
Height, 26 inches. Width, 16 inches.   Price, $37.50
Crated weight, 150 lbs.

PEDESTAL BASE   No. 1101
Height, 10 inches. Width at base, 40 inches. Price, $60.00
Crated weight, 590 lbs.

※ All prices throughout this catalogue are for
glazed pieces. For prices unglazed, deduct 10 per
cent. Prices do not include crating and transportation charges.

For locations of our retail salesrooms, see page 40.
Pieces shown in this catalogue on pages 4 to 34
inclusive are obtainable in any of the colors shown
in the color plate on page 2.
Pieces shown in this catalogue on pages 36 to 39
inclusive (Semi-Porcelain Pottery) are obtainable
in any of the colors shown in the color plate on
page 35.

When ordering, specify color
as well as piece number.

85

40

65

GLADDING, McBEAN & CO ·· POTTERY

' 23 '

Page 24 (lower left):

MADONA & CHILD PLAQUE   No. 5
Diameter, 14½ inches   Price, $20.00
Crated weight, 30 lbs.   Polychrome, $25.00

BAMBINO PLAQUE   No. 6
Diameter, 24 inches.   Price, $18.00
Crated weight, 80 lbs.   Polychrome, $22.50

MADONNA & CHILD PANEL   No. 9
Height, 22¼ inches. Width, 16½ inches. Price, $35.00
Crated weight, 80 lbs.   Polychrome, $45.00

MADONNA & CHILD PANEL   No. 10
Height, 15½ inches. Width, 12½ inches. Price, $20.00
Crated weight, 35 lbs.   Polychrome, $25.00

SINGING-BOY PANEL (Polychrome)   No. 26
Height, 41 inches. Width, 30 inches.   Price, $125.00
Crated weight, 490 lbs.

SINGING-BOY PANEL (Polychrome)   No. 27
Height, 41 inches. Top width, 30 inches. Price, $125.00
Crated weight, 570 lbs.

VASE   No. 37
Height, 14 inches. Top width, 17½ inches. Price, $22.50
Crated weight, 95 lbs.

VASE   No. 57
Height, 16 inches. Top width, 20 inches. Price, $25.00
Crated weight, 130 lbs.

VASE   No. 58
Height, 17 inches. Top width, 18 inches. Price, $25.00
Crated weight, 130 lbs.

※ All prices throughout this catalogue are for
glazed pieces. For prices unglazed, deduct 10 per
cent. Prices do not include crating and transportation charges.

For locations of our retail salesrooms, see page 40.
Pieces shown in this catalogue on pages 4 to 34
inclusive are obtainable in any of the colors shown
in the color plate on page 2.

Pieces shown in this catalogue on pages 36 to 39
inclusive (Semi-Porcelain Pottery) are obtainable
in any of the colors shown in the color plate on
page 35.

When ordering, specify color
as well as piece number.

37

58

57

GLADDING, McBEAN & CO ·· POTTERY

' 24 '

Page 25 (lower right):

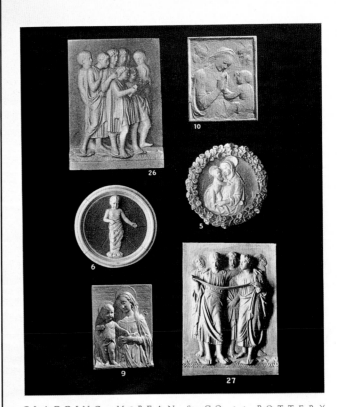

26

10

5

6

9

27

GLADDING, McBEAN & CO ·· POTTERY

' 25 '

Gladding, McBean & Co. catalog *Pottery,* 1932.

PEDESTAL	No. 1	
Height, 38 inches. Top width, 12 inches. Crated weight, 180 lbs.	Price, $30.00	
PEDESTAL	No. 2	
Height, 36 inches. Top width, 14 inches. Crated weight, 215 lbs.	Price, $30.00	
PEDESTAL	No. 3	
Height, 36 inches. Top width, 10 inches. Crated weight, 160 lbs.	Price, $25.00	
PEDESTAL	No. 4	
Height, 27 inches. Top width, 9 inches. Crated weight, 100 lbs.	Price, $20.00	
PEDESTAL	No. 15	
Height, 21½ inches. Top width, 14¾ inches. Crated weight, 175 lbs.	Price, $19.00	
PEDESTAL	No. 22	
Height, 20 inches. Top width, 9½ inches. Crated weight, 80 lbs.	Price, $15.00	
PEDESTAL	No. 33	
Height, 37 inches. Top width, 16 inches. Crated weight, 255 lbs.	Price, $57.00	
VASE	No. 72	
Height, 29 inches. Top width, 34 inches. Crated weight, 410 lbs.	Price, $60.00	
VASE	No. 86	
Height, 24 inches. Top width, 26 inches. Crated weight, 180 lbs.	Price, $30.00	
PEDESTAL	No. 108	
Height, 20 inches. Top width, 6½ inches. Crated weight, 35 lbs.	Price, $10.00	
PEDESTAL (same design as No. 15) (Not Illustrated)	No. 109	
Height, 30 inches. Top width, 15 inches. Crated weight, 220 lbs.	Price, $27.50	
VASE	No. 115	
Height, 19 inches. Top width, 26 inches. Crated weight, 145 lbs.	Price, $37.50	
DRINKING FOUNTAIN	No. 1104	
Height, 36 inches. Top width, 15 inches. Crated weight, 170 lbs.	Price, $35.00	

GLADDING. McBEAN & CO ·· POTTERY
· 26 ·

GLADDING. McBEAN & CO ·· POTTERY
· 27 ·

VASE	No. 32
Height, 29 inches. Top width, 34 inches. Crated weight, 390 lbs.	Price, $60.00
VASE	No. 63
Height, 20 inches. Top width, 23 inches. Crated weight, 180 lbs.	Price, $30.00
VASE	No. 84
Height, 24 inches. Top width, 28½ inches. Crated weight, 240 lbs.	Price, $37.50
BENCH (Legs only, pair)	No. 1005-L
Height, 15 inches. Depth, 17 inches. Crated weight, 150 lbs.	Price, $36.00
FLOWER BOX (Without legs)	No. 1010
Height, 11¼ inches. Top, 52 x 14 inches. Crated weight, 415 lbs.	Price, $60.00
FLOWER BOX (Legs only, pair)	No. 1010-L
Height, 24½ inches. Depth, 14 inches. Crated weight, 260 lbs.	Price, $47.00
FLOWER BOX (Without legs)	No. 1010-A
Height, 11¼ inches. Top, 36 x 14 inches. Crated weight, 225 lbs.	Price, $38.00
FLOWER BOX (Without legs) (Finished on four sides)	No. 1011
Height, 11¼ inches. Top, 52 x 14 inches. Crated weight, 440 lbs.	Price, $65.00
FLOWER BOX (Legs only, pair) (Finished on four sides)	No. 1011-L
Height, 26¼ inches. Depth, 14 inches. Crated weight, 275 lbs.	Price, $50.00
FLOWER BOX (Without legs)	No. 1059
Height, 14 inches. Top, 46½ x 14 inches. Crated weight, 415 lbs.	Price, $85.00
FLOWER BOX (Legs only, pair)	No. 1059-L
Height, 3 inches. Depth, 14 inches. Crated weight, 60 lbs.	Price, $17.00
FLOWER BOX (Without legs)	No. 1060
Height, 13¼ inches. Top, 49½ x 14 inches. Crated weight, 320 lbs.	Price, $100.00
FLOWER BOX (Legs only, pair)	No. 1200-L
Height, 7 inches. Bottom, 7 x 15 inches. Crated weight, 100 lbs.	Price, $25.00

Note: Any of the Legs illustrated may be used with any of the boxes.

GLADDING. McBEAN & CO ·· POTTERY
· 28 ·

GLADDING. McBEAN & CO ·· POTTERY
· 29 ·

Gladding, McBean & Co. catalog *Pottery,* 1932.

GLADDING, McBEAN & CO '' POTTERY
' 30 '

VASE	No. 46	
Height, 22 inches. Top width, 34 inches. Crated weight, 250 lbs.	Price, $45.00	
WELL HEAD	No. 64	
Height, 36 inches. Top width, 36 inches. Crated weight, 900 lbs.	Price, $145.00	
TABLE (complete)	No. 1000	
Height, 28 inches. Top, 60 x 30 inches. Crated weight, 775 lbs.	Price, $187.50	
TABLE (Legs only, per pair)	No. 1000-L	
Height, 25 inches. Depth, 29 inches. Crated weight, 525 lbs.	Price, $94.00	
BENCH (complete)	No. 1001	
Height, 19¼ inches. Top, 60 x 16 inches. Crated weight, 450 lbs.	Price, $95.00	
BENCH (with three legs)	No. 1002	
Height, 19¼ inches. Top, 60 x 26 inches. Crated weight, 500 lbs.	Price, $117.50	
BENCH (complete)	No. 1005	
Height, 18 inches. Top, 54 x 18 inches. Crated weight, 330 lbs.	Price, $85.00	
BENCH (Legs only, per pair)	No. 1005-L	
Height, 15 inches. Depth, 17 inches. Crated weight, 150 lbs.	Price, $36.00	

.*. All prices throughout this catalogue are for glazed pieces. For prices unglazed, deduct 10 per cent. Prices do not include crating and transportation charges.

For locations of our retail salesrooms, see page 40.

Pieces shown in this catalogue on pages 4 to 34 inclusive are obtainable in any of the colors shown in the color plate on page 2.

Pieces shown in this catalogue on pages 36 to 39 inclusive (Semi-Porcelain Pottery) are obtainable in any of the colors shown in the color plate on page 35.

When ordering, specify color as well as piece number.

GLADDING, McBEAN & CO '' POTTERY
' 31 '

VASE	No. 83	
Height, 20 inches. Top width, 18 inches. Crated weight, 130 lbs.	Price, $22.50	
VASE	No. 113	
Height, 21 inches. Top width, 24 inches. Crated weight, 135 lbs.	Price, $36.00	
VASE	No. 129	
Height, 31 inches. Top width, 12 inches. Crated weight, 190 lbs.	Price, $40.00	
VASE	No. 135	
Height, 46 inches. Top width, 13 inches. Crated weight, 235 lbs.	Price, $85.00	
VASE	No. 146	
Height, 29 inches. Top width, 15 inches. Crated weight, 130 lbs.	Price, $40.00	
VASE	No. 148	
Height, 31 inches. Top width, 10 inches. Crated weight, 70 lbs.	Price, $32.50	
VASE	No. 150	
Height, 30 inches. Top width, 18 inches. Crated weight, 225 lbs.	Price, $55.00	
VASE	No. 154	
Height, 27 inches. Top width, 31 inches. Crated weight, 210 lbs.	Price, $40.00	
VASE	No. 156	
Height, 26 inches. Top width, 25 inches. Crated weight, 230 lbs.	Price, $37.50	

.*. All prices throughout this catalogue are for glazed pieces. For prices unglazed, deduct 10 per cent. Prices do not include crating and transportation charges.

For locations of our retail salesrooms, see page 40.

Pieces shown in this catalogue on pages 4 to 34 inclusive are obtainable in any of the colors shown in the color plate on page 2.

Pieces shown in this catalogue on pages 36 to 39 inclusive (Semi-Porcelain Pottery) are obtainable in any of the colors shown in the color plate on page 35.

When ordering, specify color as well as piece number.

GLADDING, McBEAN & CO '' POTTERY
' 32 '

GLADDING, McBEAN & CO '' POTTERY
' 33 '

Gladding, McBean & Co. catalog *Pottery,* 1932.

Gladding, McBean & Co. catalog *Pottery,* 1932.

238
227
182
183
140
70
54
41
167
168
137
39
55
177
105
SEMI-PORCELAIN POTTERY

GLADDING, McBEAN & CO ' ' POTTERY

' 38 '

BAMBINO *Height,* 11 inches.	*Crated weight,* 10 lbs.	No. 7 *Price,* $6.00 Polychrome, $8.00
BAMBINO *Height,* 11 inches.	*Crated weight,* 10 lbs.	No. 8 *Price,* $6.00 Polychrome, $8.00
BOWL *Height,* 4½ inches.	*Crated weight,* 25 lbs. *Top width,* 16 inches.	No. 18 *Price,* $5.00
PEDESTAL *Height,* 2¾ inches.	*Crated weight,* 10 lbs. *Top width,* 8½ inches.	No. 21 *Price,* $1.75
VENUS BOOK ENDS *Height,* 6¾ inches.	*Crated weight,* 10 lbs. *Width,* 4½ inches.	No. 23 *Price,* $5.00
MONK BOOK ENDS *Height,* 6¾ inches.	*Crated weight,* 12 lbs. *Width,* 4½ inches.	No. 34 *Price,* $5.00
VASE *Height,* 9 inches.	*Crated weight,* 35 lbs. *Top width,* 12 inches.	No. 39 *Price,* $5.00
VASE *Height,* 3 inches.	*Crated weight,* 12 lbs. *Top width,* 8½ inches.	No. 41 *Price,* $2.50
VASE *Height,* 7½ inches.	*Crated weight,* 15 lbs. *Top width,* 11 inches.	No. 54 *Price,* $5.00
VASE *Height,* 6 inches.	*Crated weight,* 25 lbs. *Top width,* 16 inches.	No. 55 *Price,* $6.50
POT *Height,* 9½ inches.	*Crated weight,* 20 lbs. *Top width,* 14½ inches.	No. 70 *Price,* $5.50
VASE *Height,* 4½ inches.	*Crated weight,* 15 lbs. *Top width,* 12 inches.	No. 105 *Price,* $5.00
VASE *Height,* 7 inches.	*Crated weight,* 10 lbs. *Top width,* 5 inches.	No. 137 *Price,* $4.00
VASE *Height,* 5⅜ inches.	*Crated weight,* 5 lbs. *Top width,* 4⅛ inches.	No. 140 *Price,* $2.50
POT *Height,* 9 inches.	*Crated weight,* 10 lbs. *Top width,* 10 inches.	No. 167 *Price,* $3.50
POT *Height,* 7 inches.	*Crated weight,* 10 lbs. *Top width,* 7¾ inches.	No. 168 *Price,* $2.50
BOWL *Height,* 4 inches.	*Crated weight,* 12 lbs. *Top width,* 13 inches.	No. 170 *Price,* $6.00
BOWL *Height,* 3¼ inches.	*Crated weight,* 6 lbs. *Top width,* 10½ inches.	No. 171 *Price,* $3.50
BOWL *Height,* 2½ inches.	*Crated weight,* 6 lbs. *Top width,* 8 inches.	No. 172 *Price,* $2.00
BOWL *Height,* 3½ inches.	*Crated weight,* 5 lbs. *Top width,* 11 inches.	No. 173 *Price,* $2.00
BOWL *Height,* 2¾ inches.	*Crated weight,* 5 lbs. *Top width,* 8½ inches.	No. 174 *Price,* $1.75
VASE *Height,* 3½ inches.	*Crated weight,* 6 lbs. *Top width,* 8 inches.	No. 177 *Price,* $3.50
HANGING STRAWBERRY JAR *Height,* 11 inches. *Top width,* 6 inches. *Crated weight,* 14 lbs.		No. 182 *Price,* $8.00
BASKET *Height,* 7½ inches.	*Crated weight,* 30 lbs. *Top width,* 12 inches.	No. 183 *Price,* $7.50
VASE *Height,* 10¾ inches.	*Crated weight,* 50 lbs. *Top width,* 14¾ inches.	No. 227 *Price,* $5.00
POT *Height,* 5¾ inches.	*Crated weight,* 15 lbs. *Top width,* 11¾ inches.	No. 234 *Price,* $3.00
VASE *Height,* 8 inches.	*Crated weight,* 25 lbs. *Top width,* 13 inches.	No. 238 *Price,* $6.50

7
34
23
8
234
21
18
173
174
170
171
172
SEMI-PORCELAIN POTTERY

GLADDING, McBEAN & CO ' ' POTTERY

' 39 '

GLADDING, McBEAN & CO.

Founded 1875

SAN FRANCISCO, LOS ANGELES, SEATTLE, SPOKANE, PORTLAND, OAKLAND

*

Pottery on display and for sale at our retail salesrooms:

SAN FRANCISCO, 445 Ninth Street

LOS ANGELES, Los Feliz Boulevard and S. P. tracks, Glendale

SEATTLE, 1500 First Avenue S.

SPOKANE, North 1102 Monroe Street

PORTLAND, 454 Everett Street

OAKLAND, Twenty-second and Market Streets

*

All prices throughout this catalogue are for glazed pieces. For prices unglazed, deduct 10 per cent. Prices do not include crating and transportation charges.

All pieces shown in this catalogue on pages 4 to 34 inclusive are obtainable in any of the colors shown in the color plate on page 2.

All pieces shown in this catalogue on pages 36 to 39 inclusive (Semi-Porcelain Pottery) are obtainable in any of the colors shown in the color plate on page 35.

When ordering, please specify color as well as piece number.

Printed by Taylor & Taylor, San Francisco

' 40 '

Gladding, McBean & Co. catalog *Pottery,* 1932.

Development of a new shape in the terra cotta garden ware line. This new shape is #135 and later appears in the 1932 *Pottery* catalog. This image is from the unprocessed Gladding, McBean & Co. collection of the California State Library. In an interoffice memorandum dated August 29, 1929, from J. M. Quirolo to Athol McBean, he wrote "referring to your letter to M. Stanton a few weeks ago regarding the purchasing of a large vase similar to the one on the enclosed photo, will state that we were unable to purchase one similar to the one in the photograph, so we have made a model, of which I am enclosing a photograph. Mr. Stanton says it is very good and has graceful lines. If you think it is all right, will you kindly give us your OK so we can go ahead and make a mold, for we are sure it is going to be a good seller."

Then on September 27th, J. E. Stanton in an interoffice memorandum to M. F. Johansen at the Lincoln Plant wrote "enclosed please find letter addressed to Mr. McBean in reference to large plaster model of vase that Joe Quirolo sent to you with an order to make two. In the enclosed cut, you will notice that there are two or three sinkages or lines about this vase. Mr. McBean is desirous of having these out on mould. The order that Mr. Quirolo sent you is to be made like plaster mould without these sinkages."

When the final decision was made, the lines or sinkages disappeared and shape #135 would be manufactured without them. Athol McBean had the final word as to what would be added to the line as well as its design.

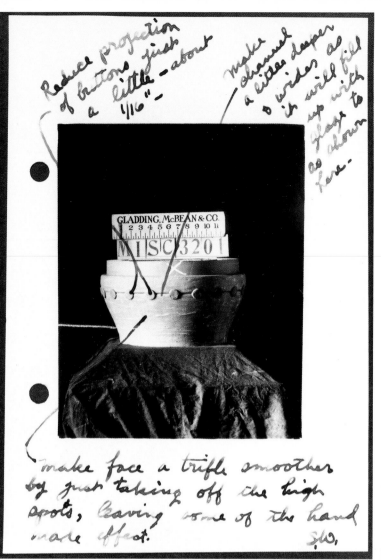

For a special order, this piece was made and according to specifications "make face a trifle smoother by just taking off the high spots, leaving some of the hand made effect, reduce projection of buttons just a little – about 1/16, and make channel a little deeper & wider as it will fill up with glaze to as shown here." The project number was assigned MISC3201 and was for a customer named Bliss. From the unprocessed collection of the Gladding, McBean & Co. at the California State Library, this document is dated November 1929 on the reverse side.

From the unprocessed Gladding, McBean & Co. collection of the California State Library, this image is of a fountain. The base is the No. 1100 Birdbath without the frogs on the rim; the standing boy with fish is Statuette No. 1108. The piece is numbered 1108X.

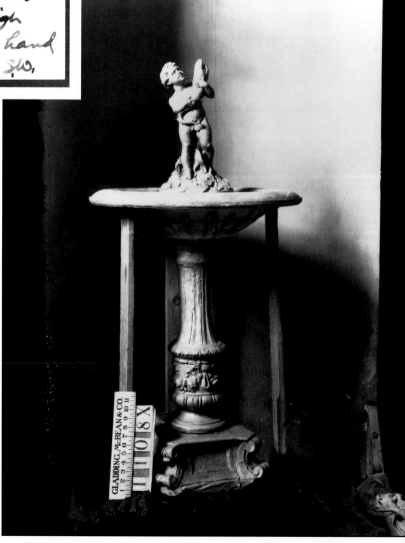

Shown is the No. 18 Bowl, height 4.5", top width 16" on the No. 21 Pedestal, height 2.25", top width 8.5". Later when Gladding, McBean & Co. produced this in Malinite, it would be named the opium bowl with stand. $195-425 for bowl and pedestal, $95-125 for pedestal alone.

The No. 21 pedestal made of semi-porcelain on the left compared to the #81A stand for opium bowl made of Malinite in gunmetal.

No. unknown, footed bowl, semi-porcelain. $125-145.

No. 137 semi-porcelain Vase. $375-450.

Semi-porcelain Bowl, number unknown. $275-375.

No. unknown, footed bowl, semi-porcelain. $125-145. This bowl would later be made in Malinite and included in the El Patio Table Ware line.

No. 45 Vase, terra cotta, height 26", top width 13". $285-425.

No. 1 Pedestal, terra cotta, height 38", top width 12". $325-450.

No. 307 semi-porcelain Vase, height 14", top width 5-3/8". $285-425.

No. 41 semi-porcelain Vase, height 3", top width 8.5". $145-245. Made in three sizes, this is the smallest.

No. 1110 Frog, terra cotta, height 8", width 15". $450-550.

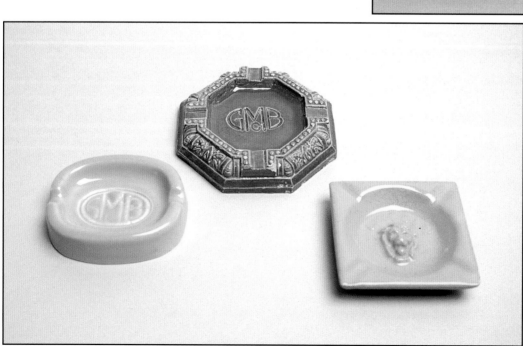

Company giveaway ashtrays. These were given to business associates to promote Gladding, McBean & Co. When they were issued is unknown. Left to right: oval GMcB ashtray, $75-85; GMcB terra cotta ashtray, $95-125; lion ashtray is embossed with a lion and the word "Lincoln" with the backside embossed with GMcB, $125-145. All were products of the Lincoln Plant.

No. 55 semi-porcelain Vase, height 6", top width 16". $245-425. Made in three sizes, this is the largest.

This is the Spanish series. There were eight styles of tile in the series, each decorated differently. There are two sizes, 6" x 6" tiles and 4.25" x 4.25" tiles. $45-55 per tile.

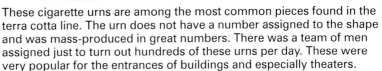

These cigarette urns are among the most common pieces found in the terra cotta line. The urn does not have a number assigned to the shape and was mass-produced in great numbers. There was a team of men assigned just to turn out hundreds of these urns per day. These were very popular for the entrances of buildings and especially theaters.

This is the Dutch series. There were five styles of tile in the series, each decorated differently. There are two sizes, 6" x 6" tiles and 4.25" x 4.25" tiles. $45-55 per tile.

This is the other Dutch series. There are two Dutch series, this one being a design in a circle. There were five styles of tile in each of the two series, each decorated differently. There are two sizes, 6" x 6" tiles and 4.25" x 4.25" tiles. $45-55 per tile.

Note the Hermosa tile series Kitchen used in this kitchen. This photograph was from company files from the Glendale Plant and was used to demonstrate the use of Hermosa tiles.

This is the Colonial series. There were five styles of tile in the series, each decorated differently. There are two sizes, 6" x 6" tiles and 4.25" x 4.25" tiles. $45-55 per tile.

The Mexican series. There were eight styles of tile in the series, each decorated differently. There are two sizes, 6" x 6" tiles and 4.25" x 4.25" tiles. $45-55 per tile.

The Kitchen series. There were four styles of tile in the series, each decorated differently. There is only one size, 4.25" x 4.25" tiles. $45-55 per tile.

Octagon tea trivet tiles were made at the Glendale Plant for different patterns. On the right is for the Tiger Flower Table Ware. The tile on the left is a Dutch design, while the tile in the middle is a promotional tile given to business associates to promote Hermosa tile.

Tile boxes for Hermosa tile given to sales associates and tile dealers. When complete with sample tiles, $85-95. Box only, $25-35. Tiles each, $4-5.

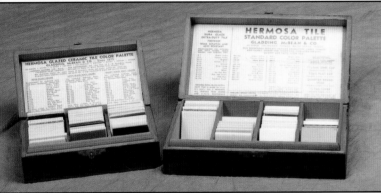

The most popular Animals series. There were five styles of tile in the series, each decorated differently. There are two sizes, 6" x 6" tiles and 4.25" x 4.25" tiles. $65-75 per tile. Other series were the Cowboys, Williamsburg, and Gloucester. The Cowboy series is another very popular series. There were five styles of tile in the series, each decorated differently. There are two sizes, 6" x 6" tiles and 4.25" x 4.25" tiles. $85-95 per tile. The Williamsburg series had five styles of tile in the series, each decorated differently. There is only one size, 6" x 6" tiles. $45-55 per tile. The Gloucester series had six styles of tile in the series, each decorated differently. There are two sizes, 6" x 6" tiles and 4.25" x 4.25" tiles. $45-55 per tile.

This is a model house display, probably in a department store. This was most likely made to promote Gladding, McBean & Co. tiling products as well as home furnishings.

Chapter 4
Introduction of Household Art Ware & Tableware 1934

On January 8, 1934, the minutes of the meeting of Production and Engineer Departments of Gladding, McBean & Co. made these recommendations: The Auburn, Vernon and Alberhill plants to be permanently abandoned after removal of all equipment to save money that is being expended for watchmen, insurance, and taxes. All Taylor plant products transferred to the Renton plant and that the Renton plant is to be the main plant for the Northern Division and the Seattle area. In the Southern Division, the Los Angeles plant would continue to operate and eventually take over production of architectural terra cotta from the Glendale plant. The Los Angeles plant would be used for the manufacture of firebrick and refractories, face brick, enamel brick, handmade roof tile and floor tile, glazed roof tile, and architectural terra cotta. The Glendale plant would continue as the base of operations for the Southern Division of Gladding, McBean & Co. The Central Division, which included only the Lincoln plant, would continue with the manufacture of quarry tile, terra cotta, and sewer pipe.

One of the most significant changes would be the establishment of the newly created Pottery Department, which, "will be installed in the Terra cotta section of the Glendale Plant, using the MacDougal Kiln in part for burning and the Terra cotta Muffle Kilns for certain shapes. The ultimate layout of this Department will depend upon the rapidity of its growth. For the present, it can be handled comfortable along with the Terra cotta but, should it reach proportions that would require all of the Terra cotta sections as noted above, the latter product can be transferred to the Los Angeles Plant. The Pottery Department contemplates transferring the manufacture of Garden Pottery from the Lincoln Plant to the Glendale Plant. Ultimate expansion of the Tile Department will make necessary the removal or abandonment of the MacDougal Kiln and its replacement by another Tunnel Kiln more suitable for the burning of Pottery Ware."

The company would move towards promoting and expanding its market for quarry tile, Hermosa tile, and its newest endeavor: pottery. Of interesting note is that the committee "definitely recom-

Frederic J. Grant. *Courtesy of Frederic Grant, Jr. and the Grant Family.*

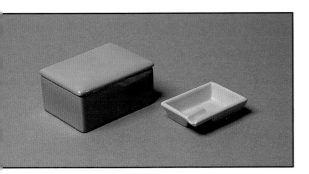

El Patio Table Ware. Cigarette box #72, $45-65, shown with ashtray #100, $16-24. These were also offered later in the Catalina Art Ware line and catalog.

El Patio Table Ware. These are the #91 ashtrays in chartreuse satin, $18-22, satin gray, $26-28, and coral satin, $18-22. This shape is in the Capistrano Ware line as well as the El Patio dinnerware line. These were also offered later in the Catalina Art Ware line and catalog.

mends against engaging in the operation of a plant manufacturing Chinaware or other similar products at Vernon either on a partnership basis or otherwise."

On January 15, 1934, Frederic J. Grant was hired as Manager of the new pottery department at the Glendale plant. A complete line of art pottery, colored tableware, and cooking ware was to be produced. Before her marriage, Mr. Grant's wife, Mary K. Grant, had been Art Director at R. H. Macy Co. in New York City. It was agreed that Mrs. Grant would style the new pottery lines, but would hold no official position in the pottery department and would not be on the payroll. Mrs. Grant was not put on the payroll until March 16, 1938.

In April of 1934, only art ware and flowerpots were in production. Roy Yourstone was hired as the first Salesman and during this month sold his first order of pottery to the Leamington Florists in Oakland, California.

On July 2, 1934, the first mimeographed Franciscan Pottery Price List and General Sales Instructions was published. The trade name of "Franciscan Pottery" was chosen to be emblematic of California. El Patio was the only dinnerware pattern that was listed. Eight solid colors were available. The original El Patio colors were White, Golden Glow, Redwood, Glacial Blue, Mexican Blue, Tahoe Green (later renamed Dark Green Gloss), Flame Orange, and Yellow. Pottery mixing bowls and casseroles were also available.

Art ware lines included Cielito Ware and Coronado Ware in which various shapes were offered in a variety of colors. Also available was the Tropico Garden Pottery that included flowerpots for indoor and outdoor use as well as garden pottery for lawns and porches. There were 66 items in the Tropico Garden Pottery in eight colors. Most of the garden pottery items were the smaller pieces that had been formerly made at the Lincoln plant. The molds had been shipped to the Glendale plant and were produced in the "Malinite" body. All of the larger garden pottery items continued to be manufactured in the Lincoln plant in the terra cotta body.

By November, there was the first exhibit of Franciscan Pottery in a museum. Earlier in the year, the director of the Metropolitan Museum of Art in New York City had invited Gladding, McBean & Co. to manufacture two special art ware pieces for their exhibit of modern industrial contemporary art. Gladding, McBean & Co. was the only American pottery invited to exhibit. The company submitted a large glazed pottery bowl, satin gray on the outside, lined with salmon gloss, and a lemon yellow vase lined with gloss gray, with a gloss gray band at the feet. Both pieces' whereabouts are unknown.

El Patio is distinctive for its cup shape with pretzel-shaped handles. After the original eight colors were introduced, White, Golden Glow, Redwood, Glacial Blue, Mexican Blue, Tahoe Green (later renamed Dark Green Gloss), Flame Orange, and Yellow. El Patio was offered in up to eighteen colors over the time of production from 1934 to 1953 when El Patio was discontinued. Flame Orange was priced separately at a higher price throughout production. The following table lists the colors that were offered with the glaze number that was assigned to the glaze as well as the time period the glazes were used. Gladding, McBean & Co. assigned glaze numbers to all glazes that were produced for their ware. The initials M.P. and then a number designated the glaze. It is unknown at this time what the initials M.P. stand for. Yellow (Gloss) was renamed Bright Yellow in 1948.

El Patio Table Ware. The #20 glacial blue salad or punch bowl is nine quarts and was furnished with either a plain or crimped top. An early piece from the time El Patio was introduced, it was discontinued prior to 1942. The punch bowl is hard to find, so expect it to be in the $150-225 price range.

White	M.P. 1	1934-1947
Glacial Blue/Turquoise	M.P. 2	1934-1950
Yellow (Gloss)	M.P. 3	1934-1947
Dark Green Gloss	M.P. 4	1934-35
Matt Ivory	M.P. 5	1942-1950
Golden Glow	M.P. 11	1934-1947
Redwood	M.P. 12	1934-1947
Flame Orange	M.P. 13	1939-1947
Mexican Blue	M.P. 14	1934-1947
Coral Satin	M.P. 15	1942-1950
Apple Green	M.P. 18	1939-1942
Maroon	M.P. 19	1948-1950
Coral Gloss	M.P. 21	1942-1950
Turquoise Satin	M.P. 27	1942-50
Yellow (Gloss)	M.P. 33	1939-1948
Chartreuse (Satin)	M.P. 45	1942-50
Satin Gray	M.P. 76	1948-1950
Bright Green	M.P. 78	1948-1950
Grape	M.P. 89	1948-1950

In the first sales catalog in July 1934, El Patio was offered in the following shapes. The number preceding the item is the stock number. Stock numbers were assigned to all shapes produced by Gladding, McBean & Co.

1	Cereal Dish
2	Bread & Butter Plate (6.5")
3	Wine Cup (4 ounces)
4	Beer Mug, Full Pint size
5	Soup Bowl
6	Cream Pitcher
7	Luncheon or Salad Plate (8.5")
8	Handled Baking Dish
8A	Lid for Handled Baking Dish
9	Sugar Bowl
10	Cup & Saucer
11	Coffee Jug, Earthenware Handle (38 oz.)
11a	Stopper for all Jugs
12	Spaghetti or Enchilada Dish
13	Large Dinner Plate (10.5")
14	Vegetable Dish
15	Tall Pitcher (3 quart)
16	Serving Plate (12.5")
17	Coffee Jug, Hardwood Handle
	a " " Iron Frame
	b " " Chrome Plated Frame
	c " " Aluminum Frame
	d " " Brass Frame
	e " " Alone for Replacing
18	Lidded Baking Dish (2.5 quart)
19	Salad Bowl
20	Punch or Large Salad Bowl (9 quarts)
21	Buffet Supper Plate (17" Diameter)
22	Water Tumbler
23	Coaster for Water Tumbler
24	Salad Bowl
25	Teapot (38 oz.) [Six-cup]
26	Tea Tile
27	Oatmeal Dish
28	Oval Platter (10" x 13")
29	Hors d'oeuvre Dish (3 compartments)
30	Sherbet or Cocktail Dish
31	Lidded Cookie Jar (Suggested the jar & lid to be sold in different colors)
32	Cup with Iron Frame
	a Cup with Nickel Frame
	b Set of six cups with Iron Frames, Jug with Iron Frame, and Iron and Glass Tray with pottery of any combination of colors except flame)
	c Set of six cups with Nickel Frame, Jug with Aluminum Frame, and Tray of Duraluminum in any colors except Flame)
	e Cup only
33	Teapot (6-cups)
34	Beer Stein
35	After Dinner Cup and Saucer [note: pretzel handled]
36	14" Sandwich Platter
37	Small Dinner Plate (9.5")
38	Lidded Baking Dish (1.5 quart)
39	Bouillon Cup

El Patio Table Ware. The #22 golden glow bud vase, $38-45, was sold also as a drinking tumbler and was also in the Tropico line. The #3 small vase (not pictured) was sold as a wine cup, $22-36 and is the same shape. Next to the #22 bud vase is the #133 candlestick in golden glow, $22-38 pair.

After 1934 and until 1953, Gladding, McBean & Co. added the following shapes over the years, while discontinuing others. When an item number was reused, the item was discontinued that first was assigned that number.

12	Buffet Service Cup and Saucer [note: number reused]
12	Jumbo Cup & Saucer [note: number reused]
12a	Jumbo Saucer
16	Small Bowl
21	Butter Dish with Lid [note: number reused]
31	Ice Lipped Pitcher, 2.5 quart [note: number reused]
34	Gravy or Sauce Boat [note: number reused]
34	Gravy Boat, Fast Stand [original #34 & #34a discontinued]
34a	Relish or bottom for Gravy or Sauce Boat #34
36	Round Platter or Chop Plate (16") [note: number reused]
39	Large Tumbler for Iced Tea, etc. [note: number reused]
40	Marmalade Jar & Lid
41	Round Platter or Chop Plate (17")
42	Small Vegetable Dish
43	Short Tumbler
51	Bowl Footed
57	Oval Platter (12")
58	Oval Platter (14")
61	Syrup or Milk Jug, Covered
62	Milk Jug, Covered
63	Cocktail Pitcher
64	Chili Bowl
65	Round Platter or Chop Plate (14")
67	Hot Water Pot
68	Egg Cup
69	Toast Cover
70	Salt & Pepper per pair
72	Cigarette Box with Lid
75	Coaster (same shape as the Rancho coaster)
77	Oval Vegetable Dish
79	Vegetable Round, 1.5 quart or Salad Bowl
84	Monk Toby Jug
88	Dessert Plate
90	Large Dinner Plate (10.5") [note: redesigned Large Dinner Plate #13]
91	Round Ashtray
96	Candlestick
97	Miniature Coffee Jug (16 oz.) with Stopper
98	Artichoke Plate
99	Pitcher, Ball Shaped
100	Individual Ashtray, Divided
133	Candlestick
140	Cigarette Box & Lid
250	Tab Handled Soup, can use #8A Lid
251	#261 with 3, 4, or 5 removable compartments
254	Large Creamer [shaped like #25 & #256 Teapot, no lid]
255	Large Sugar with Lid [companion to #254 creamer]
256	Individual Teapot (2-cup)
257	Small Individual Creamer [open, no lid]
258	After Dinner Coffee Pot
259	After Dinner Cup and Saucer [new style]
261	Serving Dish 12" (used as the tray for the #251)
264	Cream Soup Bowl with two handles and Saucer
265	Buffet Supper Tray 14", 4 trays & round container, removable
267	Baker & Lid 9"
267a	Liners for Baker
270	Small Individual Sugar [open, no lid made]
	Snack Plate, Round with cup well

El Patio Table Ware. The pitchers of El Patio. Left to right: Franciscan Monk Toby pitcher #84 in coral, $75-85; glacial blue #31 water pitcher, 2.5 quart, $75-95; flame orange, 1 quart pitcher #60, $55-65; celestial white #15 beverage pitcher 3.5 quart, $75-95; and the coral #63 cocktail pitcher 1.5 quart, $55-75.

Opposite page: El Patio Table Ware. To the left is the very rare black #17A coffee jug with metal stand with stopper 11A, $155-175 (with lid), $75-95 (without lid). Not all coffee jugs were ordered with lids. The lids had to be ordered separately, which is why so many do not have lids. In the background is the #36 medium chop plate in eggplant, $45-55. Eggplant is one of the most desirable and yet hard to find colors in El Patio. Center is the #22 bud vase and/or drinking cup in an unknown glaze in blue, $38-45. This matches the handled coffee jug in the same glaze and perhaps was sold as a special set. Front is a pair of very scarce ruby #70 salt & pepper from the Ruby Art Ware line, $75-85 and to the right is a very hard to find dark green #62 guernsey jug, lidded $65-75.

By December 15, 1948, Gladding, McBean & Co. discontinued almost all of the shapes except for standard pieces used for a short set. By 1953, El Patio was discontinued entirely.

El Patio Table Ware. The coffee jug in El Patio came in various shapes. Left to right: Celestial white #17 coffee jug with wood handle, $45-75. The coffee jug was also sold handless as the #17E, $45-55. The lid to the coffee jug is #11A, $18-22 and was sold as the stopper to all of the jugs. Next to it is the #11 coffee jug with earthen ware handle, $55-85 (with lid), $45-55 (without li in a very unusual glaze. This glaze can also be found on the #22 bud vase and/or drinking cup and may have been ordered with the coffee jug a set with 4 tumblers from Barker Brothers or another department store or specialty shop. The far right is the #17A coffee jug with metal frame again in an unusual glaze of white and violet, $6 75 (with lid), $45-55 (without lid). In front is the #11A stopper in Mexican blue, $18-22. These are all uncommon glazes on El Patio.

El Patio Table Ware. The coffee cups of El Patio. The pretzel handle was a design by Mary Grant and was to give El Patio its own look. Left to right: #12 jumbo cup and saucer in maroon, $45-65 (with saucer), $35-38 (cup only) and was advertised as being excellent for buffet service. Next to it is the #259 after dinner cup and saucer in yellow, $26-32. The golden glow #252 teacup & saucer is a very hard to find shape, $28-32. Note that the #259 and #252 do not have pretzel handles. In glacial blue is the #35 after dinner cup and saucer in which the cup has a pretzel handle, $26-32. To the far right is the #10 cup and #10a saucer with the pretzel handle, $12-15. Not pictured is the #253 coffee cup and saucer (price not yet determined). The cup is slightly taller than the #252 cup.

El Patio Table Ware. Left to right: The number unknown divided relish chop plate in light yellow is usually found in golden glow, so other colors are harder to find, $45-55 (golden glow or redwood), $55-65 (all other colors). Next to the relish is the #98 artichoke plate in coral, $45-48. The middle well was for the artichoke, the large well for the left over leaves after eating, and the small well for the butter.

El Patio Table Ware. Left to right: In flame orange is the #34 gravy, which was discontinued prior to 1942, $28-32. The flame orange glaze in El Patio was a premium glaze that was charged at 10% more than any other glaze. In the background is the #57 small platter in satin ivory, $28-38. In front of the platter is the #34A oval saucer for the gravy boat in glacial blue, $16-22. In coral satin is the #34B gravy with fast stand, $26-32. This was the gravy boat that replaced the #34 and #34A gravy and oval saucer after 1942.

El Patio Table Ware. Left to right: #20 salad or punch bowl, 9 quarts in apple green, $150-225. In glacial blue is a #71 flower bowl from the Tropico line. Note the punch bowl is taller with straighter sides and should not to be confused with the #71 flower bowl, $95-125. The Tropico line was made to coordinate with El Patio and to compliment it with vases and bowls.

El Patio Table Ware. Left is the #77 oval vegetable in apple green, $22-28, in the early style and to the right is the #77 oval vegetable in coral restyled, $22-28. In the center is the #5 soup bowl in glacial blue, $16-22. The #5 soup bowl was restyled in 1939. The tab handles were replaced with vertical stepped handles.

El Patio Table Ware. Left to right: The #99 water jug, ball shape in flame orange, $45-65; the #31 water pitcher 2.5 quart in glacial blue, $75-95; and the #63 cocktail pitcher in coral, $55-75. In 1942, all of the other pitchers were discontinued and these three pitchers became the only ones offered in stock, with the #63 cocktail pitcher being discontinued prior to 1948.

El Patio Table Ware. The Franciscan Monk Toby Jugs #84. Left to right: bright yellow, coral, glacial blue, and maroon. $125-165 each.

El Patio Table Ware. Left to right: Gray satin #70 salt & pepper, $18-22; Mexican blue #68 eggcup, $28-32; light yellow #30 sherbet, $16-22; flame orange #70 salt & pepper, $18-22; and in front is the #264 cream soup and saucer in apple green, $26-32. The #68 eggcup was discontinued prior to 1939.

El Patio Table Ware. Left to right: #258 after dinner coffee pot in apple green, $75-125; #25 teapot, 6-cup in bright yellow, $65-85, sitting on the #26 tea tile in golden glow, $18-22; and the #33 teapot, 6-cups in Mexican blue, $125-145. The #258 after dinner coffee pot and the #33 teapot was discontinued prior to 1942.

El Patio Table Ware. Front: #270 small individual sugar, $22-28 and #257 small creamer, $28-32, in apple green. Back: #9 sugar bowl with lid, $22-28 and #6 creamer in Mexican Blue, $16-22. Note the #9 and #6 have pretzel handles and the sugar was sold with the lid. A lid was never manufactured for the #270 small individual sugar.

El Patio Table Ware. Left to right: #250 soup with #8A lid in golden glow, $22-32 (with lid), $14-22 (without lid); #18 large casserole 2.5 quart in glacial blue, $85-125; and the #38 small casserole 1.5 quart in redwood, $55-85. The #250 soup replaced the #5 soup prior to 1939.

El Patio Table Ware. #8 baking dish in glacial blue with #8a lid, $22-28 with lid, $12-18 without lid. The baking dish could be ordered without lids. The #8 baking dish was also in the specials line and was sold to the Sperry Flour Company as a premium ware.

El Patio Table Ware. Left to right: #62 coral Guernsey jug, lidded 1 pint, $55-75 and #62 Guernsey jug lidded in dark green, $65-75. When you twist the lid, it has a "V" shaped slot cut into the lid to let the liquid out.

Rare colors in El Patio Table Ware. Left to right: Celestial white #247 small cream, $38-55; #270 small individual sugar, $38-45, for breakfast tray service; unusual undocumented duo-tone brown glaze exterior with celestial white interior #67 hot water pot or syrup jug base with a domed lid (not common for this piece), $85-125; #35 after dinner cup and saucer in glacial blue and celestial white was a duotone combination offered in the El Patio line and also in the El Patio Nuevo line, $45, #97 celestial white miniature coffee jug, 16 oz. with stopper, $65-85; and #259 after dinner cup and saucer in ruby, $75, which is in the Ruby Art Ware line as well as in El Patio. Rare colors in El Patio are celestial white, ruby, clear glaze (very rare), a dark green, and black.

El Patio Table Ware. Left to right: #39 large tumblers for ice tea: flame orange, apple green, glacial blue, and golden glow, $28-32 each. Plates: #2 plate, bread & butter, 6.5" in apple green, $6-8; #4 plate, desert, 7.5" in Mexican blue, $9-14; #88 plate, luncheon or salad, 8.5" in bright yellow, $10-14; #7 salad plate, 8.5" in coral satin discontinued in 1939 and replaced by #88, $10-14; #37 small dinner, 9.5" in maroon (also known as the lunch plate by collectors), $12-16; and #13 plate, large dinner, 10.5" discontinued in 1939 and replaced with #90 plate new style dinner, $18-26 (hard to find). The sizes varied from those produced prior to 1939 and those produced after. Also, #2, #7, #37, and #13 were made in regular weight for the home and also in extra heavy weight with rolled rims for tea room or restaurant use. Between restyling and different rims, it is easy to understand how difficult it is to match plates.

El Patio Table Ware. Left to right: number unknown small bowl in golden glow, $12-16; #16 Mexican blue cereal bowl discontinued prior to 1939, $16-18; #16 flame orange cereal bowl, $12-16; #27 cereal dish in glacial blue, $12-14; and #1 fruit dish in redwood, $6-8.

El Patio Table Ware. Back left is the #24 salad bowl low style in apple green, $38-48. To the front is the #14 round vegetable dish in apple green, $22-26 and to the right is the #79 salad bowl, 1 quart in apple green, $22-26.

El Patio Table Ware. Chop plates: #261 all purpose serving dish, 12" in apple green, $26-32; #36 sandwich plate coupe shape, 14" in bright yellow, $26-32; and #41 torte or large sandwich, 16" in celestial white, $65 (celestial white and other rare colors), $45-55 (other colors). Not pictured is the #21 buffet supper platter, 17.5", $55-65. At the sides are the #96 candlesticks in Mexican blue, $38-45 pair and in front is an apple green #29 relish dish with handle, $28-32.

El Patio Table Ware. Coffee set #32B consisting of iron and glass tray, six cup and frames and coffee jug and frame in flame orange. This set was sold together as a set, $145-165. The #32 cup with metal handle was also furnished with a wooden handle and sold separately, $12-18 each.

El Patio Table Ware. Left to right: The one quart #60 pitcher in flame orange, $55-65, with the #59 one pint pitcher in redwood, $45-55.

El Patio Table Ware. #251 glacial blue buffet supper tray with #241 removable trays in bright yellow, flame orange, and celestial white. The value is $85-135 for a complete set with compartments, $38-42 for the tray, and $12-16 for the compartments. The #265 buffet supper tray has a center round dish that is removable with 4 trays.

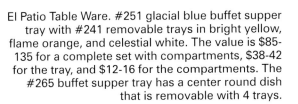

El Patio Table Ware. The #69 toast cover in light yellow, $75-85, on the #4 salad plate, 7.5" in light yellow, $9-14.

Tropico Garden Pottery

The Tropico Garden Pottery line was introduced in April of 1934. In the July 1st, 1934 Franciscan Pottery Price List and General Sales Instructions, "Numbers bearing the suffix (T) are made from terra cotta body. Otherwise all pottery is made from Malinite." The following items were offered.

Available in Regular Colors and Special Colors.

44	4" Flare Top Flower Pot
44a	4" Pot and Saucer
45	5" Flare Top Flower Pot
45a	5" Pot and Saucer
46	6" Flare Top Flower Pot
46a	6" Pot and Saucer
47	7" Flare Top Flower Pot
47a	7" Pot and Saucer
48	8" Flare Top Flower Pot
48a	8" Pot and Saucer
50	10" Flare Top Flower Pot
50a	10" Pot and Saucer

Regular Colors – Light Blue, Yellow, White, Green, Brown, Matt Green, Mexican Blue.
Special Colors – Flame Orange, Mottled Pink, Mottled Turquoise.

51	Chinese Flower Bowl (9.5") Colors: Turquoise, White, Matt Green, Verde Green, Yellow, Golden Glow, Flame Orange.
52	Flower Bowl (Old #105) Same colors #51
53	Flower Bowl (Old #55) Same colors #51
54-T	Large Vase (Old #303) Terra cotta Colors
55-T	Large Vase (Old #305) Terra cotta Colors
56-T	Large Vase (Old #301) Terra cotta Colors
57	Small Frog, Gloss or Matt Green, with or without hole in mouth for fountain
58	Large Frog, New Shape (like above)
59	Sitting Girl Figure (Old #94)
60-T	Sitting Bow with Fish (Old #1107)
61-T	Standing Boy with Fish (Old #1108)
62	Small Basket, Hand Made (Old #66)
63	Large Basket, Hand Made (Old #53)
64-T	Porch Jardinière or Palm Pot (Old #225) 12", 14", 16", or 18"
65-T	Umbrella Stand or Vase (Old #11)
66-T	Large Flaring Vase (Old #14)
67-T	Small Oil Jar (21") (Old #45A)
68-T	Medium Oil Jar (26") (Old #45)
69-T	Large Oil Jar (33") (Old #88)
70-T	Pedestal 27" high (Old #4)
70A-T	Bird Bath to fit Pedestal #70

Regular Colors & Flame Orange when indicated by an asterisk *

71	Flower Bowl (same colors #51)
72-T	Sand Jar (Old #143)
73-T	Sand Jar (Old #126)
74	4" Roll Top Flower Pot *
74a	4" Pot and Saucer *
76	6" Roll Top Flower Pot *
76a	6" Pot and Saucer *
78	8" Roll Top Flower Pot *
78a	8" Pot and Saucer *
80	10" Roll Top Flower Pot *
80a	10" Pot and Saucer *
81	Opium Bowl, any color but Flame (Old #18)
81a	Base for Opium Bowl (Old #21)
82-T	Saucer, For Bird Bath or Large Pots, (Old #240) 16", 20", or 27"
83	Bowl, any color except Flame, 8.5" (Old #174) or 11" (Old #173)
84-T	Boy on Turtle (Old #145)
85	Pet Feeding Dish
86-T	Bird Bath and Pedestal (Old #1098)
87-T	Porch Jardinière (Old #132)
88-T	Jardinière, two sizes (Old #167), 10" Wide (Old #168)

Plain Color Only & Flame Orange when indicated by an asterisk *

89	Grecian Vase, Handled (6")*
90-T	Sand Jar, Deep Type (Old #410-G)
90-A-T	Sand Jar, Shallow Type (Old #410-G)
91	Ash Tray, any listed color *
92	Jardinière, Chinese Bulge Shape, any color *
93	Flower Vase (9.5" Tall) for Florist Trade *
94	Flower Bowl, Square design (similar to #120 Cielito)

In the 1935 catalog, Tangerine would be added to the colors offered instead of Flame Orange. Also, all terra cotta garden ware was separated into a catalog of its own, no longer being a part of the Franciscan Pottery line.

On December 22, 1936, Frederic J. Grant sent this memorandum to Atholl McBean,

It is not my plan to discontinue Tropico Ware but to separate it in the mind of the trade from Franciscan. Next year it will have a separate price sheet based on net prices with no guaranteed list and no exclusive accounts.

Looking ahead, it is my thought to make flowerpots and the cheaper florist items in a cheap stoneware body instead of the expensive Malinite. I had in mind developing a little unit at Lincoln along with the birdbaths and garden ware. With a cheaper body we can compete successfully with the stoneware manufacturers and at the same time keep a small line of better grade flowerpots in Malinite. I have talked this over several times with Mr. Ortman, who seemed to feel we had plenty of space at Lincoln. I have the map available to handle the department and it is only a question of getting the necessary equipment and gets [allows] a little free time to get the department established. — Frederic J. Grant

On December 2, 1937, in a memorandum sent from F. B. Ortman to Mr. Smith, Mr. Johansen, Mr. Potter, Mr. Grant, Mr. Daly, and Mr. Dunas, he stated,

After a discussion of the subject in San Francisco last week, followed by a further discussion and analysis of figures in this office, it has been decided that the manufacture of garden pottery at Lincoln for stock will be discontinued . . . Mr. Grant will price this material as well as that now in stock at Glendale, at close-out prices and will endeavor to liquidate the entire stock as far as possible during the Spring and Summer months of next year.

Beginning January first orders will be accepted for garden pottery of Lincoln manufacture, that is, hand pressed in plaster molds, by the terra cotta department at prices indicated in the catalog and will be handled in each instance on a made-to-order basis as a terra cotta order and a part of the sales of the terra cotta department . . . Mr. Grant will arrange to retain certain shapes and colors which can be used as samples and which therefore must not be sold from stock.

Henceforth, terra cotta garden pottery manufactured at the Lincoln plant was slowly phased out. This ended a tradition for many years, until later in the 1990s when terra cotta garden pottery was reintroduced by the Pacific Coast Building Product's Gladding McBean division in Lincoln, California.

Tropico Garden Ware – Flower Pots. #44 flower pot, 4", $28, with #44a saucer, $22, in flame orange. In the Tropico Art Ware line is the #55 medium wall pot in glacial blue, $65-75. Not pictured are two other sizes of wall pots, #54 small wall pot and #56 large wall pot. Both are in the same price range.

Tropico Garden Ware was discontinued in 1937.

Tropico Garden Ware – Flower Pots. Flowerpots #44 apple green, 4", $28; #45 yellow matt, 5", $28; #46 white, 6", $30; #47 glacial blue, 7", $32; #48 glacial blue, 8", $35; and #50 yellow gloss, 10", $45. Note: these are the only sizes of flowerpots offered in the Tropico Ware line. Not pictured: #80 flowerpot with rolled edge. All flowerpots could be purchased with saucers #44a-#50a separately.

Tropico Garden Ware. Flowerpot saucer #50a for flower pot 10" #50 or #80 in glacial blue. $45-65.

Tropico Art Ware. This is the #57 small frog, $125-150, in glacial blue. There are two sizes with the #58 large frog not shown, $150-175. These shapes were also in the Tropico Garden Ware line; however, instead of being made in Malinite, they were semi-porcelain.

Tropico Art Ware. The #286 azalea pot in celestial white, $45-55 and the #284 cactus pot in celestial white, $28-35. There were two sizes of the azalea pot, not pictured is the #285, which is slightly shorter, $45-55. There were also two sizes of the cactus pot, not pictured is the smaller #283, $12-18.

Tropico Art Ware. Left to right: #293 florist stock vase, 12", $145-225 and #93 utility flower vase, $45-65.

Tropico Art Ware. Left to right: #51 satin ivory flower bowl Chinese design, 9.5", $45-55; #92 apple green jardinière, $38-45; #93 satin ivory utility flower vase, $45-65; #89 yellow gloss handled vase Grecian, $45-55; and in front #81, a stand for opium bowl in matt black, $75-85.

Tropico Art Ware. Left to right: #288 white jardinière, $35-38; #289 white jardinière, $35-38.

Tropico Art Ware. Left to right: #291 glacial blue jardinière, $45-48; #288 white jardinière, $35-38; #289 white jardinière, $35-38; and #290 glacier blue jardinière, $38-45.

Tropico Art Ware. Left to right: #292 satin ivory jardinière, $36-38; #294 apache orange bulb vase, $35-38; #292 yellow gloss jardinière, $36-38; and #294 glacial blue bulb vase, $35-38.

Ruffled bowl. The exact line or shape number is not known however– it may be in either the Tropico or El Patio line.

Cielito Ware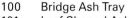

In the July 1st, 1934 Franciscan Pottery Price List and General Sales Instructions, Cielito Ware was described as an, "Entire line modeled along pure Chinese lines. Glazed in a brilliant Turquoise Blue emphasized by clear white lining."

The following were the first shapes introduced in the line.

Cielito Art Ware in the rare ruby glaze. This is the #116 bottle shape vase, 9.5", $225-245. All shapes in ruby are a higher value than those in the standard glazes. In 1935, color combinations included glacial blue lined with white, matt ivory lined with glacial blue, Chinese yellow lined with white, and ruby lined with celestial white.

100	Bridge Ash Tray
101	Leaf Shaped Ash Tray
102	Vase, Beaker Shape
103	Vase, Inverted Pear Shape
104	Vase, Ball Shape
105	Vase, Bottle Shape
106	Candlestick
107	Vase, Wide Mouthed Beaker
108	Bowl, Petal Shaped, Small
109	Handled Vase
110	Vase
111	Lidded Box
112	Bowl, Deep Shape
113	Vase, Wide Mouthed Beaker
114	Vase, Flare Top Beaker
115	Vase, Long Neck Pear Shape
116	Vase, Bottle Shape
117	Vase, Beaker Shape
118	Base, Cylindrical
119	Footed Compote
120	Square Bowl
121	Bowl, Petal Shape, Large
122	Vase, Ball Shape
123	Vase, Ball Shape with Neck and Foot
124	Opium Bowl with Metal Stand Complete Bowl Alone
125	Flower Bowl with Metal Stand
126	Flower Bowl, Oval
130	Cactus Bowl
131	Low Bowl
132	Vase, Round
133	Candlestick
134	Candlestick, matches #126
135	Vase, Low
136	Vase, Slender Neck
137	Vase, Round
138	Vase, Round, Low
139	Vase, Tall Flaring Top
140	Cigarette Box & Lid

Cielito could be ordered in the following solid glazes as well as solid ruby.
M.P. 1 White Gloss
M.P. 2 Turquoise or Glacial Blue
M.P. 3 Yellow
M.P. 4 Dark Green Gloss
M.P. 5 Satin Ivory Matt
M.P. 6 Celestial White
M.P. 7 Transparent Gloss
M.P. 8 Pastel Green Matt
M.P. 9 Pastel Blue Matt
M.P. 10 Dark Green Matt
M.P. 11 Golden Glow
M.P. 12 Redwood
M.P. 13 Flame Orange
M.P. 14 Mexican Blue
M.P. 16 Chinese Yellow
M.P. 18 Apple Green

Cielito Ware #115 Vase, Chinese yellow lined with white, $145-155.

In 1935, Cielito Ware was offered in a number of different color and texture combinations including Ruby. Besides Ruby, Cielito Ware was offered in Flambé and Ox-blood. Each piece was described in the catalog of 1935 as a "ceramic gem." Ruby would be discontinued in 1936. One of the most popular color combinations was Chinese Yellow and White. Note special orders could be made and you will find Cielito Ware in a variety of colors. The Cielito Ware line would be discontinued in 1937. Later on, these shapes would be the basis on which Gladding, McBean & Co. would apply many different glaze treatments, and market them as different lines. The Ox-Blood and Angeleno Ware lines used some of the same shapes as the Cielito Ware line.

Cielito Ware, Chinese yellow lined with white. Left to right: #105 bottle shape vase, 6", $75-95; vase with handles also used as a lamp base, $145-245; #131 low bowl shaped vase, $45; and #106 candlesticks, $145-225 pair.

Cielito Ware #124 opium bowl with detachable stand in glacial blue, $85-125, for the bowl and $125-145 for the extremely rare and delicate base. The opium bowl was sold as "excellent for floral arrangement. Furnished with metal stand or black matt pottery base."

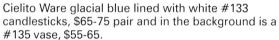

Cielito Ware glacial blue lined with white. Left to right: #103 vase (or small lamp base), $65-85; #138 low vase, $75-85.

Cielito Ware glacial blue lined with white #133 candlesticks, $65-75 pair and in the background is a #135 vase, $55-65.

Cielito Ware glacial blue lined with white. Left to right: #131 low bowl shaped vase, $45; #116 bottle shape vase, 9.5", $125-145; #107 vase, $45-65; and #136 vase, $45-65.

Cielito Ware glacial blue lined with white. #122 ball shape vase 8.25" x 9.5". $185-245.

Cielito Ware glacial blue lined with white. Left to right: #113 vase, $125-145; #118 vase, $125-145; and #102 vase, $75-95.

Cielito Ware glacial blue lined with white. Left to right: # 137 vase, $45-75; #112 wide mouth vase, $65-95; and #132 round vase, 4.5", $55-75.

Cielito Ware glacial blue interior and satin ivory exterior: #108 bowl petal shape, 8.5" diameter, $75-85.

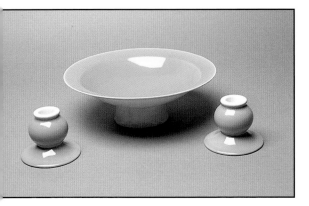

Cielito Ware #133 glacial blue lined with white candlesticks, $65-75 pair, with #119 satin ivory lined with glacial blue footed comport, $85-125.

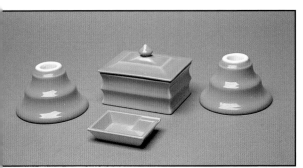

Cielito Ware glacial blue lined with white. Left to right: # 134 glacial blue lined with white candlesticks, $85-125 pair; # 140 covered cigarette or candy box, $95-145; with #100 satin ivory lined with glacial blue ashtray, $32-38.

Coronado Ware

From the July 1st, 1934 Franciscan Pottery Price List and General Sales Instructions: "Extremely interesting shapes glazed in three satin textured colors: Ivory, Pastel Green and Pastel Blue. The highest quality possible in pottery."

150	Ball Shaped Vase (4.5" x 3")
151	Plain Wide Mouthed Vase (6.5")
152	Footed Vase (5.5")
153	Low Candlestick (4")
154	Plain Wide Mouthed Vase (9.5")
155	Lancastrian Vase (5" x 8")
156	Wide Mouth Vase with Swirl Base (7.5")
157	Ball Vase, Unique Design (5.5")
158	Cornucopia with foot (6.75")
159	Lidded Box, with foot (4.5")
160	Large Bulge Vase (9")
161	Wide Mouth Vase with Swirl Base (10.5")
163	Low Bowl (13" wide)
164	Deep Bowl (11.5" wide)
165	Flat Bowl with Inside Design (13")
166	Comport with Swirl Foot (5" x 10.25")
167	Vase, Diablo Shape (10")
168	Bowl 9"
169	Low Oval Flower Bowl 14"
170	Compote 1-3/8"
171	Bud Vase 6-1/8"
172	Low Bowl 2-5/8"
173	Vase 5.5"
174	Vase, Footed 6"
175	Vase, Footed 6-5/8"
176	Vase 5-5/8"
198	Ashtray, Individual
200	Chop Plate for Flowers
214	Relish Dish 9.5"
222	Cigarette Box

Coronado Ware. Left to right: #161 matt green vase, 10", $145-225, in rare colors and $125-145 in common colors and #156 ivory satin vase, 7.5", $85-95.

In the 1935 picture catalog, Coronado Ware was described as "an art line using a swirl adapted from the Spanish of the early Mission period, and thus typically Californian." The colors too changed their names to Matt Ivory, Matt Green, and Matt Blue, although they were the same colors as offered in 1934. Coronado Ware was discontinued in 1942.

Special orders would be accepted and you will find Coronado Ware in a deep yellow and in a matt gray. It is not known whether these colors were ever included in the catalogs as standard colors offered.

Coronado Ware in satin ivory. Left to right: #166 footed comport, 5" x 10.25" hard to find, $225-295 and #170 compote or candy dish footed, 7.5" x 3.5", $45-65.

Coronado Ware. Rare blue #165 flat bowl or deep plate, 13", $125-145 in rare colors and $85-125 in common colors, displayed with in rare blue #155 Lancastrian style vase, 5" x 8" inside, $125-145 in rare colors and $85-95 in common colors.

Coronado Ware. Left to right: #176 coral satin bud vase, $85; #157 ivory satin vase unique design, 5.5", $85-95; #153 turquoise gloss candlestick, $35-45; and #172 ivory satin rose bowl, $45-65.

Coronado Ware in ivory satin. Left to right: #152 footed vase, 5.5", $55-65; #175 vase, $85; and #175 bud vase, $85.

Coronado Ware. Left to right: #167 rare yellow gloss vase, 10", $145-165 in rare colors and $125-145 in common colors; #171 ivory satin hourglass bud vase, $85; #160 ivory satin vase, 9", $145; and #173 ivory satin vase, $55-75.

Coronado Ware. Left to right: #167 rare yellow gloss vase, 10", $145-165 in rare colors and $125-145 in common colors; #155 rare color Lancastrian style vase, 5" x 8", $125-145 in rare colors, $85-95 in common colors; #161 matt green vase, 10", $145-225; and #154 yellow gloss vase, 9.5", $125-165.

#157 gray satin vase, unique design, 5.5" in a very rare color for Coronado Ware, $155-175.

Coronado Ware. Back left to right: #151 ivory satin vase, 6.5", $55-65; #154 matt blue vase, 9.5", $125; and #158 ivory satin footed cornucopia, 6.75", $55-75. Front: Cigarette box ivory satin (# 222), $145-165.

Coronado Ware. Left to right: Coral satin #163 low bowl, 13" diameter, $85 with #164 matt blue deep bowl, 11.5" diameter, $85, inside; #169 matt green oval bowl, 9" x 13", $85; and #168 ivory satin low bowl, 9", $45-55 with a #155 rare blue Lancastrian style vase, 5" x 8", $125-145 rare colors and $85-95 common colors, inside.

Coronado Ware. Rare #159 lidded box, 4.5" in ivory satin, $225.

97

Chapter 5

First Picture Catalogue Published on "Franciscan Pottery" 1935

On April 15, 1935, Gladding, McBean & Co. published their first picture catalog on Franciscan Pottery. Measuring 4.25" x 7", it contained 23 pages. New lines introduced were El Patio Nuevo, Cocinero Ware, and Coronado Table Ware. El Patio Nuevo was offered in Turquoise and White; Chinese Yellow and White; Apple Green and White. The Cocinero cooking ware line listed 25 pieces in four colors. The new line of Ruby Art Ware was introduced late in 1935 and consisted of vases and an after dinner coffee service.

The entire Franciscan Pottery line went on sale to the public in the Glendale plant's pottery yard, which had formerly only sold Lincoln garden pottery. Mostly first grade was sold, but some seconds were sold at reduced prices.

El Patio Nuevo

The plates in El Patio Nuevo were offered with white wells and colored rims and backs "offering a new glaze technique." Three different color combinations were offered.

Combination M – Turquoise (M.P. 2) and White (M.P. 1)

Combination Y – Chinese Yellow (M.P. 16) and White (M.P. 1)

Combination G – Apple Green (M.P. 18) and White (M.P. 1)

The interior of the hollow pieces would be white, while the exteriors would be the alternate color.

The shapes offered were:

1	Fruit
2	Bread & Butter Plate
7	Luncheon Plate
13	Large Dinner Plate
24	Salad Bowl, 3 quart
25	Teapot (about 6 cups)
26	Tea Tile
27	Cereal Bowl
36	Chop Plate 14"
41	Sandwich Platter 16"
250	Onion Soup (Sold with or without lid)
251	Removable Compartments for Trays (For hors d'oeuvres, etc.)
252	Tea Cup and Saucer
253	Coffee Cup and Saucer
254	Large Creamer
255	Sugar with Lid
256	Small Teapot (2 cups)
257	Small Creamer
258	After Dinner Coffee Pot
259	After Dinner Cup and Saucer
260	Sherbet, Cocktail, or Egg Cup
261	Serving Dish 12"
262	Ash Tray
263	Ash Tray, Individual
264	Cream Soup and Sacuer
265	Buffet Supper Tray (These Supper Trays come in two sizes)
266	Casserole 7"
267	Casserole 9"
267A	Removable Compartments for 9" Casserole
268	Liqueur Jug
269	Vegetable Dish
270	Small Individual Sugar (For breakfast tray service)
	Snack Plate with Cup Well

El Patio Nuevo was discontinued in 1936. El Patio Nuevo is a very hard to find pattern today.

El Patio Nuevo in Chinese yellow and white. Number unknown, round snack plate with cup well, $32-45; #252 cup, $22; number unknown covered jug, $65-85; small individual sugar, $38-45; and small creamer, $38-45.

El Patio Nuevo was furnished in the colors of glacial blue (exterior) with a celestial white (interior), as well as the duo-tone combinations of Chinese yellow and celestial white, and apple green and white. Glacial blue #265 buffet supper tray came in two sizes. The larger welled version fits the #251 removable compartments for trays for hors d'oeuvres, mayonnaise, cheese, etc. The #251 trays are in white. The value is $85-135 for a complete set with compartments, $38-42 for the tray, and $12-16 for the compartments.

El Patio Nuevo in Chinese yellow and white. Small creamer, $38-45; small teapot 2 cups, $65-75; #260 sherbet, cocktail, or eggcup, $28-35; and #252 teacup and saucer, $28-36.

Coronado Table Ware

In the 1935 catalog: "the swirl motif of the Coronado decorative pottery has been adapted in a handsome table service line. All the shapes have been handled in a pleasing, formal manner and incorporated in the line are such unusual items as after dinner coffee service, tea service, salad sets and serving dishes.

A very striking ensemble of table service, candlesticks and centerpiece may be arranged using the white matt and turquoise glazes."

Original colors were Matt Ivory (M.P. 5), Matt Green (M.P. 8), and Matt Blue (M.P. 9). The original pieces offered in 1935 were:

180	After Dinner Cup and Saucer
181	Tea Cup and Saucer
182	Bouillon Cup
183	Creamer [note: footed]
184	Sugar [note: footed]
185	Tea Pot [note: footed]
186	Plate, Bread & Butter, 6.5"
187	Plate, Dessert, 7.5"
188	Plate, Salad, 8.5"
189	Plate, Dinner, 9.5"
190	Plate, Large Dinner, 10.5"
191	Crescent Salad Plate
192	Oval Platter, 13" x 10"
193	Fruit Dish
194	Vegetable Dish (#168 in the art ware line is also used for this purpose)
195	Salad Bowl
196	Sherbet or Cocktail
197	After Dinner Coffee Pot
198	Ash Tray

Coronado Table Ware. #197 tall coffee pot in coral introduced in the 1950s, $225-245; #185 restyled teapot in yellow, $55-75; #183 restyled sugar bowl in copper, $55-65, $22-28 other colors; and #184 restyled creamer in maroon, $28-36, $22-28 other colors.

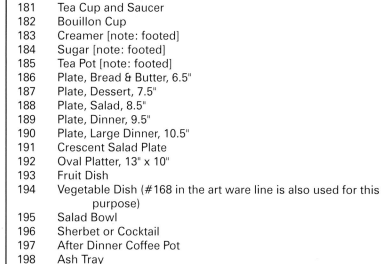

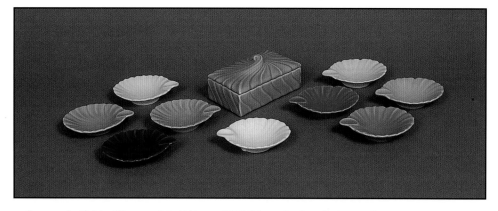

Coronado Table Ware and Art Ware. #222 Cigarette box in turquoise, $145-165. Ashtrays #198: Left to right: in turquoise, maroon, yellow, coral, matt ivory, copper, bright yellow, apple green, and matt blue. Common colors, $16-22, $18-28. for copper, maroon, apple green, or the not pictured chartreuse.

Other colors were offered in addition to the original colors. Satin glazes added were Turquoise (M.P. 27), Yellow (M.P. 43), and Coral (M.P. 15). Matt Green (M.P. 8) and Matt Blue (M.P. 9) were discontinued shortly after they were introduced and prior to 1942. Gloss glazes were added in Turquoise (M.P. 2), Yellow (M.P. 3), Coral (M.P. 21), and in about 1942, Maroon (M.P. 19). Maroon is the most popular of the glazes today.

Soon after introduction, the footed sugar, creamer, and teapot would be discontinued. A restyled sugar, creamer, and teapot were designed, cutting off the foot. The exact reason is unknown as to why this was done, as the footed pieces are extremely desirable now. One reason may be the cost in manufacture as the foot had to be manually applied to the unglazed body of the piece.

After introduction and until Coronado was discontinued in 1954, the following pieces were added:

182A	Cream Soup Saucer [#182 Bouillon renamed Cream Soup]
183	Sugar [restyled]
184	Creamer [restyled]
185	Teapot (6-cup) [restyled]
199	Onion Soup with Lugs
199A	Lid for Onion Soup
200	Large Chop Plate, 14"
201	Casserole with Lid
202	Pitcher
203	Oval Vegetable
204	Oval Platter, Large, 15.25" x 11.5"
205	Gravy Boat, Fast Stand
206	Footed Creamer (Old)
207	Footed Sugar (Old)
208	Footed Teapot (Old)
209	Nut Cup, Footed
210	Salt & Pepper
211	Vegetable
212	Cereal
213	Chop Plate, 12.5"
214	Relish Dish
215	Jam Jar with Lid
216	Tumbler
217	Oval Platter, Small
219	Butter Dish, Covered
220	Jumbo Cup
221	Jumbo Saucer
222	Cigarette Box with Lid
223	Rim Soup
	Crescent Shaped Snack Plate with Cup Well

Coronado Table Ware. #183 original creamer in matt ivory, $32-55; #184 original sugar in matt ivory, $32-55. Same set in turquoise (glacial blue). The footed cream and sugar are very rare and hard to find as they were discontinued soon after being introduced and were restyled.

A restyled coffee server #197 was introduced in the 1950s, and was offered for a very short time. This is very scarce and very desirable today. In 1936, the #400 candlestick, #402 candlestick, #407 & #408 centerpiece set, #412 square bowl, #415 pansy jar rectangular, and #419 large oval bowl from the Capistrano Art Ware line were also offered in the Coronado Table Ware line. For these shapes, see Capistrano Art Ware in Chapter 6.

Coronado Table Ware. #197 after dinner coffee pot in coral, #180 after dinner cup and saucer sets in: Left to right: matt ivory, turquoise, coral, bright yellow, copper, turquoise (satin), maroon, apple green, and light yellow. $28-32 for common colors, $32-45 for maroon, copper, and apple green.

Coronado Table Ware. Three versions of cups and saucers. Left to right: #220 jumbo cup and #221 jumbo saucer in maroon, $55-65 set for common colors, $55-75 set for maroon, copper, apple green; #180 after dinner cup and saucer in apple green, $32-45; and #181 tea cup and saucer in coral, $8-10 common colors.

Coronado Table Ware. #193 fruit dish in maroon, $12-16; #212 cereal in turquoise, $16-18; and #196 sherbet or cocktail in apple green, $18-22.

Coronado Table Ware. #191 crescent salad plate in coral, $45-55 and #223 rim soup in maroon, $32-38.

Coronado Table Ware. Plates: Left to right: #188 salad, 8.5" in copper, $16-18; #189 dinner, 9.5" in maroon, $22-28; #190 large dinner, 10.5" in gray, $22-32; #187 salad plate, 7.5" in bright yellow, $10-15; and #186 bread & butter, 6.5" in apple green, $6-8.

Coronado Table Ware. This is the crescent buffet or snack plate with cup well. The colors pictured are coral, apple green and matt ivory. $55-65. Cup is optional.

102

Coronado Table Ware and Art Ware. Left to right: #159 lidded box, 4.5" in ivory satin, $225 and #215 condiment jar with lid (usually referred to as a jam jar), $65-75.

Coronado Table Ware. Left to right: #182 originally called a bouillon cup, later renamed a cream soup with #182A cream soup saucer in matt ivory, $22-26 for the cup, $18-20 for the saucer; #209 nut cup, footed in coral, $45-55; #216 tumbler in turquoise, $45-65; and #198 ashtray in copper, $18-28.

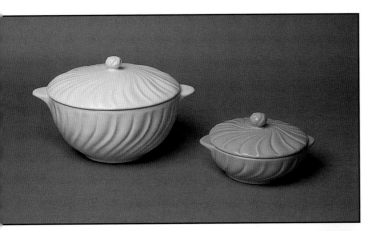

Coronado Table Ware. Left to right: #201 casserole with lid in matt ivory, $75-85 and #199 onion soup with lugs with a #199A lid for onion soup, $38-45 with lid, $16-18 without lid. The lid was purchased separately, so many lug soups were sold without a lid.

Coronado Table Ware. Oval Platters: Left to right: #204 large oval platter, 15.25" x 11.5" in matt ivory, $38-45; #192 oval platter, 13" x 10" in maroon, $36-38; and #217 small oval platter in turquoise, $28-38.

Coronado Table Ware. Chop plates: Left to right: #200 large chop plate, 14" in turquoise (satin), $45-55 and #213 chop plate, 12.5" in yellow, $22-32.

Coronado Table Ware. #202 pitcher in coral matt, $45-65; #214 relish dish, $22-26 in yellow; and #205 gravy boat with fast stand, $38-55 in unusual colors and $28-36 in common colors.

Coronado Table Ware. #210 salt & pepper in light yellow, $22-26 and #219 butter dish covered in coral matt, $36-45.

Coronado Table Ware. #203 oval vegetable in coral matt, $28-36 and #211 vegetable in matt ivory, $36-38.

Unusual pieces in Coronado Table Ware include the restyled salt & pepper set in matt ivory, $55-65 pair. Any items in chartreuse are rare, including this creamer, $55-65. This relish is in the very rare matt blue, $55-75.

Unusual pieces in Coronado Table Ware. Besides the bright yellow, the ruby cup and saucer and Mexican blue after dinner saucer demonstrate different glazes that have been found on Coronado Table Ware. Special orders were made and accepted by Gladding, McBean & Co. and include these pieces. Since an order could be made for an individual set, you may never find a piece in glazes that were not offered to the public. These sets and pieces are one of a kind. Other sets that have been found include a set in transparent gloss — which appear white due to the Malinite body.

Ruby Art Ware, number unknown, covered dish. $225-245.

Ruby Art Ware

The brilliant red of this ware makes it very collectible today. This was a very short line consisting of vases and an after dinner coffee service. All shapes used were from the Cielito Art Ware and El Patio Table Ware lines. Of particular note is that the Ruby glaze could be special ordered and applied onto any shape. Only the pieces listed below belong in the Ruby Art Ware line. Ruby Art Ware consisted of the following pieces. The line was discontinued in 1936.

R-104	Vase Ball Shape
R-105	Vase Bottle Shape
R-114	Vase Beaker Shape
R-115	Vase
R-116	Vase Flask Shape
R-119	Compote Footed
R-122	Vase Large Ball Shape
R-132	Vase
R-133	Candlestick
R-135	Vase Low Bottle Shape
R-136	Vase Slender Neck
R-137	Vase
24	Flower Bowl (or serving bowl)
25	Tea Pot
70	Salt & Pepper
254	Creamer
255	Sugar & Lid
258	After Dinner Coffee & Lid
259	After Dinner Cup & Saucer
352	Fish Ash Tray

Ruby Art Ware #R-119 footed comport. $145-175.

Comparison of the flambé glaze and the ruby glaze. Left to right: Encanto Art Ware #608 vase in the flambé glaze and the #R-105 vase bottle shape. The flambé glaze is slightly more orange than the ruby glaze.

Ruby Art Ware: Left to right: #R-115 vase, $225-275 and #R-105 vase bottle shape, $125-175.

Introduced in 1935, Cocinero Ware was described in the catalog as, "a new utility ware suitable for table service as well as for the modern kitchen. Modeled in a graceful, shell-like motif. No stilt marks on inside of bowls. Available in four colors: white, yellow, apple green, and glacial blue."

Later other colors were added including redwood, tangerine, maroon, flame orange, coral gloss, and Mexican blue. The glaze color tangerine was only used in the Cocinero Ware line. Cocinero Ware was discontinued in 1938.

The original pieces offered were:

Cocinero Cooking Ware. Left to right: #315 turquoise gloss covered casserole, $125-145 and #317 apple green ramekin with lid and plate (also furnished without lid), $75-85 set of three pieces.

300	Pitcher (Capacity 1 pint)
301	Pitcher (Capacity 1 quart)
302	Pitcher (Capacity 2 quarts)
304	Custard Cup
304x	Wire Frame with six Custard Cups
305-	
310	Mixing Bowl Set (6 pieces, 5" diameter to 10" diameter)
312	Large Bowl for Mixing or Punch 12"
316	Pie Plate
315	Casserole and Lid 8"
317	Ramekin, with Lid & Plate (also furnished alone without lid)
318	Ramekin, with Lid and Plate
319	Ramekin (without lid)
320	Handled Batter Bowl (Capacity 2 quarts)
321	Range Shaker, Furnished in "Salt", "Pepper", "Sugar", "Flour"
322	Mug for Punch or Eggnog

Cocinero Cooking Ware. Left to right: #301 tangerine pitcher one quart, $85-95; #302 apple green pitcher two quarts, $125-145; and #300 pitcher one pint in white, $75-85.

Cocinero Cooking Ware: #317 apple green ramekin with lid and plate (also furnished without lid), $75-85 set of three pieces.

Cocinero Cooking Ware. Left to right: #305-310 mixing bowl set – 6 pieces, 5" diameter to 10" diameter. Colors pictured are yellow gloss, white, redwood, Mexican blue, and glacial blue. $45 small to $85 large.

Cocinero Cooking Ware. Left to right: Nested #305-310 mixing bowl set – 6 pieces, 5" diameter to 10" diameter. $45 small to $85 large.

Cocinero Cooking Ware. Left to right: #321 range shaker furnished in "Sugar," "Flour," "Salt," and "Pepper." Glacial blue sugar with blue imprint "Sugar," white sugar with embossed "Sugar," white flour with embossed "Flour," apple green embossed "Salt," and apple green pepper embossed "Pepper." All are $75-85 each.

Cocinero Cooking Ware. Left to right: #304 apple green custard cup, $16-22; #304 glacial blue custard cup, $16-18; #316 yellow matt pie plate, $55-75; #304 yellow gloss custard cup, $16-18; and #304 white custard cup, $16-22.

Cocinero Cooking Ware: #320 handled batter bowl, capacity 2 quarts in yellow gloss, $125-145. Pictured with custard cups in various colors, $16-22.

This is the #312 large bowl for mixing or punch, $145-225, with the #322 mug for punch or eggnog, $32-45. The punch bowl is in yellow gloss and the mugs are in apple green and white.

Chapter 6

Name of "Franciscan Pottery" Changed to "Franciscan Ware" 1936

Given away to business associates to promote Franciscan Pottery, the ashtray on the right was given out prior to January 1st, 1936. Since the term pottery had a bad image, being considered crude, the name was changed to Franciscan Ware, which is used on the ashtray on the left. The hole in the ashtray on the left was for removing the ash from a cigarette while it was burning instead of flicking the ash into the tray. Both ashtrays are $145-165 each.

Another giveaway was this ashtray (#100 shape) with "Franciscan Pottery" on the front surface, $125-145.

On January 1st, 1936 the name of "Franciscan Pottery" was changed to "Franciscan Ware." The term *pottery* connoted certain crudeness according to plant correspondence. At the same time, Gladding, McBean & Co. invented the dinnerware "Starter Set." It was first listed in the price list of January 1st, 1936 under the name "Starter Set" and was shown as being packed in an individual carton. The first starter set consisted of the following pieces: cup, saucer, dinner plate 9", bread & butter plate 6", and fruit bowl.

With other tile makers, Gladding, McBean & Co. participated in the "Model American Village" homes. The Village consisted of three period homes, modern, Cape Cod, and Tudor on permanent exhibition at Atlantic City. These were opened to the public in July of 1938.

Another wonderful tile installation in 1936 was the Jay Paley House swimming pool in Beverly Hills. In the swimming pool, Gladding, McBean & Co. incorporated the signs of the Zodiac created by their own design department. The roof of the house was Gladding, McBean & Co.'s hand-made shingle tile in a light blue color blending with the pool.

Buildings continued to be constructed and, though the 1930s were tough and slow, by 1936 demand was growing for building materials. Gladding, McBean & Co. was meeting the demand for sewer pipes for new streets, roofing materials for buildings and houses, and tile for decoration in the interior and exterior of buildings. Bathrooms and kitchens were beginning to have a worn, out-dated look, and ready for a remodel.

Gladding, McBean & Co. heavily promoted their art ware and tableware through such media as film shorts for movie theaters and schools, magazine and newspaper advertisements, and press releases.

Franciscan Ware was sold in Department Stores throughout the U.S.A. The quality of the ware was very high. Besides being durable, the glazes were brilliant and did not craze. Sales were beyond what management had hoped.

Initially a venture to add profits to the bottom line, Franciscan Ware became a leader in American made pottery. The Glendale plant was remodeled and new equipment was added to accommodate the demand for Hermosa Tiles and Franciscan Ware.

Gladding, McBean & Co. did not introduce any dinnerware lines; however, two art ware lines were introduced in 1936: Capistrano Art Ware and Florist Specials.

Capistrano Ware

Capistrano Art Ware consisted mostly of low bowls for flower arranging. Flower arranging became a pastime in the late 1930s, lasting through the 1940s. Experts would give seminars and write numerous books about the subject. Two curious items in this line are a charming goose on a pedestal base vase (#86) and two sizes of a sunbonnet bowl (#87), which is shaped exactly like a sunbonnet. Otherwise, the line was designed with very clean lines as to not distract from the flower arrangement. Candlesticks were in the line to accommodate the carefully arranged flower centerpiece.

Glazes available were solid Satin Ivory (M.P. 5), solid celadon (M.P. 24), solid Chanteuse (M.P. 38), solid Mauve (M.P. 67), and solid Oatmeal (M.P. 32). In two toned, Satin Ivory (M.P. 5) lined with Glacial Blue (M.P. 2), Satin Mauve (M.P. 67) lined with Satin Ivory (M.P. 5), Coral (M.P. 15) lined with satin Pastel Green (M.P. 8), Satin Buff Pink (M.P. 46) lined with Satin Turquoise (M.P. 27), Deep Yellow (M.P. 23) lined with Oxblood Red (M.P. 22), Coral (M.P. 21) lined with satin ivory (M.P. 5), Apple Green (M.P. 18) lined with satin ivory (M.P. 5), Coral (M.P. 21) lined with light blue (M.P. 25), Maroon (M.P. 19) lined with Chartreuse satin (M.P. 45), Blue satin (M.P. 65) lined with Eggplant (M.P. 29), and Gunmetal (M.P. 51) lined with Dark Yellow (M.P. 33).

Shapes in this line included the following:

Capistrano Ware. Left to right: #412, rectangular bowl in a two-toned combination with a glacial blue interior and a satin ivory exterior, 8.25" x 4.25" x 3.25", $28; #441, low, rectangular flower bowl in 5" x 9", $26; also available in the same shape as #441 but not shown are #442, 7" x 12", $28; and #443, 10" x 15", $35.

86	Goose on Pedestal Vase
87	Sun Bonnet Bowl (note: two sizes -- small & large)
133	Candlestick
142	Bowl Rectangular 6" x 9"
143	Bowl Rectangular 7.5" x 10.25"
144	Bowl Rectangular 9" x 11.75"
145	Bowl Oval 10.5" x 15.25"
146	Bowl Leaf Shape 9.75" x 14"
147	Bowl, Oval 6" x 10"
242	Bowl Rectangular, very low, footed 4.5" x 6.5"
400	Candlestick with flutings
401	Square Dish or ashtray
402	Candlestick 4"
403	Round Vase
404	Lid for #403
405	Vase, Ball & Cylinder
406	Square Vase 4.5" x 3.25"
407	Centerpiece, semi-circular
408	Square Bowl
409	Round Vase
410	Vase or Bowl, low round
411	Square Jar or Flower Pot 6.25" x 4.25"
412	Rectangular Bowl 8.25 x 4.5" x 3.25"
413	Round Vase, flared
414	Low Square Bowl 8.5" x 2.5"
415	Long Rectangular Pansy Jar, 10" x 3.75" x 3.25"
416	Bowl, fluted
417	Jar, round flaring
418	Hexagonal Bowl 8-5/8" x 10" x 5-1/8"
419	Large Oval Bowl 15.75" x 7.75" x 3.5"
420	Fruit Bowl, flaring
421	Bowl, large rectangular
422	Square Bowl 9.75" x 4"
423	Bowl with six grooves
424	Bowl with grooves, large
425	Vase, tall cylinder & ball
426	Vase, tall cylinder & ball
428	Tall Square Vase 10"
429	Jardinière (old #296)
430	Bowl, round flaring 8"
431	Bowl, oval
440	Bowl, rectangular 3.5" x 7"
441	Low Rectangular Flower Bowl 5" x 9"
442	Low Rectangular Flower Bowl 7" x 12"
443	Low Rectangular Flower Bowl 10" x 15"
444	Tall Footed Vase 12"

Capistrano Ware was discontinued in 1942.

Capistrano Ware in yellow and maroon. Left to right: #422, square bowl, 9.75" x 4", $32 and #442, low rectangular flower bowl, 7" x 12", $28.

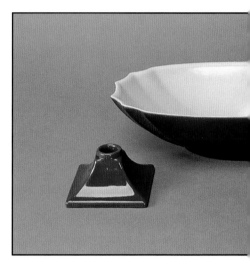

Capistrano Ware, #402 maroon gloss lined with yellow matt candlesticks square, 4", $35 pair and #419 large oval bowl, 14.75" x 7.75" x 3.25", $48.

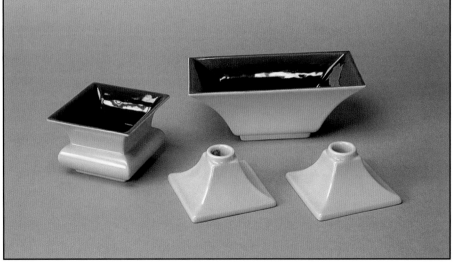

Capistrano Ware in the rare and desirable color of blue lined with plum. Left to right front: square candlesticks #402, 4", $38. Left to Right back: #406, square vase, 4.5" x 3.25", $38 and #412, 8.25" x 4.25" x 3.25", $42.

112

Capistrano Ware, satin coral lined with light satin green. Front: leaf shape bowl, $28. Back: #146 leaf shape bowl, 9.75" x 14", $28.

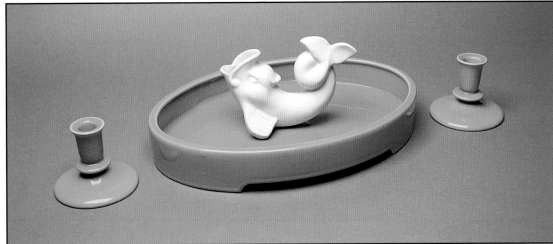

Tropico Line #96 candlesticks in glacial blue, $28 with Nautical Ware #C-641 satin ivory dolphin table piece, 5.5", $125-175 in the center of the Capistrano Ware #145 glacial blue oval low bowl, 10.5" x 15.25", $32.

Capistrano Ware #428 satin ivory exterior with a glacial blue interior tall square vase, 10", $48-55 and #414 satin ivory exterior with a glacial blue interior low square bowl, 8.5" x 2.5", $28-32 with Avalon Art Ware # C-607 ivory matt candelabra 3 branch curved base, $45 and #C-382 ivory matt candelabra 3 branch, straight base, $45.

Capistrano Ware #429 jardinière in satin ivory, $65-75. This shape was also in the Tropico line as shape #296 and was known as the florist stock vase.

Capistrano Ware #418 hexagonal bowl, 8-5/8" x 10" x 5-1/8", with a satin mauve exterior and ivory satin exterior, $75-85.

Included in the Capistrano Art Ware line is this #86 goose on pedestal vase. The goose planter can be found marked either with "Franciscan" or "Catalina Pottery." This is one of the most unusual shapes ever produced by Gladding, McBean & Co and has hand-painted beak and eyes. $75-125.

Capistrano Art Ware. #87 bonnet vase, satin ivory comes in two sizes, this is the larger of the two. $75-85 large, $38-45 small. These have been found in satin ivory, glacial blue, and coral satin.

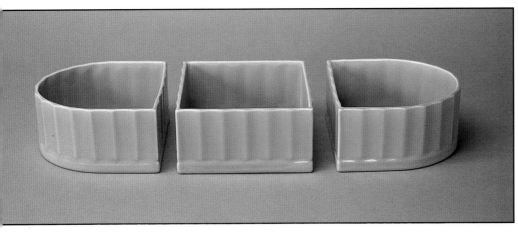

Capistrano Art Ware. This three-compartment table centerpiece is in apple green. Each piece is $35-45 each. The end pieces are shape #407 and the square centerpiece is #408. A complete set in a matching color way would be $125-155.

Here is the same three-compartment table center-piece in three various color combinations. Left to Right: Solid apple green, satin ivory with a coral interior, and satin ivory with an apple green interior. Each piece is $35-45 each.

Capistrano Art Ware ivory satin bowl #424 with an apple green interior, $65-85.

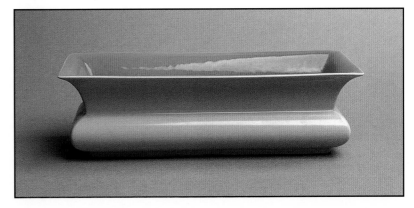

Capistrano Art Ware #415 large rectangular pansy jar, 10" x 3.75" x 3.25" in satin gray with a flambé interior.

115

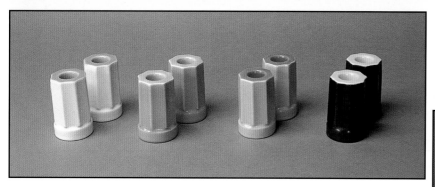

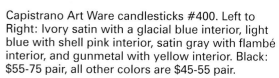

Capistrano Art Ware candlesticks #400. Left to Right: Ivory satin with a glacial blue interior, light blue with shell pink interior, satin gray with flambé interior, and gunmetal with yellow interior. Black: $55-75 pair, all other colors are $45-55 pair.

Light blue with shell pink interior Capistrano Art Ware. #133 candlesticks, $45-65 pair with the #426 vase, $65-75.

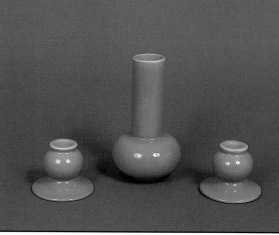

Capistrano Art Ware. A wonderful centerpiece set in gunmetal lined in yellow with #400 candlesticks, $55-75 pair and #410 round bowl, $95-125.

Capistrano Art Ware. This is a great color combination with a light blue exterior lined with a shell pink interior. Left to Right: #400 candlesticks, $45-55 pair; #409 vase, $75-85; and # 424 fluted bowl, $85-95.

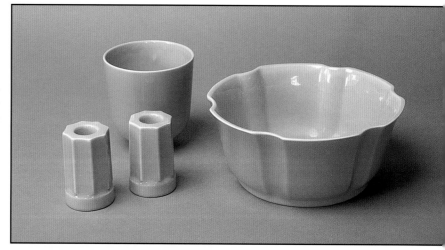

Light blue with shell pink interior Capistrano Art Ware. Left to Right: #430 round bowl, $85-125; #413 vase, $85-95; and #431 oval bowl, $75-95. In front: #133 candlesticks, $45-65. pair.

Florist Special. Right to left: #275 flower pot in satin ivory, $55-75; #272 large leaf design vase, $125-145; #275 leaf design flower pot in coral, $45-65; and in front #273 leaf design wall pocket, $85-125. The correct name for the green glaze has not been identified.

orist Special. Left to Right: Although the Duotone ble Ware #C-85 large bowl (with satin ivory exterior d glacial blue interior, $125-145) is not in the Florist ecial line, the shape is like the #271 vase. The #271 se in coral, $55-75 and in satin ivory, $55-75. The 346 coral gloss pineapple pitcher is in the Kitchen are line; however, it goes very well with the floral apes in the Florist Special line, $125-225.
he #271 vases can be used as tumblers; however, they tually are vases. Beware of fake tumblers that re-mble the #271 vases.
he new shapes being roduced are not ways marked, but hen marked are arked "Bauer." Not to e confused with Bauer ottery produced from e 1930s to the 1960s, ese are new repro-uctions produced by a ompany that is now sing the Bauer logo nd name. It is interest-g that this is a ranciscan shape and ot a vintage Bauer esign. One way to entify a fake is they re slightly larger in eight than the ranciscan and ranciscan examples re usually marked ther "Made in USA" or atalina Pottery" in ack or dark blue ink.

Florist Special

The Florist Special line included vases and flowerpots to be sold in florist shops. New shapes were introduced including the leaf shaped flowerpot, vase, tall vase, and wall pocket. All other shapes were previously used in other lines. Solid glazes included Satin Ivory (M.P. 5), White (M.P. 1), Light Yellow (M.P. 3), Glacial Blue (M.P. 2), and Apple Green (M.P. 18). The leaf shaped vases were offered in duotone glazes. Flowerpots #44-48 and flowerpot saucers #44a-48a were also in the line. The line was discontinued in 1941.

Shapes in this line are as follows.

92	Jardinière
93	Flower Vase 9.5"
95	Small Cactus Pot
271	Small Vase, Leaf Design 5.25"
272	Large Vase, Leaf Design 12"
273	Wall Pocket, Leaf Design
275	Jardinière, Leaf Design
276	Jardinière, Leaf Design
277	Jardinière, Leaf Design
278	Jardinière, Leaf Design
283	Flower Pot 2.5"
284	Flower Pot 3"
285	Azalea Pot 6.5"
286	Azalea Pot 7.75"
287	Jardinière 5.25"
288	Jardinière 6.5"
289	Jardinière 7"
290	Jardinière 7.5"
291	Jardinière 8.5"
292	Jardinière 6.25"
293	Jardinière Stock Vase 12"
294	Bulb Bowl 5"
295	Jardinière, round
296	Jardinière, square

Chapter 7
Acquisition of Catalina Island Pottery 1937

On January 15, 1937, Gladding, McBean & Co. introduced the first hand-decorated earthenware. The pattern produced was named "Padua." The ware was decorated under glaze on the El Patio shape and glazed with a clear glaze. Decoration was in yellows and browns, and consisted of many bands with stylized flower center decoration. Up to ten bands were on the dinner plate. Later this pattern would be referred to in price lists as Padua I.

The year 1937 saw the company once again become profitable. Gladding, McBean & Co. paid off a loan of $600,000 that was borrowed to keep the company afloat during the rough times of 1930-32. The University of Washington in Seattle, Washington, used Gladding, McBean & Co.'s architectural terra cotta and brick for their new Condon Hall. In May of 1937, Gladding, McBean & Co. supplied the terra cotta tile for the J.C. Penny in Los Angeles. Building contracts increased, as the economy grew stronger.

Gladding, McBean & Co. Building, San Francisco. "Tall windows, fluted pilasters of warm gray ceramic veneer and blue spandrels have been judiciously combined to give the company's new home the feeling of modernity and the usefulness of light. To shed still more light on the West's most modern tile and Franciscan ware display rooms, huge windows line an attractive courtyard at the rear of the building. The ceramic veneer, the Windsor shingle tile that tops the three-story structure and the many other clay products are seen in practical use throughout the building are all from the company's kilns." – *Shapes of Clay*, October 1937.

University of Washington, Condon Hall, Seattle, Washington. Architect: A.H. Albertson with Joseph Wilson and Paul Richardson, Associates. The building is faced with brick and medium buff ceramic veneer.

Jay Paley Swimming Pool, Beverly Hills, California. Paul Williams, Architect. "The signs of the Zodiac, with their graceful, symbolic spears of deep, aquamarine blue, are a most unusual and original architectural treatment. The colorful pool, with its blue-green floor and walls, its steps of brilliant yellow ceramic tile and its commanding central design, is a noteworthy decorative tile achievement of the company's artists." – *Shapes of Clay*, October 1937.

The company prospered and built new headquarters in San Francisco at Ninth and Harrison Streets. The building was built of materials that Gladding, McBean & Co. produced from its ceramic veneer to its Windsor shingle tile roof. The building was a showcase of what Gladding, McBean & Co. manufactured. Showrooms were elegantly appointed to show off the new pottery lines that were introduced. Store buyers and merchandisers could visit the showroom and order the newest in art ware or tableware. Architects could consult with the design departments for commercial or residential buildings for just the look they had in mind.

From the journal *Ceramic Industry*, in a column named "The Roving Reporter on the West Coast," H. V. Kaeppel (Herb) wrote:

Among the best informed men in the pottery and whiteware field in Los Angeles is Lee Bennett, director of research for Gladding, McBean & Co. Bennett and his assistant, B. M. Burchfield, have done some excellent work particularly in glazes. One thing that distinguishes the pottery made here from the conventional type is the character of the glaze. Bennett tells me that it is applied in thickness ranging from 10 to 15 thousandths of an inch, which is probably three times as heavy a coat as is found on ordinary ware . . . Franciscan and Catalina, both made by Gladding, McBean & Co., are one-fire

wares. Most of the ware produced in other potteries is two-fire. –*Ceramic Industry*, December 1937.

On April 1, 1937, Gladding, McBean & Co. purchased Catalina Pottery, the Catalina Clay Products division of the Santa Catalina Island Company. Included in the purchase were all cases and molds, the complete inventory of dinnerware and art ware, much of the plant equipment and the right to the name "Catalina Pottery." This purchase added 174 pieces of dinnerware and art ware to the lines produced by Gladding, McBean & Co.

New lines were developed adding the shapes from the Catalina Pottery. Additional pieces were sculpted and added to the lines as well as using shapes previously used by Gladding, McBean & Co. The lines to market the shapes from Catalina Pottery were Avalon Art Ware, Aurora Art Ware, Encanto Art Ware, and Terra Cotta Specialties. A special ink stamp was developed to capitalize on the Catalina Pottery trademark. Art ware pieces were ink stamped "Catalina Pottery" with the ink stamp "Made in USA". These lines were marketed as Catalina Pottery.

Based on the popularity of the Catalina Pottery tableware, Gladding, McBean & Co. put into production the line Rancho Table Ware, based on Catalina shapes. This line was marked with an ink stamp or impressed "Rancho," "Rancho Catalina," "Catalina Pottery," and "Catalina." Most, but not all, pieces bear the "Made in USA" ink stamp.

Avalon Art Ware. Left: #C-314 candleholder, $35-45 pair. Foreground: #C-608 candleholder, $35-45 pair. Background: #C-311 vase fluted, 8", $75-85.

To determine whether Gladding, McBean & Co. made an art ware or tableware item on the mainland look for the "Made in USA" or "Catalina Pottery" maker's marks rather than the "Catalina Island" mark. These pieces are definitely mainland produced Gladding, McBean & Co. products. Catalina pottery, made on the island, is marked "Catalina Island," and was manufactured by the Catalina Clay Division of the Santa Catalina Island Company.

Later in August, Gladding, McBean & Co. introduced four new hand-decorated under glaze dinnerware patterns: Mango, Willow, Del Mar, and Del Oro. Gladding, McBean also introduced a new solid color dinnerware line named "Montecito Table Ware" with new shapes.

As a new venture, Gladding, McBean & Co. made lamp bases for lamp companies to use in their manufacture of lamps. As far as is known, Gladding, McBean & Co. never made complete lamps with metal work and shades. No company information has been found.

Avalon Art Ware

Avalon Art Ware was introduced in 1937 and discontinued in 1942. Colors available were Matt Ivory (M.P. 5) and a two-toned combination of Matt Ivory exterior lined with a Turquoise Satin interior. The "C-" prefix to the shape number indicates that the item was from a Catalina mold. All of the items in Avalon Art Ware are on Catalina Pottery shapes. Gladding, McBean & Co sculpted no new pieces.

C-202	Bowl, Oval, 15"
C-204	Bowl, Oval, 18"
C-234	Bowl, Flat, 13.5"
C-304	Vase, 6.5"
C-305	Vase, 8"
C-307	Vase, 12"
C-310	Vase, Flat Fan Shape, 7.5"
C-311	Vase, Fluted, 8"
C-312	Vase, Bulge Foot, 7.75"
C-314	Candleholder
C-382	Candelabra, 3-branch strait base
C-603	Vase, Round, Scroll Foot, 5"
C-604	Vase, Round, Scroll Foot, 6.5"
C-607	Candelabra, 3-branch curved base
C-608	Candelabra
C-703	Bowl, Flat Oval, 14.75"
C-709	Bowl, Star Shape, 9.5"
C-724	Compote, 8"
C-725	Compote, 13"

Avalon Art Ware. Left to right: #104 vase, small, $35-55; #110 vase, 7.75", $75-85; and #137, $45-55.

Avalon Art Ware. #C-610 ribbed vase, 7.75", $85-95. This shape is also used in the Aurora Art Ware line and the Catalina Art Ware line.

Avalon Art Ware. Candlesticks #400, $55-65 pair; compote #119, footed compote, $65-85. The compote is in the Ruby Art Ware line and in the Cielito Ware line. It is also in the El Patio dinnerware line. Glazes for the compote have been found in yellow, glacial blue, ruby, celestial white, and satin ivory.

Aurora Art Ware

Aurora Art Ware was introduced in 1937 and discontinued in 1942. All Aurora Art Ware has fluted shapes from the vases to the plates and bowls. Aurora can be found in either two-tone glazes, with the exterior one color and the interior another or in solid glazes. The "C-" prefix to the shape number indicates that the item was from a Catalina mold. All items in the Aurora Art Ware line were from Catalina Pottery shapes.

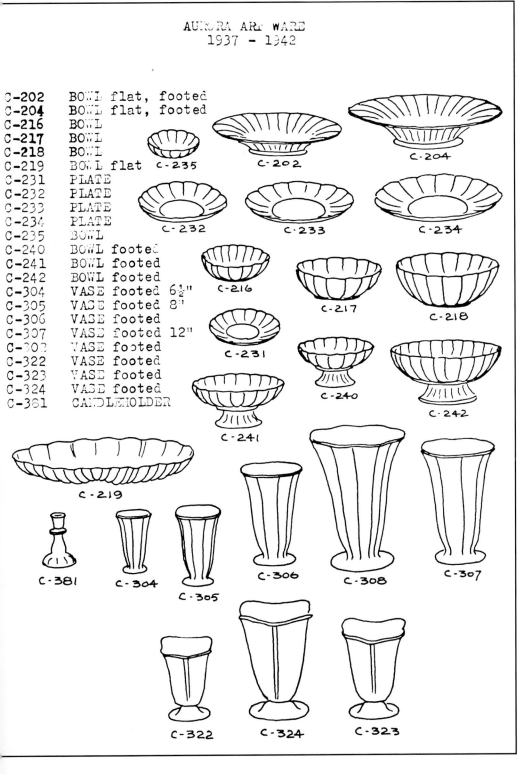

AURORA ART WARE
1937 - 1942

C-202   BOWL flat, footed
C-204   BOWL flat, footed
C-216   BOWL
C-217   BOWL
C-218   BOWL
C-219   BOWL flat   C-235
C-231   PLATE
C-232   PLATE
C-233   PLATE
C-234   PLATE
C-235   BOWL
C-240   BOWL footed
C-241   BOWL footed
C-242   BOWL footed
C-304   VASE footed 6½"
C-305   VASE footed 8"
C-306   VASE footed
C-307   VASE footed 12"
C-308   VASE footed
C-322   VASE footed
C-323   VASE footed
C-324   VASE footed
C-381   CANDLEHOLDER

C-202	Bowl, Oval, 15"
C-204	Bowl, Oval, 18"
C-216	Bowl
C-217	Bowl
C-218	Bowl
C-219	Bowl
C-231	Plate
C-232	Plate
C-233	Plate
C-234	Bowl, Flat, 13.5"
C-235	Bowl
C-240	Bowl, Footed
C-241	Bowl, Footed
C-242	Bowl, Footed
C-304	Vase, 6.5"
C-305	Vase, 8"
C-306	Vase, Footed
C-307	Vase, 12"
C-308	Vase, Footed
C-322	Vase, Footed
C-323	Vase, Footed
C-324	Vase, Footed
C-381	Candleholder

This is a page from a report that was done for the Glendale Plant during 1962. Aurora Art Wares all have fluted shapes. Aurora can be found in two-toned glazes with glacial blue lined with white or white lined with glacial blue. Solid colors were also made. The shapes reappear in the Rancho Table Ware line and are marked "Rancho." The shapes are all from the Catalina Island Pottery. The only way to identify a piece as in the Aurora Art Ware line is by the shape.

Catalina Art Ware

The line with the most art ware shapes produced by Gladding, McBean & Co. is in the Catalina Art Ware line. This line was introduced in 1937 and was not discontinued until 1942. At various times from 1937-42, pieces were added and discontinued.

Although, the "C-" prefix to the shape number indicates that the item was from a Catalina mold, not all shapes were from Catalina products that were made on the island by the Catalina Clay Products Division of the Santa Catalina Island Company.

One of the examples of pieces added to the line and sculpted by Gladding, McBean & Co. was the peasant head, shape #C-801. Gladding, McBean & Co patented this shape, which was uncommon for them to do. It was sculpted and designed by Dorr Bothwell, an artist in her own

right. Dorr Bothwell was a painter and considered to be a pioneering printmaker. She was exhibited in many museums such as the Los Angeles County Museum of Art and the Metropolitan Museum of Art. Of interesting note, she sailed alone at age 26 to Samoa where she had begun painting. When she returned to San Francisco in 1930, she sang Samoan songs on the radio and demonstrated Samoan dance at art world parties. She was contracted by Gladding, McBean & Co. to design some new contemporary shapes to be added to the Catalina Art Ware line. She is also credited with designing the reclining Samoan girl, shape #808 as well as other shapes in the Catalina Art Ware and Terra Cotta Specialties lines.

Art ware in the Catalina Art Ware line included the following shapes.

C-202	Bowl, Oval, 15"
C-204	Bowl, Oval, 18"
C-219	Bowl
C-231	Plate
C-234	Bowl, Flat, 13.5"
C-235	Bowl
C-236	Bowl, Giant Clam Shell, 16"
C-237	Bowl, Clam Shell, medium, 11"
C-238	Bowl, Clam Shell, small
C-304	Vase, 6.5"
C-305	Vase, 8"
C-307	Vase, 12"
C-310	Vase Flat Fan Shape, 7.5"
C-311	Vase Fluted, 8"
C-312	Vase Bulge Foot, 7.75"
C-314	Candleholder
C-317	Bowl, 10" Deep
C-326	Vase Shell
C-330	Vase, 6.5"
C-331	Vase, 4"
C-332	Vase, 5" Wide Mouth
C-333	Vase, 7"
C-334	Fancy Bowl, 9"
C-335	Vase, 6.75"
C-336	Candleholder
C-337	Bowl
C-338	Vase, 11.5" Tall Narrow
C-339	Vase, 9.5" Flaring
C-340	Bowl, 10" Low
C-341	Bowl Curve Top
C-342	Vase, 7.5" Oval
C-349	Bowl, 18" Long Narrow
C-350	Sea Shell Cornucopia
C-351	Sea Shell Vase
C-352	Double Clam Shell Vase
C-353	Shell Vase
C-354	Shell Vase
C-360	Oval Bowl Fish Pattern
C-361	Small Fish Vase

Catalina Art Ware, satin ivory. Left to right: (number unknown) bust of lady, $225-325 and #C-805 lady with hat, $195-245. These were offered in the Terra Cotta Specialties line and are in the same value range.

Catalina Art Ware, satin ivory. Left to right: #C-801 bust of peasant girl, $65-75 and #C-803 girl with fan, $75-95.

Catalina Art Ware: #C-807 Samoan mother & child in satin ivory (Design Patent #D-83,373) designed by Dorr Bothwell, $125-175. In Terra Cotta Specialties, $145-225.

Catalina Art Ware, satin ivory. Left to right: #C-806 bird on base, $145-175 and #C-802 bird, $85-125. In the Terra Cotta Specialties line, $145-225 for the bird.

Catalina Art Ware: #C-809 turbaned head of Malayan woman. This piece is unmarked and may not have been included in the Catalina Art Ware line. According to factory information this piece was listed as being made in the Terra Cotta Specialties line and not in the Catalina Art Ware line. This piece was designed by Dorr Bothwell. $175-350. In Terra Cotta Specialties: $285-395.

Catalina Art Ware: #C-725 compote, 13", $65-75.

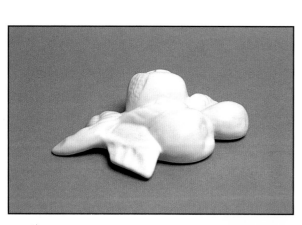

Catalina Art Ware: #C-812 fruit and nut table ornament, $125-145. There is also the #810 grape table ornament, which is not pictured. These were used on the table top for decoration. Some have been found with the 1939 San Francisco Golden Gate International Exposition sticker on them. As far as known, this shape was created by Gladding, McBean & Co. and is not a Catalina Island Pottery shape.

Catalina Art Ware: #C-801 bust of peasant girl, designed by Dorr Bothwell for Gladding, McBean & Co. This is one of the few pieces that Gladding, McBean & Co. ever U.S. design patented. The U.S. design patent number is 114,804. The bust can be found hand-painted either in maroon and brown or blue and maroon. Colors found have been coral matt, turquoise matt, matt ivory, and pastel green matt. $65-75 for matt ivory, $95-125 for all other colors. You will also find the bust in the Terra Cotta Specialties line, $125-145.

Encanto Art Ware

Derived from images of plant life and sea life, Encanto Art Ware was introduced in 1937 by Gladding, McBean & Co. The shapes are all heavily embossed, each one with its own design and motif. This was the most creative of the lines produced by Gladding, McBean & Co. The line was discontinued in 1939, but the shapes would be revived as the art ware line Polynesia.

Polynesia was an embossed hand-painted version of Encanto.

Color variations will be found in two-toned and solid color glazes. Glazes used were Celadon (M.P. 24), Flambé (M.P. 39), Matt Ivory (M.P. 5), Coral Gloss (M.P. 21), White (M.P. 1), and Oxblood (M.P. 40).

The following shapes were produced.

Encanto Art Ware, flambé glaze. Left to right: #618 round vase, 6.75", $265; #620 vase, $265; and #603 ball vase, 3.5", $165.

Encanto Art Ware, flambé glaze. Left to right: #608 ball vase narrow, $125-165; #617 ball vase, $225-265; and #605 flaring vase footed, $125-165.

601	Bud Vase
602	Bud Vase
603	Ball Vase, 3.5" (same as 376)
604	Small Pot, 3.5" (same as 377)
605	Footed Vase, 4.75" (same as 378)
606	Vase, 5" (same as 379)
607	Vase, 4.75" (same as 380)
608	Ball Vase, 3.5" (same as 381)
609	Oval Vase
610	Cigarette Box (same as 375)
611	Flat Oval Vase with Fish
612	Oval Vase, 5" x 4" (same as 382)
613	Round Footed Vase with Fish
614	Vase, 6" x 5" diameter (same as 383)
615	Cylinder Vase Small
616	Oval Bowl, 8" x 4" (same as 384)
617	Round Vase with Fish
618	Round Vase, 6.75" (same as 385)
619	Cylinder Vase, 9" Medium (same as 387)
620	Vase, 7.75"
621	Oval Bowl, 10" x 5" (same as 386)
622	Cylinder Vase Large
623	Vase Large (1934 Museum Expo Piece)
624	Round Bowl, 14" (same as 388)

Encanto Art Ware. Left to right; #606 vase, 5" in matt ivory, $65-75 and #610 cigarette box, $75-125. The lid on the box is in the coral gloss glaze with a satin ivory glaze on the base. Other colors found in the Encanto Art Ware line are solid celadon and solid celestial white.

Encanto Art Ware #623 vase, cylindrical, 8" in satin ivory, $225-275.

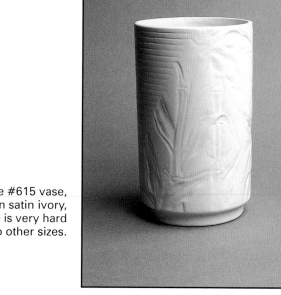

Encanto Art Ware #615 vase, cylindrical, 6.75" in satin ivory, $125-145. This size is very hard to find compared to other sizes.

Encanto Art Ware. Left to right: #609 oval bowl small in coral lined with gray, $85-95 and #616 oval bowl medium in satin ivory, $85-95. There are three sizes of the oval bowl, #609 small, #616 medium, and #621 large.

Encanto Art Ware coral lined with gray. Left to right: #609 oval vase, $125-135; #606 vase, $75-85; #602 bud vase, $85-145; and #601 bud vase, $85-145.

Encanto Art Ware. Left to right in center of #624 satin ivory low bowl, $145-225: #612 vase in celadon, $85-95; #614 vase in coral lined in satin ivory, $135-165; and #608 vase in satin ivory, $75-95.

Encanto Art Ware. Left to right: #605 vase in satin ivory, $75-85 and #621 oval bowl, large in celadon, $75-95.

Encanto Art Ware. This vase comes in three sizes. Pictured is the #619 in coral lined with gray, 9", $145-225. The three sizes are small #615, medium #619, and large #622. All are in the same price range.

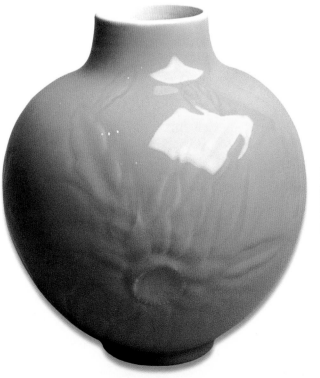

Encanto Art Ware. #618 round vase in glacial blue lined with white: $225-265. Not listed as a color combination in the factory information, this is very rare and unusual piece.

Terra Cotta Specialties

Terra Cotta Specialties have a special stained Malinite clay body giving the appearance of unglazed terra cotta. All of the shapes may have been designed by Dorr Bothwell with the exception of the #C-219 bowl. This is one of the most desired lines made by Gladding, McBean & Co. and is very collectible today. The special stained Malinite body was glazed with either Turquoise (M.P. 2) or Maroon (M.P. 19) in combination with Gunmetal (M.P. 51) or, as with the case of the reclining Samoan girl, with a sea green color (M.P. unknown). The line was discontinued in 1940.

These are the shapes offered in the line; however, the special stained Malinite clay body has been found on other items not listed here.

C-219	Bowl
C-703	Bowl, Flat Oval, 14.75"
C-801	Bust of Peasant Girl
C-802	Bird C-803
C-803	Bust of Girl With Fan
C-804	Large Head of Girl
C-805	Lady With Hat
C-807	Samoan Mother & Childs
C-808	Reclining Samoan Girl
C-809	Turbaned Head of Malayan Woman

Terra Cotta Specialties #C-805 bust of lady with hat, $195-245. All of the Terra Cotta Specialties were produced with a special stained Malinite body. Besides finding shapes trimmed with yellow and turquoise glazing, you will also find these shapes in maroon gloss trim.

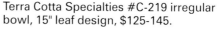

Terra Cotta Specialties #C-219 irregular bowl, 15" leaf design, $125-145.

Terra Cotta Specialties #C-801 bust of peasant girl, $125-145.

Montecito Ware. Left to right: Turquoise #550 teapot, $75-95; eggplant #552 after dinner coffee pot, $85-95; and coral #553 hot water or chocolate pot, $75-95. The hot water or chocolate pot was discontinued prior to 1939.

Montecito Ware. Front to back: #593 turquoise coffee jug, handled with stopper, $85-95; #570 medium platter hexagonal, 13" long in satin ivory, $55-65; and #571 large hexagonal platter, 17" long in coral, $65-75. The #593 coffee jug was only sold with a stopper. Hence, if the coffee jug is without a stopper, it is incomplete and would be $45-48.

Montecito Table Ware

Montecito Table Ware was displayed at Justin Tharaud, Inc. on March 3, 1937. Justin Tharaud represented Gladding, McBean & Co.'s pottery product lines in New York City. This marketing strategy, having other companies represent their wares, was new to Gladding, McBean & Co., but would prove to be highly successful.

"For formality, there is Montecito with its suavity of line and beauty of contour. The classic simplicity of the shapes is a perfect foil for the unusually beautiful colorings and the color harmonies possible to achieve have never been available in tableware of any type." –Gladding, McBean & Co.'s brochure "Color Counts, Franciscan Ware."

The original colors of Montecito were Eggplant (M.P. 29), Coral (M.P. 15 – Satin Coral), Turquoise (M.P. 2), Celadon Green (M.P. 24 – Celadon), Yellow (M.P. 3), Satin Gray (M.P. 20), and Satin Ivory (M.P. 5 – Matt Ivory).

Montecito was made in the following shapes.

501	Fruit
502	Cereal
506	Plate, Bread & Butter, 6.5"
507	Plate, Dessert, 7.5"
508	Plate, Salad, 8.5"
509	Plate, Dinner, 9.5"
510	Plate, Large Dinner, 10.5"
512	Chop Plate, 12.5"
514	Chop Plate, 14.5"
520-21	Cup and Saucer
522-23	After Dinner Cup and Saucer
524-525	Cream Soup and Saucer
526	Lidded Soup
530	Sherbet or Cocktail
531	Tumbler, Footed
533	Small Tumbler
540	Creamer
541	Sugar and Lid
543	Individual Creamer
544	Individual Sugar
546	Creamer, New Style
550	Teapot, 6-cup
552	After Dinner Coffee Pot
522-523	After Dinner Cup and Saucer
553	Hot Water or Chocolate Pot
554	Individual Teapot
560	Vegetable Dish, Round
570	Platter, Hexagonal, 13"
571	Hexagonal Platter, Large, 16"
580	Salad Bowl, Footed
581	Hexagonal Bowl, handled
582	Casserole with Lid, 7.5"
590	Gravy Boat, Fast Stand
591	Salt & Pepper, per Pair
592	Toast Cover
593	Coffee Jug, Handled, with stopper, 50 oz.
594	Ash Tray

Throughout the time that Montecito was made, many pieces were discontinued. Prior to 1939, the #540 creamer, #581 hexagonal bowl with handles, #553 hot water or chocolate pot, and #554 individual teapot were discontinued. All of these items are scarce and very hard to find.

In 1938, Montecito was offered in two-tone glazes. The flatware was solid color and the hollowware two-toned. Flatware pieces are glazed in Oatmeal (M.P. 32), Coral (M.P. 15), Turquoise (M.P. 27), and Green (M.P. 62). The four-color combinations used on the hollowwares were Satin Oatmeal and Maroon Gloss (M.P. 32/19), Satin Coral and Turquoise Gloss (M.P. 15/77), Satin Turquoise and Coral Gloss (M.P. 27/21), and Satin Green and Yellow Gloss (M.P. 3/62).

Montecito and Two-Toned Montecito were discontinued in 1942.

Montecito Ware. Left to right: #520 cup and #521 saucer in eggplant, $35-45 set; #594 ashtray in yellow, $26-28; and #522 after dinner cup and #523 after dinner saucer in copper, $42-45.

Montecito Ware. Left to right: #530 sherbet or cocktail in copper, $22-28; #502 cereal, suitable for soup in light blue, $28-34; and #501 fruit in eggplant, $12-18.

Montecito Ware. Front: #591 salt & pepper; left: turquoise #552 after dinner coffee pot, $85-95; right: #520 cup and #521 saucer in satin ivory, $35-45 set; plates front to back: #506 bread & butter plate, 6.5" in coral, $5-8; #507 dessert plate, 7.5" in satin gray, $10-12; #508 salad plate, 8.5" in eggplant, $12-16; #509 dinner plate, 9.5" in shell pink, $18-22; #510 large dinner plate, 10.5" in yellow, $26-30; #512 chop plate, 12.5" in copper, $35-45; and #514 chop plate, 14.5" in celadon, $45-75. You will find the salt & peppers with one hole, two holes, and three holes for pouring either salt or pepper.

Montecito Ware. Left to right: #582 casserole with lid in copper, 7.5", $125-145 and #526 lidded soup in satin ivory, $45-65. Both pieces are hard to find.

Montecito Ware. Front: #560 round vegetable dish in yellow, $45-55. Back, left to right: #580 footed salad bowl in light blue, $75-85 and #562 round vegetable dish in eggplant, $45-55. The #562 replaced the #560 round vegetable dish prior to 1942.

Montecito Ware. Front to back: #544 individual sugar, $22-28 and #543 individual creamer, $22-26 in satin ivory; #540 creamer, $22-28; and #541 sugar and lid, $26-30 in yellow; #512 chop plate, 12.5" in coral, $35-45; and #514 chop plate, 14.5" in celadon $45-75. Sugars were furnished with a lid, and a sugar without a lid is incomplete.

Montecito Ware. Left to right: #592 rare and hard to find muffin or toast cover, $55-75, sitting on a #507 dessert plate, 7.5" in coral, $10-12; #531 footed tumbler in yellow, $28-45; and a #524 cream soup and #525 cream soup saucer in eggplant, $45-55 set.

Montecito Ware. Front to back: #590 fast stand gravy boat in satin ivory, $38-45 and #570 medium platter hexagonal, 13" long in turquoise, $55-65.

Montecito Table Ware, flambé glaze. "'Adieu to Bachelorhood' was the title of a complete bachelor buffet setup in Chinese red Franciscan Pottery at the May Co.'s down-town store in April. The group sold well for at least 10 days." "Making the Rounds of the Markets," *Ceramic Industry*, January 1942. Left to right: #510 large dinner plate, 10.5", $85-95; #509 dinner plate, 9.5", $75-85; #520 cup and #521 saucer, $65-75; #531 footed tumbler, $75-85; and #506 bread & butter plate, 6.5", $35-55.

Montecito Table Ware, flambé glaze. Left to right: #591 salt & pepper, $75-85 pair; #593 coffee jug with wooded handle and stopper, $125-155.

Two-Tone Montecito. Front to back: #541 sugar and lid, $26-30; #552 after dinner coffee pot, $75-95; #540 creamer, $22-28 in satin coral and turquoise gloss; #570 medium platter hexagonal, 13" long in turquoise, $55-65. Hollow ware was two-toned and flatware was solid colored.

Two-Tone Montecito. #520 cup and #521 saucer in yellow and plum, $35-45 set; #531 footed tumbler in satin coral and turquoise gloss, $28-45; and #522 after dinner cup and #523 after dinner saucer in satin oatmeal and maroon gloss, $42-45.

Two-Tone Montecito. Left to right: #525 cream soup saucer in satin coral and turquoise gloss, $45-55 set; #502 cereal, suitable for soup in yellow and plum, $28-34; and #501 fruit in satin coral and turquoise gloss, $12-18.

Two-Tone Montecito. Left to right: #590 fast stand gravy boat in satin turquoise and coral gloss, $38-45 and #562 round vegetable dish in satin coral and turquoise gloss, $45-55.

Montecito Ware. Extremely rare and hard to find #581 handled hexagonal bowl in satin gray. The hexagonal bowl was discontinued prior to 1939. Value undetermined.

Never before had Gladding, McBean & Co. manufactured a hand-painted tableware. The new hand-painted pattern was Padua. New machinery had to be purchased for use in lining the new tableware. Lining is the process where the piece is placed on a turntable and a line is made using a paint-brush. The pottery department at the Glendale plant had to be updated. New employees were hired to hand-paint the tableware. Most of these new employees were art students and housewives seeking part-time employment. Most housewives found this work to be perfect for them as they could go to work when they sent their children to school and return when the children arrived home after school. Many of the new employees were relatives of the existing plant workers. Mothers and daughters would work together and continue to do so over many years.

In 1939, Padua was restyled as a new pattern called Padua II. Padua was renamed Padua I. The new pattern had a new glaze treatment with an over glaze of Celadon (M.P. 24); whereas, Padua had a clear over glaze (M.P. 7). The same under glazed brown and yellow hand-painted treatment of Padua was applied to Padua II.

Padua is on the same shape as El Patio, however, not all shapes in El Patio were offered in Padua or Padua II.

Padua II is very scarce and hard to find today. Padua II was probably made on in the pieces that were offered in 1942. Barker Brothers Department Stores offered Padua in either Buff or Celadon and the pattern was sold under the pattern name Freesia.

Padua I and Padua II were offered in only these shapes in January 1942.

2	Plate, Bread and Butter, 6.5"
4	Plate, Dessert, 7.5"
37	Plate, Dinner, 9.5"
90	Plate, Large Dinner, 10.5"
65	Plate, Chop, 12-3/8"
10	Cup and Saucer
1	Fruit
16	Cereal, or Soup
14	Vegetable Dish
6	Creamer
9	Sugar, Lidded

Additional shapes were added later in 1942 and included the following:

7	Plate, Salad 8.5"
17	Coffee Jug & Stopper
23	Coupe Dessert Plate
24	Salad Bowl
25	Tea Pot & Lid
26	Tea Tile
30	Sherbet
32	Cup with Iron or Wood Handle
36	Plate, Chop 14"
38	Casserole and Lid
42	Serving Bowl
67	Hot Water Pot
68	Egg Cup
69	Toast Cover
70	Salt & Pepper
88	Salad Plate 8"
250	Onion Soup 5"
256	Individual Tea Pot
257	Individual Creamer
270	Individual Sugar
S-27	Dinner Plate
S	

By December 1942, Padua I and Padua II were discontinued.

Padua. Front to back: left, fruit #1, $12-16; right, #10 cup & saucer, $16-22; #2 bread & butter plate, 6.5", $8-10; #7 salad plate, 8.5", $12-18; #37 dinner, 9.5", $16-22; and #90 service or large dinner plate, 10.5", $22-26.

Padua. Left to right: #32 cups in metal holders, $26-28; #17 carafe without stopper, $38-45; stopper, not pictured, $12-15; under carafe, # 26 round footed tea tile, $35-45; #9 sugar with lid, $26-28; and #6 creamer, $24-26. The sugar was furnished with a lid, so a lidless sugar is incomplete. Closer image of the tea tile and the mugs shown with a carafe with metal handle, $65-75.

Padua. Front to back: #16 soup or cereal bowl, $22-28; # 23 coupe dessert plate, $24-26; #65, 12" chop plate, $28-38; and # 36, 14" chop plate, $38-48.

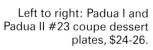

Left to right: Padua I and Padua II #23 coupe dessert plates, $24-26.

Padua. #24 salad bowl, $45-65.

Padua II. Plates: #88 salad plate, 8.5", $28-32; #4 dessert plate, 7.5", $22-26; and #2 bread & butter plate, $10-15.

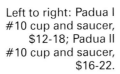

Left to right: Padua I #10 cup and saucer, $12-18; Padua II #10 cup and saucer, $16-22.

Padua II. Left to right: #4 dessert plate, 7.5", $22-26 and #6 creamer, $26-36.

Gladding, McBean & Company continued to produce the tableware offered previously by the Catalina Pottery Division of the Santa Catalina Island Company. This tableware was already a well respected and desired line purchased by store buyers from across the county. Gladding, McBean & Co. renamed this line Rancho Table Ware. From the Catalina Pottery brochure: "All of California's romantic charm is brought to you in the glowing colors and delightful shapes of Rancho Ware." To stress the difference between Catalina Island produced ware, the brochure went on to say that "important from the practical standpoint is the exceptionally tough and durable body that will not leak or craze." One of the problems with the Catalina Island ware produced by the Santa Catalina Island Co. was that it was easily chipped, was not durable, and crazed due to a two-fire kiln process, whereas, Rancho Ware was made with a one-fire process with a Malinite body. Rancho Ware today is as beautiful as the day it was produced and can be used for everyday entertaining. The Avalon Table Ware line was the old Catalina Island "Rope Edge" table ware; no new pieces were ever made by Gladding, McBean & Co. Only the stock left from the purchase of the Catalina Pottery was sold.

Gladding, McBean & Co. redeveloped the glazes used by Catalina Pottery for the Rancho Ware. Rancho Ware was offered in a variety of colors including Catalina Red (M.P. 73), Catalina Dark Blue (M.P. 79), Catalina Sand (M.P. 81), Catalina Red Brown (M.P. 83), Catalina Turquoise (M.P. 77), Dark Yellow (M.P. 33), Catalina Green (M.P. 88), Satin Coral (M.P. 15), Coral (M.P. 21 Gloss), Transparent (M.P. 7), Pastel Green (M.P. 8), and Ivory White (M.P. 2).

This following is a list of shapes found in Rancho Ware.

C-0	Plate, Bread & Butter
C-1	Plate, Salad
C-2	Plate, Dinner
C-3	Plate, Large Dinner
C-4	Plate, Chop, 12"
C-6	Plate, Chop, 14"
C-10	Plate, Chop, 16", Medium
C-12	Plate, Chop, 17", Large
C-15	Fruit, Tab Handled
C-16	Cereal or Soup, Tab Handled
C-17	Vegetable, Tab Handled
C-18	Salad Bowl
C-19	Vegetable, Oval
C-20	Cup and Saucer
C-22	Creamer
C-23	Sugar with Lid
C-24	Teapot
C-25	Platter, Oval
C-27	Coffee Carafe with Wooden Handle
C-29	Pitcher
C-30	Pitcher, inset handle
C-31	Lid for C-30
C-34	Pitcher
C-35	Tumbler
C-37	Tumbler, Short
C-39	Mug, Handled
C-40	Cup and Saucer
C-41	Mug, Demitasse
C-42	Cream Soup Cup & Saucer
C-44	Chowder Bowl & Lid
C-45	Individual Condiment Dish
C-46	Onion Soup, Covered
C-47	Casserole, Covered & Metal Frame 7"
C-48	Casserole & Lid
C-49	Plate for Casserole
C-50	Cereal
C-51	Salad Bowl, Tab Handled
C-54	Tray, Oval, used for Individual Cream & Sugar
C-59	Individual Creamer
C-60	Individual Sugar
C-62	Vegetable, Round
C-65	Salt and Pepper, Gourd Shape, Pair
C-67	Salt and Pepper, Tulip Shaped, Pair
C-70	Vinegar Cruet — Gourd Shape
C-72	Condiment Jar with Lid, Gourd Shape
C-74	Condiment, Nut Cup, Gourd Shape
C-75	Salt & Pepper, Fish
C-77	Oval Vegetable
C-80	Coaster for C-35

Also used in the Rancho Ware line, and found marked Rancho Ware, are the following shapes. All of the shapes are fluted.

Avalon Table Ware was discontinued in 1938, and Rancho Ware in 1941.

C-217	Salad Bowl, Fluted
C-218	Bowl, Bread & Butter, Fluted
C-231	Plate, Salad Plate, Fluted
C-234	Bowl, Flat, 13.5", Fluted Large Chop
C-235	Bowl, Cereal, Fluted

Custom designed cup & saucer made as a special. Although the trim colors are Padua, the cup and saucer are in the Rancho shape. Value undetermined.

Rancho Ware. Front to back: #C-47 casserole with lid in coral, $45-55; #C-25 oval 12" platter in satin ivory, $32-38; #C-6 chop or buffet plate, 12" in dark yellow, $45-55; and #C-10 medium chop plate, 14" in Catalina dark blue, $45-55. Not pictured is the #C-12 large chop plate, 16", $55-65.

Rancho Ware. Left to right: #C-47 casserole with lid and stand in apple green, $45-55 and #C-47 casserole with lid and stand in coral, $45-55.

Rancho Ware. Front to Back: #C-15 fruit in satin coral, $10-16; left, #C-16 tab handled cereal or soup in Catalina green, $12-18; right, #C-50 cereal or soup in Catalina turquoise, $12-18; #C-0 bread & butter plate, 6.5" in satin ivory, $8-10; #C-1 dessert plate, 7.5" in Catalina red, $12-14; #C-2 salad plate, 8.5" in Catalina green, $12-14; #C4 large dinner, 10.5" in Catalina dark blue, $26-28.

Rancho Ware. Front to Back: #49 plate for casserole in Catalina green, $38-55 and #C-51 salad bowl in dark yellow, $55-75.

Rancho Ware. Left: #C-74 nut dish, gourd shape in Catalina turquoise, $26-28. Right: #C-65 gourd salt & pepper in dark yellow, $38-55. Center: #C-60 sugar, #C-59 creamer, sitting in a #C-54 tray, $22-26, all in Catalina sand. To the back is a #C-1 dessert plate, 7.5" in Catalina red, $12-14.

142

This is the Rancho Ware C-44 chowder bowl with lid in satin ivory, $85-125.

Rancho Ware. Left to right: C-20 Catalina blue cup & saucer, $18-22; #C-3 Catalina blue dinner or luncheon plate, $22-26; #C-46 satin ivory individual casserole with Catalina blue lid, $38-45; #C-45 Catalina blue small dish, $18-22; and #C-35 Catalina blue tumbler, $28-35.

Rancho Ware. Front: #235 bowl in unknown green, $28-32. Back: #234 chop plate, 14" in Catalina turquoise, $65-85. To the right: #C-35 tumbler in Catalina red, $28-35 and #C-37 small tumbler in Catalina red, $18-26.

Rancho Ware. Front to back: #C-23 sugar, $26-28 and #C-22 creamer, $26-28 in satin ivory; #C-1 dessert plate, 7.5" in Catalina red, $12-14; and #C-6 chop or buffet plate, 12" in dark yellow, $45-55.

Rancho Ware. #C-218 bowl in green, $45-65.

Rancho Ware. Left to right: Mexican blue #C-217 bowl and #C-216 bowl. Mexican blue glaze in Rancho is very rare. No price determined.

Rancho Ware. Left to right: #C-27 coffee jug with lid in Catalina turquoise, $45-55 and #C-29 pitcher in Catalina sand, $65-85.

Rancho Ware. This is the #C-30 pitcher in dark yellow, $35-45 as is without the #C-31 lid. The lid is very scarce, so with a lid this pitcher is valued $85-125. These were sold with lids, so without a lid it is incomplete.

Rancho Ware #C-24 teapot in satin ivory, $145-225.

Rancho Ware #C-80 coaster in Catalina sand, $16-22. This shape was also used in the El Patio Table Ware line as #75 coaster and later used in the Max Schonfeld Kaolena Specials line.

Original Rancho Ware brochure, $45-65.

Del Mar

One of the most desirable patterns today is Del Mar. Del Mar is Spanish for "Of the Sea." Del Mar is lined with white featuring picturesque hand-painted sailboats.

Expect to find the following pieces:

Plate, Bread and Butter, 6.5"
Plate, Dessert and Salad, 7.5"
Plate, Salad, 8.5"
Plate, Luncheon, 9.5"
Plate, Large Dinner or Service
Plate, 10.5"
Soup Bowl
Teapot & Lid
Plate, Chop, 12-3/8"
Cup and Saucer
Vegetable Dish
Creamer
Sugar, Lidded
Salad Bowl

Del Mar was very short-lived, being discontinued in 1938.

Del Mar is an extremely hard to find and rare pattern. Left to right: 9.5" dinner plate, $75-85 and salad or dessert plate, 7.5", $45-55.

Del Oro

Del Oro is Spanish for "Of the Sun." In a brilliant yellow banding with a clear over glaze, this pattern was very elegant in its presentation. Del Oro was made on the Montecito shapes.

Expect to find the following pieces:
Candlestick
Fruit
Cereal
Plate, Bread and Butter, 6.5"
Plate, Dessert, 7.5"
Plate, Salad, 8.5"
Plate, Dinner, 9.5"
Plate, Large Dinner or Service Plate, 10.5"
Plate, Chop, 12-3/8"
Plate, Chop, 14"

Cup and Saucer
After Dinner Cup and Saucer
Cream Soup Cup and Saucer
Sherbet
Tumbler
Creamer
Sugar & Lid
Tea Pot & Lid
After Dinner Coffee Pot
Baker, Round
Hexagonal Platter, Small
Hexagonal Platter, Large
Salad Bowl
Hexagonal Bowl with Handles
Gravy Boat
Salt & Pepper
Dish

Del Mar was very short-lived, being discontinued in 1939.

Del Oro is hard to find. This is a coffee carafe without a stopper, $75-95.

Del Oro. Left to right: salad or desert plate, 7.5", $28-32 and after dinner cup and saucer, $38-45.

Mango is hand-painted with mangos and lined in deep yellows and browns. Mango is on the Monticeto shape. It is not known if all Montecito shapes were used for Mango.

Pieces found in Mango are the following:

Plate, Bread and Butter, 6.5"
Plate, Dessert, 7.5"
Plate, Salad, 8.5"
Plate, Dinner, 9.5"
Plate, Large Dinner or Service Plate, 10.5"
Plate, Chop, 12-3/8"
Cup and Saucer
Jumbo Cup and Saucer
Fruit
Cereal, or Soup
Baker or Vegetable Dish, Round
Creamer
Sugar, Lidded
Tea Pot
Salad Bowl
Hexagonal Platter
Small Creamer
Small Sugar Bowl & Lid

Mango was discontinued in 1938 and is very hard to find today.

Mango creamer, $45-55.

Mango. Left front: cup & saucer, $26-32. Left back: bread & butter, 6.5", $16-18 and dessert, 7.5", $18-22. Right front: cereal or soup, $26-32. Right back: salad, 8.5", $22-24; luncheon, 9.5", $26-32; and large dinner, 10.5", $32-42.

Mango 14" chop plate, $75-95.

Willow

Willow is partially decaled and then hand-painted and lined. Two variations are found, one under glaze decoration on Yellow and the other under glaze decoration on Oatmeal. Willow is on the Montecito shape. Willow does have a restyled cup, however it is not known if this cup shape was ever made in the Montecito Table Ware line. Willow was discontinued in July of 1940.

This is a list of items that were made:

Plate, Bread and Butter, 6.5"
Plate, Dessert, 7.5"
Plate, Salad, 8.5"
Plate, Dinner, 9.5"
Plate, Large Dinner, 10.5"
Plate, Chop, 12-3/8"
Plate, Chop, 14"
Cup and Saucer
Fruit
Cereal, or Soup
Vegetable Dish
Salad Bowl
Creamer
Sugar, Lidded
Tea Pot & Lid

Willow, underglaze on oatmeal. Left to right: cup and saucer, $22-28; luncheon plate, 9.5", $22-32; bread & butter plate, 6.5", $10-14; and dessert or salad plate, 7.5", $14-22.

Willow, underglaze on oatmeal. Left to right: vegetable dish, $45-65; chop plate, 12-3/8", $65-85; sugar with lid, $45-55; and creamer, $45-55.

Willow, underglaze on oatmeal. Left to right: salad bowl, $125-145; 14" chop plate, $85-125; and vegetable dish, $45-65.

Lamp Bases

Lamp bases were made for different companies to be used in the manufacture of lamps for household and commercial use. One of which is known is the Colonial Lamp Company. Not all lamp bases are marked. If the vase has a drilled but not glazed hole, then it is a vase that was made into a lamp. Only the glazed over holes were bases made by Gladding McBean for lamp bases. Different shapes were used from various lines, however new shapes were designed and sculpted for the use of just a lamp base. Lamp bases continued to be made to 1951 in earthenware and china bodies.

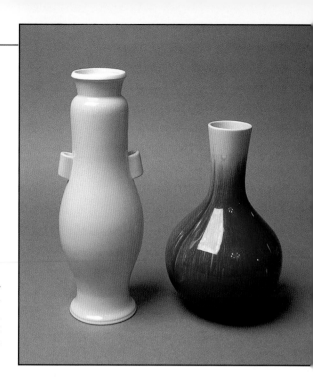

Lamp bases. Left to right: lamp base in duotone Chinese yellow over celestial white, $255-310 and oxblood bottle shape lamp base #S-91, $255-310. The shape to the right has never been found in a vase, as it usually has a glazed-over hole in the base, while the shape to the left has been found as a vase without a glazed-over hole.

Gladding McBean produced lamp bases for companies to use with their hardware and lamp shade businesses. Many shapes were produced from the general Cielito art ware shapes with holes that were glazed over. Pictured is the #116 vase, bottle shape, 9.5" in an oxblood glaze. The vase is to the left while the lamp base is to the right. Note that the mark "Made in USA" is offset from the glazed-over hole. Not all lamp bases are marked. If the vase has a drilled but not glazed hole, then it is a vase that was made into a lamp. Only the glazed-over holes were bases made by Gladding McBean for lamp bases. Factory-made lamp bases, complete with original hardware, are about 20-30% more than vases. The vase is $225 and the lamp base is $245-290.

Lamp Base, shape #S-92 made as a special for the Spirit of India and could have sold at the Golden Gate Exposition of 1939 and 1940 in San Francisco. Original hardware, no shade, $265-325.

This lamp base shape resembles the #C-290 vase shape; however, notice the top of the vase shape, which is the #L-15 shape. Made only as a lamp base shape, this lamp features original hardware and the original shade, $325-345. Most lamps have been refitted with new hardware or shades, which should not detract from their value. However, if the lamp is fitted with original hardware and shade, expect to pay more. The only way to determine original hardware is by verifying this with the original owner. Rust and wear to the metal hardware detracts from the value.

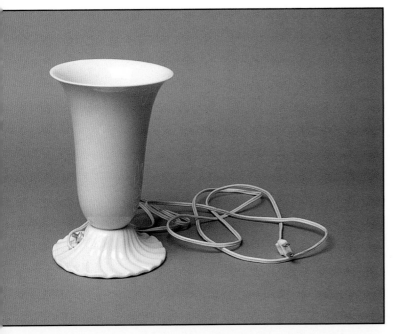

A classic lamp based on the Coronado shape vases #161 & #156. This lamp was only made in the fine china clay body. The lamp parts are marked Colonial Lamp Co. Probably the Colonial Lamp Co. ordered this lamp shape from Gladding McBean specifically for their distribution. Usually found with an over glaze of either light tan glaze or a very light turquoise glaze on the ivory china body. This lamp has also been found in a clear glaze over the ivory china body. This lamp has been rewired. $225-245.

Chapter 8

Hotel Ware and Specials as a New Business Venture 1938

After a prosperous year in 1937, Gladding, McBean & Co. enjoyed the success brought on by the growth in the pottery division. 1937 was the year Gladding, McBean & Co. introduced the most patterns in art ware and tableware during their history. To continue with this success, Gladding, McBean & Co. added to their art ware line Ox-Blood Art Ware, and to their tableware line Hawthorne, and Fruit.

A new line was marketed using the kitchenware shapes of the El Patio dinnerware line and was named Kitchen Ware. Gladding, McBean & Co. also looked to new ventures, supplying hotel ware to the hotel supply companies. Though the company produced specials for various organizations and companies, a large order was placed for premium and give-away wares for the Sperry Flour Company.

Ox-blood. #123 large vase, 11" x 9.75" diameter, $350-$450.

Ox-blood. Left to right: #115 vase, 10.5", $225; lamp base, $275; #116 bottle shaped vase, 9.5", $225.

Ox Blood Art Ware

Ox-blood. Left to right: #C-289 wide mouth vase, 9", $225; #114 vase with flaring top, 8.75", $275; #C-290 vase, 11", $275.

On August 1, 1938, Gladding, McBean & Co. introduced the "Chinese Ox-Blood" glaze on 15 items of art ware in what company documents referred to as "pure Chinese shapes." This reduced red copper glaze at the time had never been produced in the United States except on a laboratory scale. The chemists of Gladding, McBean & Co created a glaze that could be used on the "Malinite" body in their "Prouty" tunnel kilns. The line was named "Ox Blood Art Ware." Oxblood is glaz M.P. 40.

The following are the shapes that were produced in the Ox Blood Art Ware Line.

16	Bowl, small	C-281	Vase, 6" Footed
79	Bowl, round	C-282	Bowl, 7.5" Low Square
104	Ball Shape Vase	C-283	Bowl, 10" Round
105	Vase, Small Bottle Shape	C-284	Vase, 8.25"
114	Vase, 2.75" Flaring	C-285	Vase, 9"
115	Vase, 10.5"	C-286	Vase, 11"
116	Vase, 9.5" Bottle Shape	C-287	Bowl, 16"
122	Vase, 9.5" Ball Shape	C-288	Vase
123	Vase, 11" Large	C-289	Vase, 9" Wide Mouth
140	Vase, Low	C-290	Vase, 11"
141	Vase, 7.25" Beaker Shape	C-293	Vase, 5.5" (Rose Bowl)
C-277	Vase, 4.5" Low	C-300	Vase, 5" Small
C-278	Vase, 6"	C-806	Bird on Base
C-279	Vase, 4.5" Square		

This was a very popular glaze for the employees. Many employees had various other shapes not in the Ox Blood Art Ware line made for their personal use. Usually you will find these without factory marks; however, many of these pieces are ink stamped "Catalina Pottery" or "Franciscan Ware."

Ox-blood. Left to right: #105 bottle shape vase, 6", $145; #140 vase, low, $165; #132 round vase, 4.5", $145; #C-300 small vase, 5", $95.

Ox-blood. Left to right: #387 cylinder vase, 9", $325 and #C-806 bird, $350-375.

Ox-blood. #C-278 vase, 6", $285-325.

Ox-blood. #C286 vase, 11" flaring, $775-850.

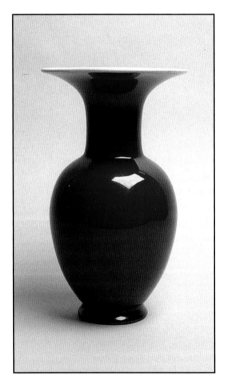

Ox-blood. #C-289 vase, 9" wide mouth, $275-295.

Ox-blood. #122 vase, 9.5" ball shape, $275-285.

Ox-blood. #C-293 vase, 5.5" large round, $225-255.

Ox-blood. #C-279 vase, 4.5" square, $225-255.

Ox-blood. #141 vase, 7.25" beaker shape, $195-245.

Ox-blood. Left to right: #79 bowl, round, $145-165; #16 bowl, small, $95-125.

155

Hawthorne is on the Montecito shape with an under glaze decoration with a clear over glaze. Hawthorne is banded and lined with copper. Hawthorne was discontinued in 1942.

Pieces found in Hawthorne are the following:
Plate, Bread and Butter, 6.5"
Plate, Dessert, 7.5"
Plate, Salad, 8.5"
Plate, Dinner, 9.5"
Plate, Large Dinner or Service
    Plate, 10.5"
Plate, Chop, 12-3/8"
Cup and Saucer
Fruit
Cereal, or Soup
Vegetable Dish
Creamer
Sugar, Lidded
Casserole, Covered
Individual Casserole with lid
Individual Cream
Individual Sugar
Coffee Pot
Tea Pot
Demitasse Cup and Saucer
Salad Bowl
Platter, Hexagonal, 13"

Hawthorne. Left to right: vegetable bowl, $75-95; octagonal platter, 13", $85-125; coffee pot, $125-145; sugar with lid, $45-65; creamer, $45-55; and shaker, $28-32 each.

Hawthorne. Left to right: bread & butter plate, 6.5", $15-18; fruit bowl, $18-22; salad plate, 7.5", $22-28; dessert plate, 8.5", $22-28; dinner plate, 9.5", $28-32; dinner plate, large, 10.5" $28-35; cup and saucer, $45-55.

Fruit is a decaled dinnerware set that is banded in blue with a blue over glaze on the Montecito shape. Another variation was banded in brown with a clear over glaze. This variation has not been found, but was listed in documentation found. Fruit was discontinued in 1942.

Plate, Bread and Butter, 6.5"

Plate, Dessert and Salad, 7.5"

Plate, Dinner, 9.5"

Plate, Large Dinner or Service Plate, 10.5"

Plate, Chop, 12-3/8"

Plate, Chop, 14"

Cup and Saucer

Fruit

Cereal, or Soup

Vegetable Dish

Creamer

Sugar, Lidded

Salad Bowl

Tea Pot & Lid

Platter, Hexagonal, 13"

Small Creamer

Small Sugar Bowl with Lid

Fruit salad bowl, $95-145 and Fruit octagonal platter, 13", $95-125.

Fruit 14" chop plate, $95-145.

Fruit salad plate, 7.5", $32-36.

Kitchen Ware

Kitchen Ware was a new line marketed by Gladding, McBean & Co. using the kitchenware shapes from El Patio. No new shapes were made. The colors available were the same as those of El Patio. It was suggested and marketed as a multi-colored set using a different colored lid for the cookie jar and encouraging store buyers to mix various colored custards. This line included a cookie jar, covered casserole, individual covered casserole, and custard and mixing bowls in various sizes. There are two types of mixing bowls, one is ribbed (335-340) and the other is straight flared, no ribbing (360-363).

Shapes included in the Kitchen Ware line are the following:

Kitchen Ware. Left to right: #31 lidded cookie or pretzel jar in light yellow, $125-225; #341 custard cup in apple green, $18-22; and #15 beverage pitcher, 3.5 quart in celestial white, $75-95. Note the ribbing to the sides of the El Patio kitchenware. The cookie jar and beverage pitcher were the first to be introduced with other pieces following. The beverage pitcher matches the #39 ice tea tumbler in the El Patio line with the same ribbing.

335	Mixing Bowl 4.5"
336	Mixing Bowl 5.5"
337	Mixing Bowl 6.5"
338	Mixing Bowl 7.5"
339	Mixing Bowl 8.5"
340	Mixing Bowl 9.5"
341	Custard Cup
341x	Set of 6 cups in wire frame
342	Casserole with lid & iron frame
343	Casserole only
344	Handled Batter Bowl
345	Ramekin and Lid
346	Pitcher 2 quart (shaped like a pineapple)
352	Mixing Bowl 5 quart
353	Mixing Bowl 7.5 quart
360	Mixing Bowl 1.5 pint
361	Mixing Bowl 1.5 quart
362	Mixing Bowl 2.5 quart
363	Mixing Bowl 4 quart
364	3 piece set (360-1-2)
365	4 piece set (360-1-2-3)
366	Pie Plate 10"
367	Ice Box Pitcher 2 quart*
368	Ice Box Dish 1 pint — stackable*
369	Ice Box Dish 1 quart — stackable*
370	Lid for 368 and 369*
372	Covered Butter Dish *
373	Cookie Jar & Lid*
*	Found in the Geranium pattern

Kitchen Ware. Left to right: #341 custard cup in apple green, $18-22 and #344 batter bowl in yellow, $75-95.

158

Kitchen Ware, set of mixing bowls, nested. From the inside out: #335 in glacial blue, $28-38; #336 in apple green, $32-42; #337 in light blue, $35-45; #338 in coral, $38-55; and #339 in yellow, $45-65.

Kitchen Ware, set of mixing bowls. Right to left: #335 in glacial blue, $28-38; #336 in apple green, $32-42; #337 in light blue, $35-45; #338 in coral, $38-55; and #339 in yellow, $45-65.

Kitchen Ware. #346 pineapple pitcher, 2 quart in apple green, $75-145.

Hotel Ware

Gladding, McBean & Co. on March 22, 1938 produced the first hotel ware. This was a rolled rim coupe shape on the earthenware body, glazed in gloss coral. This line was first sold to Dohrmann Hotel Supply Co. of San Francisco. Later in the year it was sold to the Southern Pacific Co. for use on the "Daylite" trains between San Francisco and Los Angeles. Colors offered were in the gloss glazes of Turquoise (M.P. 92), Green (M.P. 98), Coral (M.P. 91), Dark Yellow (M.P. 93), and Pastel Pink (M.P. 95). Hotel Ware has also been found in Coral Satin (M.P. 15).

The following shapes are found in the Hotel Ware line.

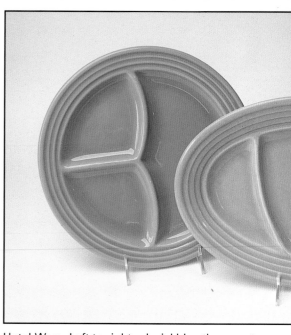

Hotel Ware. Left to right: glacial blue three part divided sectional plate #1014, $28-32 and coral three part divided oval grille platter #1075, $28-32.

1000	Butter Chip		1022	After Dinner Cup
1001	Fruit Dish		1023	After Dinner Saucer
1002	Cereal		1024	Bouillon
1004	Coupe Soup		1024a	Lid for Bouillon
1005	Plate, 5.5"		1036	Individual Gravy
1006	Plate, 6.5"		1037	Single Egg Cup
1007	Plate, 7.5"		1038	Double Egg Cup
1008	Plate, 8.5"		1042	Individual Creamer
1009	Plate, 9.5"		1071	Platter 9" Crescent
1010	Plate, 10.5"		1072	Platter 10.5" Crescent
1013	Sectional Plate		1075	Platter Grille
1014	Sectional Plate, Large		1076	Platter 6" Oval
1020	Cup		1077	Platter 7" Oval
1021	Saucer		1079	Platter 9" Oval

Hotel Ware. Left to right: apple green flat soup plate #1004, $12-18; celadon compote S-52 in the specials line and not offered in the open stock Hotel Ware line, $32-38; and apple green butter chip #1000, $16-18.

Hotel Ware. Left to right, front: coral blue trimmed after dinner coffee cup #1022 and saucer #1023, $22-32; coral after dinner cup and saucer #1022/23, $22-26; individual cream #1042 in yellow, $22-26; coral coffee cup #1020, $22-26; and cereal or soup bowl #1002, $22-26. Back: eggcup #1038 in light blue, $16-22 and eggcup in satin ivory, $16-22; the 6.5" bread & butter plate #1005 in coral, $6-10; 7.5" dessert plate #1007 in coral, $8-12; and 10.5" dinner plate #1010 in coral satin, $22-32.

Hotel Ware. Left to right: yellow oval platter, 9" #1079, $22-32 and coral oval platter #1076, small 6", $22-28.

Hotel Ware. #1071 platter, 9" crescent in coral, $25-35. This also came in a larger size as the 1072 platter, 10" crescent.

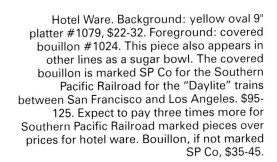

Hotel Ware. Background: yellow oval 9" platter #1079, $22-32. Foreground: covered bouillon #1024. This piece also appears in other lines as a sugar bowl. The covered bouillon is marked SP Co for the Southern Pacific Railroad for the "Daylite" trains between San Francisco and Los Angeles. $95-125. Expect to pay three times more for Southern Pacific Railroad marked pieces over prices for hotel ware. Bouillon, if not marked SP Co, $35-45.

Though not documented in the Hotel Ware line, this is a pitcher with an earthenware handle, $45-55. This pitcher has been found in yellow and glacial blue glazes and is usually found not marked. This could also be in the Specials, Pueblo, or Kitchen Ware lines.

Pueblo

The "Pueblo" line was made for ware only sold as premiums from 1938 to 1939. Pieces have been found marked Pueblo on art ware shapes. A special dinnerware line was created and marked Pueblo. These pieces all have rings around the perimeter of the plates and around the foot of hollow ware shapes. Colors offered were Coral, Yellow, Turquoise, and Green. Also found have been Satin Ivory and Maroon.

Shapes in the Pueblo line are the following:

1201	Fruit
1202	Soup or Cereal
1203	Cereal Bowl
1206	Bread & Butter, 6.5"
1207	Dessert Plate, 7.5"
1208	Salad Plate, 8.5"
1209	Dinner Plate, 9.5"
1210	Service Plate, 10.5"
1212	Chop Plate, 12"
1214	Chop Plate, 14"
1220	Cup, Ovide (SC-20)
1221	Saucer
1240	Creamer
1241	Sugar with Lid
1260	Baker
1270	Oval Platter
1280	Salad Bowl
1290	Ash Tray

Pueblo. Plates left to right: maroon #1209 dinner plate, 9.5", $12-18; matt ivory #1206 bread & butter plate, 6.5", $8-10; coral #1207 dessert plate, 7.5", $10-14; yellow #1209 dinner plate, 9.5", $12-18; and a glacial blue #1206 bread & butter plate, 6.5", $8-10.

Pueblo. Background plates left to right: matt ivory #1209 dinner plate, 9.5", $12-18; apple green #1206 bread & butter plate, 6.5", $8-10; glacial blue #1209 dinner plate, $12-18; and yellow #1206 bread & butter plate, $8-10. Foreground: #1260 baker, $28-35.

Dear Friend:

Here is that Breakfast Set you ...ered. We hope you will enjoy it thorou...ly and that your family is enjoying your p...cka...e of Wheat Hearts, too!

May I tell you about another surp...e we have? It's a new offer for those wh... have not yet tried our fine product, Sperry Pancake and Waffle Flour. The details are printed below and our friends tell us it's a most exciting offer.

Martha Meade

THIS GENUINE

Franciscan

CONDIMENT SERVICE
SALT & PEPPER • JAR & LADLE

4 SMART MATCHING ACCESSORIES THAT BRING NEW GLORY TO YOUR TABLE

FOR ONLY 50¢

AND A GROCER'S SALES SLIP SHOWING YOUR PURCHASE OF ONE PACKAGE OF

SPERRY PANCAKE AND WAFFLE FLOUR

Easily filled, the salt and pepper shakers hold one ounce each. They stand firm and sprinkle their contents correctly through the spouts, like the tiny teapots they resemble. The sauce jar holds a full three ounces of mustard or mayonnaise.

As an investment in advertising, Sperry has secured a limited shipment of these 4-piece sets direct from the Franciscan people. As long as the supply lasts they will be offered at only 50c per set—far less than retail value —as a means of acquainting you with the goodness of Sperry Pancakes and Waffles. We suggest you buy your package of Sperry Pancake and Waffle Flour today, and send for your set at once. Orders honored only while the supply lasts. . . .

FLAME ORANGE   MEXICAN BLUE

TURQUOISE   JONQUIL YELLOW

Choose your set in any <u>one</u> of the 4 lovely colors shown

HOW TO ORDER • See other side

Gladding, McBean & Co. produced premiums for Sperry Flour Company, a division of General Mills, that could be purchased for a fraction of retail cost. Premiums included condiment sets and cream and sugar sets.

This cardboard insert came with the condiment service in its original box. On the reverse side was a form to pass along to a friend, presenting that friend with the opportunity to participate in the promotion as well.

Made for the Sperry Flour Company, this is the complete condiment set sent directly by the Franciscan factory after the customer submitted the coupon from packages of Sperry Pancake and Waffle Flour, along with a grocer's receipt and 50 cents. The set consisted of a salt & pepper, jar, and ladle. The ladle was made of glass. Colors available were flame orange, Mexican blue, turquoise, and jonquil yellow. With box, salt & pepper, jar, & ladle, $145. #S-45 salt & pepper set only, $12-22. #S-47 jar only, $10-14. Sperry Flour Company was a trade name of the Western Division of General Mills, Inc.

Another promotion from the Sperry Flour Company. For 50 cents, a grocer's sales slip showing you had purchased one package of Wheat Hearts, and a completed coupon, you could have this cream and sugar sent to you directly from the Franciscan factory. The teapot was also a promotion, but it is unknown what product had to be purchased to have it arrive at your doorstep. With a domed lid, it is marked "Made in USA." Colors available for the set were Mexican blue, jonquil yellow, flame orange, and turquoise. However, the set has also been found in apple green. #S-38 cream, $18-24; #S-39 sugar, $18-22; and #S-47 tea pot, $145-185.

This is the #8 baking dish in glacial blue, used as a promotional premium for the Sperry Flour Company. These have been found in their original boxes, either as a single or as a set of two. $12-18 each. If found in original box, add 30%. Other colors that are common are brilliant yellow, Mexican blue, coral, satin coral, and flame orange.

SPECIAL OFFER

TO MAKE NEW FRIENDS FOR OUR
HOT CEREAL WHEAT HEARTS
A SET OF GENUINE
FRANCISCAN WARE

A BARGAIN in beauty offered because our experience shows that once you try our hot cereal Wheat Hearts, you'll be back for more!

And your doctor will approve your choice, because Wheat Hearts, unlike the usual hot cereals, contains pure toasted wheat germ. This is the food substance that, University tests showed, caused underweight children to grow three times faster! It makes Wheat Hearts richer in Vitamin B (for growth and appetite) than any other common table food. In this respect, one bowl of Wheat Hearts equals 80 bowls of corn cereals!

These same toasted flakes of wheat germ give Wheat Hearts that nut-like flavor. It's a taste youngsters like because it's rich . . . not flat or tasteless. Try Wheat Hearts right away . . . you'll be glad you did and the Franciscan set will be an extra reward.

Here is a colorful Cream-and-Sugar Set of exceptional smartness and in the same de luxe pottery ware honored by display at the Metropolitan Museum of New York. It's made by Franciscan . . . and has the high-lustre, the unusually brilliant color, for which Franciscan Ware is famous. A set in your choice of colors will be sent you for only 50¢ . . . far less than retail value. But since this is strictly an introductory offer, it is good only while supplies last. And only one set per family, please!

Sperry Flour Company (Trade Name)
Western Division of General Mills, Inc.

FOUR GLAMOROUS COLORS
. . . your choice of
Mexican Blue
Jonquil Yellow
Turquoise
or Flame Orange.
Size: Pitcher and bowl hold one cup each.

Copyright 1938
General Mills, Inc.

Mail Today

Sperry Flour Company, San Francisco, Calif.
I enclose 50¢ (coin, money order or stamps) and grocer's sales slip showing purchase of one package of Wheat Hearts. Please send me one Franciscan Cream-and-Sugar Set as described. I want the color checked below.

COLOR DESIRED

Mexican Blue ☐   Flame Orange ☐
Jonquil Yellow ☐   Turquoise ☐

Name

Address

City   State

S-3

This is a Sperry Flour Company advertisement from 1938 for the promotion, "To make new friends for our hot cereal Wheat Hearts – a set of genuine Franciscan Ware," with a coupon to submit. "And only one set per family, please!"

165

Chapter 9
1939 San Francisco Golden Gate International Exposition

The World's Fair began in 1939 in New York City and in San Francisco. The World's Fair in San Francisco was officially named the Golden Gate International Exposition. Gladding, McBean & Co., and especially Atholl McBean, were involved in the planning, construction, and exhibition of wares for the World's Fair. Atholl McBean joined in the planning for the World's Fair in San Francisco in 1934 as one of its Directors and would later become the Chairman of the Board of the Golden Gate International Exposition Corporation. Atholl McBean was a leader and devoted more of his time to civic matters while at the same time keeping an eye on the bottom line for Gladding, McBean & Co.

Gladding, McBean & Co. had exhibition space to show off the products of the company including terra cotta sewer pipe, sculpted ceramic veneer, tile, Franciscan Ware, and other clay products. Gladding, McBean & Co. published the "Color Counts, Franciscan Ware" brochure for their display of Franciscan Ware. Franciscan Ware shared space with Barker Brothers Department Store. New items were specifically manufactured for Barker Brothers to sell at the fair as well as in their department stores promoting the fair. Hand-painted tableware sets from the Rancho Ware shapes, a series of plates commemorating the missions of California, and two-toned Montecito that was specifically ink marked "Barker Brothers," were just some of the special items made for Barker Brothers Department Stores.

A special gold round sticker with the words Golden Gate Exposition, Barker Brothers and Gladding, McBean & Co. was used on fair souvenirs. Souvenirs found have been the C-810 Grape Table Ornament and the C-812 Fruit & Nut Table Ornament from the Catalina Art Ware line, and vases from various lines.

One of the highlights in ceramics displayed at San Francisco was the official group of 100 ceramic products selected from the National Ceramic Exhibition, which included an opium bowl of copper red glaze. The bowl featured a glaze developed and executed by Max D. Compton. Max Compton in 1939 was the Chief Ceramist for the Glendale plant.

Only one art ware line was introduced in 1939. The new line was Nautical Art Ware.

New in tableware were Geranium, Padua II, and Rancho Duotone.

On March 1, 1939, Gladding, McBean & Co. produced its first line of vitrified hotel ware. Unlike the earthernware hotel ware produced in 1938, the body could withstand the harsher treatment that is necessary for hotel use. Again this new ware was sold through Dohrmann Hotel Supply Co. Making this ware gave the Company valuable experience in manufacturing a china body and producing suitable glazes for china.

On July 10, 1939, Gladding, McBean & Co. produced special earthenware shapes for the Max Schonfeld Co. A local importer of china cologne bottles and dressing table sets, Max Schonfeld had his supplies from Germany and France cut off by the war in Europe. There were small bottle and stoppers in satin matt pastel glazes. Gladding, McBean & Co. supplied him with "blanks" and he set up his own studio to decorate the pieces with gold and fired them.

By August 1939, on a laboratory scale, Gladding, McBean & Co. developed a china casting body, of a Belleek-type, and a suitable glaze for the body. A completely new body was made and to their knowledge never before used. The decision was made to produce a few items in blanks for the Max Schonfeld Co. in their new china body and glaze. By making this ware, Gladding, McBean & Co. would partially pay for their development cost.

Gladding, McBean & Co. produced many specials for companies throughout the years. New contracts were made with Nasco, trademark of the National Silver Company, and Sunkist, a registered trademark of the California Fruitgrowers Exchange. 1939 also saw Gladding, McBean & Co. awarded its first major special order for 25,000 pieces from the Toastmaster Division of McGraw Electric Company for toast and jam sets.

Titled "India," this is a scaled down version of a actual statue that originally stood as one of pair known as "The Spirit of India" in the Court of Pacifica at the Golden Gate Exposition of 1939 and 1940 in San Francisco. Pacifica was a huge statue that measured 80 feet tall. California Governor, Culbert Olson, described the Court of Pacifica toward the end of a speech in a September 1939 live radio broadcast, "Here on Treasure Island, is the Court of Pacifica, leading into the Court of Seven Seas, The Court of Honor, and the Court of the Moon. Overlooking this scene, from her eminence, the Statue of Pacifica folds her arms in peaceful benediction upon the Treasure Island scene. Pacifica—symbol of peace—ruling theme of Treasure Island and California—America's shrine of friendship…" This was an important theme at a time when most of the world was already at war and the attack on Pearl Harbor had yet to happen.

At the foot of Pacifica stood a terraced fountain surrounded by twenty sculptures by eight different artists, four men and four women. Each statue represented one of a variety of peoples who live along the shores of the Pacific Ocean. This figure of India has a terra cotta special glazed interior with an over glaze of eggplant purple, like that found on Montecito dinnerware. The figure measures 10.25" tall and about 10.75" long. The base is marked with the artist signature "J Schnier" and "5/1" indicating it is one out of five made. Jacque Schnier was a true artist and devoted his entire life to sculpting in many mediums besides terra cotta and clay. He was one of many commissioned artists paid to create large scaled sculpture for the many "Courts" on "Treasure Island" as the Fair came to be known. At this time it isn't clear why this miniature version of India was made or who it was presented to.

CALIFORNIA WORLD'S FAIR ON SAN FRANCISCO BAY

This is a picture postcard of the statue of "Pacifica," Court of Pacifica. In the foreground are the larger-than-life size statues of India.

"Color Counts" Franciscan Ware catalog and separate price list, 1939. This was given away at the Golden Gate International Exposition. It is marked Barker Bros. and Golden Gate International Exposition, 1939. $75-125.

Bottom view of "India." The base is ink marked "Made in USA" in black. No price determined.

Nautical Art Ware was a new art ware line introduced in 1939. Many of the shapes had previously been in other art ware lines. Gladding, McBean & Co. also added new shapes to the line.

The following is a complete list of the shapes in the Nautical Art Ware line.

C-236	Bowl, Giant Clam Shell, 16"
C-237	Bowl, Clam Shell, med, 11"
C-238	Bowl, Clam Shell, small
C-326	Vase, Shell
C-350	Sea Shell Cornucopia
C-351	Sea Shell Vase
C-352	Double Clam Shell Vase
C-353	Shell Vase
C-354	Shell Vase
C-355	Shell Vase
C-356	Shell Bowl, 15"
C-357	Shell Bowl, 9.5"
C-358	Shell Vase, Murex Design
C-359	Shell Vase, Strombus
C-360	Oval Bowl, Fish Pattern
C-361	Small Fish Vase
C-362	Fan Vase, Fish Pattern
C-363	Large Vase, Fish Pattern
C-364	Large Bowl, Fish Deco
C-370	Shell Vase, Conch Design
C-371	Shell Ash Tray
C-372	Shell Ash Tray
C-373	Clam Shell, Large Double
C-374	Shell Compote, Double
C-375	Shell Bowl, Low Round
C-641	Dolphin Table Piece

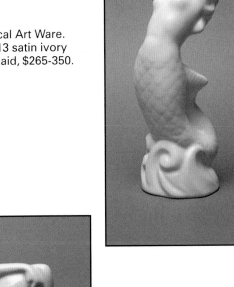

Nautical Art Ware. #C-813 satin ivory mermaid, $265-350.

The Nautical Art Ware line was discontinued in 1942. Not all shapes were available from 1939 to 1942 as many were discontinued prior to 1942.

Nautical Art Ware, ivory outside and lined with coral. Left to right: #C-236 giant clamshell bowl, 15" x 6.5", $225; #C-238 small size clamshell bowl, $45; and #C-237 clamshell bowl, medium size, 11" x 5.25", $85-125.

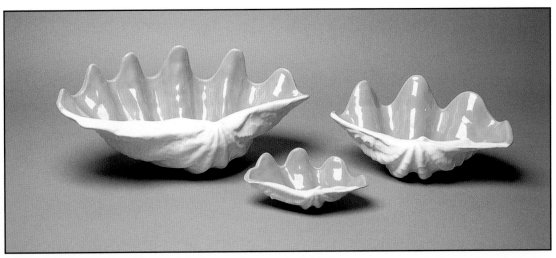

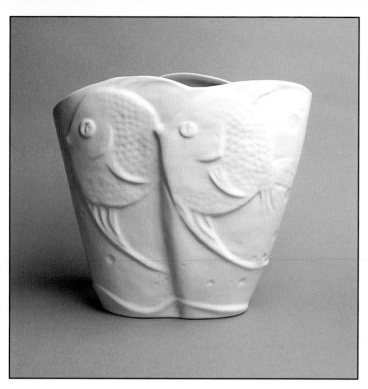

Nautical Art Ware, ivory outside and lined with glacial blue #C-363 large vase fish, deco, 9.5", $275-325.

Nautical Art Ware, ivory outside and lined with glacial blue #C-361 small fish vase, 5", $145-245.

Nautical Art Ware, ivory outside and lined with coral. Left to right: #C-355 shell vase, $145; #C-271 shell ashtray, solid color coral, $45; and #C-359 strombus shell vase, $145.

Nautical Art Ware, ivory outside and lined with satin turquoise fish bowl, $225-245.

Nautical Art Ware, ivory outside and lined with coral. Back left to right: #C-326 shell vase, $145 and #C-353 shell vase, 7.25", $125. Front: #C-374 double shell compote, $95-125.

Nautical Art Ware, ivory outside and lined with coral. Top left to right: #C-370 conch design shell vase, $145; #C-358 murex design shell vase, $145; and #C-350 seashell cornucopia, 6", $85-95. Front: #C-375 shell bowl, low round, $45-65.

Nautical Art Ware, ivory outside and lined with satin turquoise. Left to right: #C-360 oval fish bowl, 11", $225-245 and #C-363 large vase, fish, deco, 9.5", $225-285.

171

Nautical Art Ware. #C-354 ivory outside lined with coral shell vase, 5.25", $85-95, and #C-372 satin turquoise shell ashtray, $38-45.

Nautical Art Ware. Foreground: #C-641 satin ivory dolphin table piece, 5.5", $95-145. Background: #C-375 satin ivory lined with satin turquoise shell bowl, low round, $45-65.

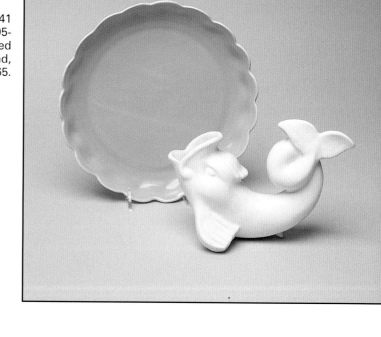

Nautical Art Ware. #C-362 fan vase, fish pattern in satin ivory lined with satin turquoise, $225-275.

Nautical Art Ware. Left to right: #C-371 satin turquoise shell ashtray, $45 and #C-352 double clamshell vase in satin ivory, $245-265.

172

Nautical Art Ware. Very rare coral exterior and gray interior #C-350 seashell cornucopia, 6", $95-125.

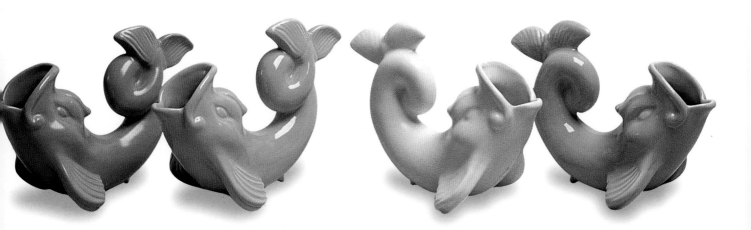

Nautical Art Ware. Left to right: unusual Rancho Table Ware color #C-641 dolphin table piece, 5.5"; coral gloss dolphin; ivory dolphin; and glacial blue dolphin. Ivory dolphin is valued $95-145. All other dolphins are valued $145-225. Dolphins are usually found in satin ivory. There is also a duo-tone dolphin with a coral interior, an ivory exterior and one featuring a satin turquoise interior with an ivory exterior. Both of the duo-tone versions are quite scarce, $145-225.

With a vivid white over glaze on Montecito shapes, Geranium is partially hand-painted and decaled with geraniums. It is lined in a brilliant red. New shapes offered in this set and not used by any other set are a refrigerator jug with lid, a large counter canister, and a butter dish. Later on, Gladding, McBean & Co. used this butter dish shape for other tableware sets. You will find a chop plate on the El Patio shape as well as the Montecito shape in the set. The cup is unusual as it is not the Montecito cup shape. For Geranium, the cup shape is from the Duo-tone Rancho Ware tableware.

Expect to find the following pieces:

Plate, Bread and Butter, 6.5"
Plate, Dessert and Salad, 7.5"
Plate, Luncheon, 9.5"
Plate, Large Dinner, 10.5"
Plate, Chop, 12-3/8"
Cup and Saucer
Fruit
Cereal, or Soup
Vegetable Dish
Creamer
Sugar, Lidded
Refrigerator Jug with Lid
Canister with Lid (Cookie Jar)
Canister, small, stacking with Lid
Canister, medium, stacking
   with Lid
Butter Dish
Geranium was discontinued in
   1942.

Geranium canister with lid, $75-125; small canister with lid, $65-85; and refrigerator jug, $125-145.

Geranium dinner plate, 9.5", $55-65 and bread & butter plate, 6.5", $22-26.

Rancho Ware Table Ware was used as the basis for Rancho Duotone. Rancho Duotone was offered in pastel blue (M.P. 9), green (M.P. 4), light yellow (M.P. 3), Maroon (M.P. 19), and coral (M.P. 15 –Coral Satin) on the interior of the hollowware shapes and on the topside of the plates. Matt Ivory (M.P. 5) was on the exterior of the hollowware shapes and on the underside of the plates.

Special pieces to this line are the leaf-shaped salad plates and a salad bowl with a leaf motif. The cups and cream soups were redesigned for this set from those originally used with Rancho Table Ware. Rancho Duotone was discontinued in 1941.

These are the shapes in Rancho Duotone.

Rancho Duotone. Left to right: #C-221 leaf plate satin ivory & satin turquoise, $38-45; #C-50 cereal bowl, $26-28, in light yellow; #C-14 fruit bowl, $12-16, in coral satin; #C-35 tumbler, $32-38, light yellow, $28-38. Plates: #C-0 bread & butter, 6" in blue, $10-12; #C-1 salad plate, 7" in ivory satin, $16-18; #C-3 dinner plate, 8.5" in rare maroon, $28-45; #C-4 large dinner, 10.5" in turquoise satin, $28-35; and #C-40 cup & saucer in blue, $28-32.

C-0	Plate, Bread & Butter, 6"
C-1	Plate, Dessert, 7"
C-2	Plate, Salad, 8.5"
C-3	Plate, Dinner, 9.5"
C-221	Plate, Leaf Design
C-40	Cup and Saucer
C-35	Tumbler
C-42	Bouillon and Saucer
C-14	Fruit, Tab Handle
C-50	Cereal, Tab Handle
C-22	Creamer
C-23	Sugar with Lid
C-6	Chop Plate, 12"
C-25	Platter, Oval, 12"
C-62	Vegetable Bowl
C-85	Salad Bowl

Rancho Duotone was discontinued in 1941.

Rancho Duotone. Left to right: #C-221 leaf plates, satin ivory & blue, satin ivory & satin turquoise, and satin ivory & sand. All are $38-45.

Rancho Duotone. Left to right: #C-62 round vegetable bowl in satin ivory & coral satin, $28-36; #C-25 12" oval platter in satin ivory & turquoise satin, $32-38; #C-23 sugar in satin ivory & sand, $26-28; and #C-22 creamer in satin ivory and sand, $26-28.

Rancho Duotone. Front to back: #C-42 cream soup and plate in satin ivory & satin turquoise, $36-45; shell or leaf plate, $38-45, in blue; and #C-3 dinner or luncheon plate, 9.5" in sand $28-35.

176

Barkertone and Barker Brother's Series

Gladding, McBean & Co. manufactured Barkertone to be sold exclusively by Barker Brothers Department Store, a Los Angeles, California, based department store. Barkertone was two-tone Montecito with a special ink stamp, which read, "Franciscan Barkertone, Made in USA." These were to be sold at the 1939 San Francisco World's Fair – Golden Gate International Exposition.

Also manufactured and to be sold by Barker Brothers was the series called "California Missions," "Winning of the West," and "California Wild-flowers." Of these, Winning of the West and California Wild-flowers have been found to be tableware sets that include the following items.

Cup and Saucer
Plate, Bread & Butter, 6"
Plate, Salad, 8"
Plate, Dinner, 9.5"
Cream
Sugar
Chop Plate, 12"

Later in 1940 and until 1945, Barker Brothers had their own brand name tableware, "Mary Louise," manufactured by Gladding, McBean & Co.

Barker Brothers Department Store's "Barkertone" tableware included this series called California Missions. There are three in the series and these include Mission San Juan Bautista, Mission San Luis Rey, and Mission San Rafael. $125-145 each.

Another series in Barkertone is this unknown pattern with a butterfly on three branches. Cup & saucer, $45-55; bread & butter, 6", $26-32; dessert plate, 7", $26-32; and dinner plate, $32-45.

This is the Barkertone series Winning of the West. Sugar with lid, $75-95; creamer, $75-85; cup, $28-36; and dinner plate, 9.5", $95-145. Each plate has a unique design on it.

Unknown Barkertone dessert plate, 7.5" with palm trees and yellow clouds, $75-85.

178

On June 6, 1939, the Dinnerware division received its first large special order for earthenware. Up until this time, the Company had produced 73 different items on special order. The largest order was for 4,000 pieces. Now they had received a special order for 25,000 pieces of a special "toast and jam" set for the Toastmaster Division of McGraw Electric Co. of Elgin, Illinois. The ware was ordered in solid colors. After this, Toastmaster ordered other toast and jam sets to be used with their Toaster services.

Also produced for Toastmaster was a batter bowl and syrup pitcher for their waffle service. The relationship between Toastmaster and Gladding, McBean & Co. would continue to last through to the 1950s.

Advertisement from *Better Homes & Gardens*, December 1940, for Toastmaster. This advertisement shows the set combinations for toasters and a waffle set using Franciscan Ware dishes. Toastmaster was the largest special order ever for Gladding McBean with over 25,000 pieces ordered. Toastmaster is a registered trademark of McGraw Electric Company, Toastmaster Products Division, Elgin, Illinois. A booklet was made available for free, titled "Entertaining Hints on How to Entertain," by Henrietta Ripperger. Complete Toastmaster sets with the correct Franciscan Ware dishes are $225-245.

Introduced in July 1941 as the Junior Toast 'n Jam Set from Toastmaster, the set included a rich walnut serving tray, jam jar, and toast plate with the newly designed Junior toaster. The Toast 'n Jam set was code named "Juet" and is catalog number 6E3. The toaster was code named "Jule" and is catalog number 1B11. The new set was priced at $8.95. The jam jar with lid and toast tray is now priced around $35-45 for the set.

Toastmaster waffle service set, batter bowl, and syrup pitcher. The third piece in the ensemble was a metal ladle with the Toastmaster symbol on it. Included with the service set was a wooden tray. All pieces in the service set were code named "Servet." The waffle iron was code named "Bake" and is #2D2. Batter bowl, $45-55; syrup, $18-26.

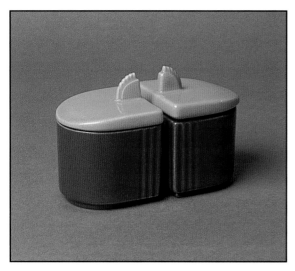

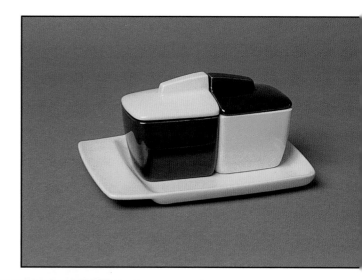

Toastmaster jam set with toast plate in yellow and green.

Toastmaster jam set in redwood and coral. This was offered with the toaster "Tweet" or also known as the two-slice toaster #1B9. Not pictured is the plate they sit on, which is coral and has the Toastmaster symbol on it. Code-named "Delu" and catalog number 6D4. Complete with under tray, $38-45.

This is one of two jam jars in flame orange and yellow, the other is turquoise and yellow. The jam jar was offered with the Toastmaster "De Luxe" Toast 'n Jam set.

Gladding, McBean & Co. manufactured specials for companies to promote their own product. Of these, the best known companies were Sunkist from the California Fruitgrowers Association of Los Angeles, California, and Nasco from the National Silver Company of New York, New York.

Items made for Sunkist are a cream and sugar set, a salad bowl, and a fruit bowl. Only the salad bowl is marked "Sunkist." All pieces have a unique melon shape.

Items marked Nasco are covered casseroles, a salad bowl, and a pie plate. Some casseroles are hand-painted in multi-colors; otherwise, pieces found thus far are in solid colors. Nasco used Franciscan Ware as inserts for its metal serving stands. Over time, many of these metal-serving stands have been separated from the Franciscan Ware.

California Fruitgrowers Exchange, Los Angeles, California, registered the mark of "Sunkist" in 1937 for items made by Gladding McBean for use as premiums and promotions. This line is associated due to the consistant melon shape among the pieces. These items are associated with the Sunkist name because the bowl to the right is marked "Sunkist." However, this same bowl can be found marked "Salad Bowl." The cream and sugar are always found marked "Franciscan." Back left to right: Large bowl in light blue, marked "Franciscan," $125-135 and bowl marked "Sunkist" in apple green, $245-255—if marked "Salad Bowl" then it is valued $75-85. Front: Sugar and creamer set in golden glow, $45-55.

Nasco salad bowl, $35-55 and Nasco pie plate with embossed design, $32-45.

181

Made for the National Silver Co. since 1934, these covered casseroles are marked "Nasco – Oven Proof." The lids are in the tulip design. Left to right: yellow, light blue, and maroon, $35-45. The stands are not Nasco, but were offered as the stand for the covered Franciscan Ware casserole.

The casserole lid on the left is from the California Pacific Exposition, San Diego, 1935 in glacial blue and can be fit on either a Cocinero or Nasco casserole bottom. Since the lid was found alone, it is not know at this time which bottom it was made for and whether or not it was made for Nasco. The lid is unmarked. The casserole to the right is the same tulip design that is found mostly in solid glazes; however, this is in the hand-painted version. Gladding McBean did manufacture hand-painted lids for Nasco casseroles.

Nasco lettuce green covered casserole in metal stand. This is in the flowers in a basket design. Stand is original to the casserole and was made by Nasco.

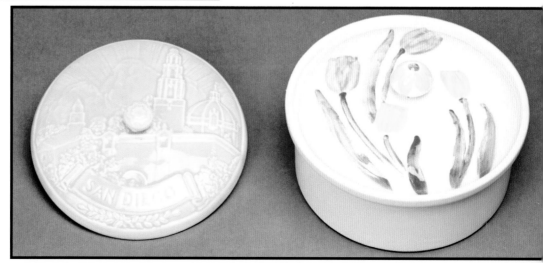

A special dinnerware line was manufactured for Silver City. Unfortunately at this time it is not known exactly how these pieces were marketed. There is a Silver City Glass Company in Meriden, Connecticut, which used silver overlay on glass. Many of these glass pieces feature a pattern that is found on Franciscan Ware El Patio shapes and on the fluted plates from the Rancho Table Ware line. However, these pieces usually are in various glazes, whereas information from Gladding, McBean & Co. indicate that the Silver City Special Line were only in the glaze of matt ivory (M.P. 5). More research is needed. The Silver City Special Line was discontinued in 1940.

The prefix to the shapes in the Silver City Special Line is "SC" for Silver City. Some of the shapes in this line come from the El Patio line or another line, and are noted in brackets, while other shapes are totally unique to this line and are not found in any other line. It is unknown at this time how these pieces were marked.

Pictured next to the El Patio friar pitcher is a wine bottle in the shape of a friar. These bottles were made for a Napa Valley winery that commissioned them. Unfortunately, the winery never used them and they remained in crates until found in the 1980s. They do come up for sale, though they are rare and unusual. Besides the friar, there are a male and female Californian Native American and a nun. Colors found are Mexican blue, coral, yellow, and turquoise. All are in the $145-225 price range.

SC-6[2]	Bread & Butter 6"
SC-9[37]	Dinner Plate 9.5"
SC-12	Tray 12"
SC-14	Tray 14"
SC-16	Tray 16"
SC-17 [251]	Chop Plate 12.5"
SC-18 [265]	Chop Plate 14"
SC-20 [1220]	Cup [from the Pueblo Line]
SC-21 [C-40a]	Saucer [from the Rancho Line]
SC-26	Punch Cup
SC-27	Individual Ashtray
SC-31	High Ball Tumbler
SC-32	Fruit or Juice Tumbler
SC-33	Cocktail Tumbler
SC-51 [61]	Guernsey Jug 1-pint
SC-52 [62]	Guernsey Jug 1-quart
SC-53 [63]	Cocktail Pitcher
SC-70	Bread Tray
SC-72	Oval Tray 12"
SC-74	Oval Tray 14"
SC-76	Oval Tray 16"
SC-85	Punch Bowl
SC-86	Punch Bowl Tray
SC-93	Coffee Jug
SC-96	Candlestick

Gladding, McBean & Co. manufactured over 73 different items on special order up until this time. The largest single order before Toastmaster was for 4,000 pieces. These specials were for companies to use as premiums and advertisement as well as one of a kind items sold by exclusive stores. For Betty Crocker, a special bowl was made and is ink backstamped "Betty Crocker." Other items included a perfume bottle for Fragrance de Heriot, Hollywood & New York, an Alpha Phi ivy leaf for new members, wine bottles for a winery, as well as other items. Mugs, cup and saucers, and ashtrays from various lines were common shapes used. Although many of these items were marked with the Gladding, McBean & Co. backstamps or Franciscan backstamp, many were marked specifically for the customer who ordered them.

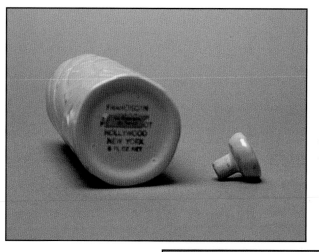

Bottom of the Fragrance de heriot perfume bottle. In blue ink is "Franciscan Ware Fragrance de heriot, Hollywood, New York, 8 fl oz net" with a gold sticker that reads "La Premiere de heriot." The top once had cork around the stopper.

Marked with the Franciscan Ware mark from 1939, this leaf shape candy dish in satin ivory, $75-85, has the symbols of Alpha and Phi. Alpha Phi's are members of a *lifelong* sisterhood, a woman's fraternity with members in the USA and Canada. In 1898, the Fraternity adopted a special badge to honor her newest members. The badge they selected is in the shape of an ivy leaf, set in silver pewter. An ever-growing vine, the ivy symbolizes the growth of the Alpha Phi sisterhood. This was probably a gift to new members.

This is a very rare and unusual perfume bottle in coral, $145-225, made for Fragrance de heriot, Hollywood & New York. The side of the bottle has an embossed script that reads "Fragrance de heriot."

This is the Jiffy Juicer in apple green, $145-165, and is marked Jiffy Juicer, Pat. Pending. Jiffy Juicers have been found in glacial blue, yellow, Mexican blue, coral, satin ivory, and flame orange.

Another Jiffy Juicer in an unidentified color. The impressed mark appears on the base. $145-165.

This is the #S-23 honey pot and #S-23a lid in light yellow, a special ordered by a company to be used as either a premium ware or to promote their product, $65-85.

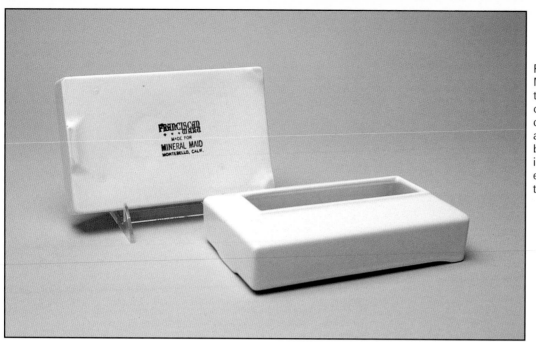

Planter, made for the Mineral Maid company in celestial white, the mark is from 1939. Shown is only the bottom; missing is the ceramic box that fits in the base and a terra cotta piece that goes between them to absorb water into the top piece. Complete examples are found and are in the $75-85 price range.

Bookend #S-12 in glacial blue made for an unknown company. This may have been made for a florist, $65-75.

Batter bowl #S-67 in coral, $75-85, made for an unknown company to be used as a premium. This batter bowl has been found in yellow, coral, and turquoise. This may have come in other colors as well.

Don the Beachcombers Rum Barrel. Unusual for a special order, $125-145.

Max Schonfeld's Kaolena China. Early pieces, Malinite body. The exact uses of these charming umbrella shapes are unknown. They could have been used either for the display of flowers, asachet, potopouri, or as hatpin holders. Both are lidded. They are on earthenware bodies rather than china and are hand-painted decorated and lined. Early pieces in Kaolena are marked with the initials MS in Script. These pieces are marked with the initials MS in script. Shape B-27, $95-125 each.

Max Schonfeld was a distributor of giftware. His company was named Max Schonfeld Co. and specialized prior to the war in 1934 in importing giftware. However, after the war began in Europe, his supplies from Germany and France were cut off. He has been described as a very affable guy with a great sense of humor. He was instrumental in promoting California ceramics by, later in the 1950s, gathering a group of companies to form "Registered California." Registered California was organized to promote ware made in California to the US and abroad to try to curtail the erosion effect of sales because of post-war imports.

Gladding, McBean & Co. produced earthenware boudoir sets and cologne bottles for Max Schonfeld. His own company embellished the ware with gold lining and decoration and fired the ware at his own establishment. Later, Gladding, McBean & Co. would produce a china body for Max Schonfeld's ware. Gladding, McBean & Co. would continue this relationship with Max Schonfeld until the late 1950s.

Here are the shapes in the China Art Ware for Max Schonfeld (blanks only) according to factory information:

Max Schonfeld's Kaolena China. Early pieces, Malinite body. Left to right: frying pan handle wall decoration marked in hand script "Made for Bullocks Wilshire," $45-55 and frying pan handle wall decoration marked with the Gladding, McBean & Co. "Made in USA" stamp as well as the Kaolena stamp, $35-45. Many pieces of Kaolena have French sayings on them, as they were to replace the imports that could no longer be imported from France. Both are hand-painted. The large pan is shape B-18 and the smaller pan is shape B-26 and were only made in Malinite and not in china.

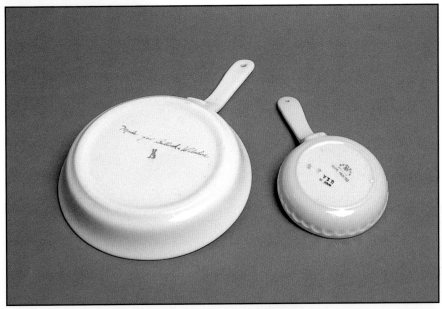

B-1	Bottle		B-44	Urn
B-2	Bottle		B-45	Stamp Box
B-3	Bottle		B-46	Powder Box
B-4	Bottle		B-47	Bottle
B-5	Jar		B-48	Perfume Bottle
B-6	Tulip Bottle		B-49	Small Bottle
B-7	Plume Bottle		B-50	Tumbler
B-8	Powder Box		B-51	Soup Dish
B-9	Bottle		B-52	Powder Box
B-10	Bottle		B-53	Cotton Picker
B-11	Bottle		B-54	Bottle
B-12	Ash Tray		B-55	Vase
B-13	Ash Tray		B-56	Shell
B-14	Barrel		B-57	Cigarette Box
B-16	Vase		B-58	Ash Tray
B-17	Vase		B-59	Pear Tray
B-18	Large Pan (only in pottery)		B-60	2-compartment Tray
B-19	Jug		B-61	Small Pan
B-20	Jar (has six styles of lids — A, B, C, D, E, & F)		B-62	Box
B-21	Ash Tray		B-63	Fruit Bowl, Fluted
B-22	Ash Tray		B-64	Grape Plate
B-23	Clock		B-65	Bottle
B-24	Box (has two styles of lids — A & B)		B-66	Lid for B-20 Box
B-25	Box (has two styles of lids — A & B)		B-67	Tray, Small Rectangular
B-26	Small Pan (only in pottery)		B-68	Tray, Round
B-27	Umbrella		B-70	Wall Pocket
B-28	Bottle		B-71	Bottle
B-29	Bottle		B-72	Bud Vase
B-30	Place Card		B-73	Bud Vase, Handled
B-31	Candy Box (has four styles of lids — A, B, C, & D)		B-75	Pan or Dish
B-32	Bottle		B-76	Shell Tray
B-33	Cache Pot		B-77	Leaf Tray
B-34	Octagon Jar		B-78	Wall Pocket
B-35	Round Jar		B-100	Cup (fits in well of B-101 Tray)
B-36	Tray		B-101	Tray (snack)
B-37	Vase		B-102	Rolling Pin
B-38	Basket		B-106	Bread & Butter Plate
B-39	Double Box		B-108	Salad Plate
B-40	Madonna		B-109	Luncheon Plate
B-41	Dish		B-111	Dinner Plate
B-42	Pitcher		B-112	After Dinner Cup, Footed
B-43	Candy Jar			

Max Schonfeld's Kaolena China. Early pieces, Malinite body. Left to right: covered box shape #B-24 with shape "B" lid, $35-39 and men's cologne bottle, shape B-9, $55-75. Both are hand-painted and are made of earthenware.

These shapes were produced for Max Schonfeld's Kaolena China; however, these pieces are marked Franciscan Fine China and were distributed by Gladding McBean. They are decorated in a light blue color over the ivory china clay body. Other pieces are found marked Franciscan Fine China on shapes produced for Max Schonfeld, including a powder box and lid in a larger size. Expect to pay $85-125 for a complete set.

Comparisons of Kaolena China and Gladding, McBean ware. The El Patio/Rancho tableware coaster was used as the shape mold for the handled frying pan wall decoration. The shell shaped dish was originally a shape made as an example of the new china body being developed by Gladding, McBean & Co. It is marked Franciscan China, Gladding, McBean & Company of California, $75-95. Kaolena shell dish, shape B-56, $22-28.

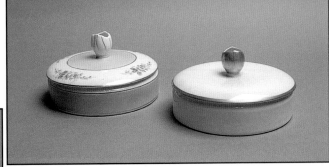

Comparisons of Kaolena China and Gladding, McBean & Co. Franciscan ware. Left to right: covered box, floral knob Kaolena, shape B-31 with lid "A," $38-45 and Franciscan China marked covered box with floral knob, $45-55.

Comparisons of Kaolena China and Gladding, McBean & Co. Franciscan ware. The three pieces on the left are Kaolena compared to the three pieces on the right, which are Franciscan China in the Fremont pattern. Large covered box, shape B-25 with lid "B," $38-55; small covered box, shape B-24, with lid "B," $28-38; and ashtray, shape B-58, $12-22. Franciscan China is priced higher.

Comparisons of Kaolena China and Gladding, McBean & Co. Franciscan ware. This covered jar is shown with the Franciscan China jar in the middle. The two other jars are marked in French "Day" and "Night," shape B-5. Both Kaolena and Franciscan China jars are $28-38 each.

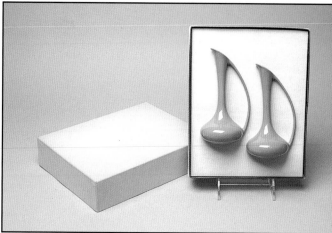

These two vases are packed in a Franciscan China box as a set of two. This vase shape is from Kaolena shape B-17. Both are marked with the Franciscan China mark, $38-45 each or $125-145 set complete with box.

Gladding McBean produced china blanks for Max Schonfeld's Kaolena China. This is a dresser set, which consists of two perfume bottles, shape #unknown, $28-35 each, and a powder box, shape B-46, $28-32. Unfortunately, the name of the decal design is unknown. The pieces are marked "Kaolena China, Made in California."

Produced for Kaolena China, this is a plate, $28-45, which has been glazed in a blue color over the ivory clay body, producing the leave and grape pattern, shape B-64. The name of the line is unknown. This is from a set of twelve plates and could have been used as dessert plates. The plate is marked "Kaolena China, Made in California."

A cream and sugar set, $26-32 each, glazed in a yellow over the ivory background of the clay body. These items are decal decorated with gold painted handles and knob. The pattern and shape number is unknown. Both pieces are marked "Kaolena China, Made in California."

Kaolena China. Left to right: wall pocket, shape B-78, $55-65; two handled urn, shape B-44 $45-55; and cache pot, shape B-33, $45-55.

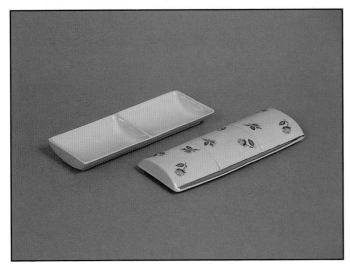
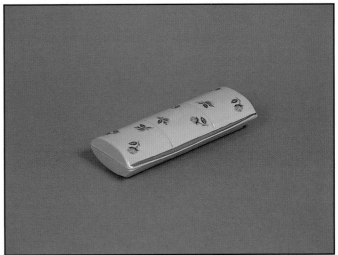

Kaolena China. Covered compartment box, shape #unknown, $45-55.

Kaolena China. Left to right front: men's cologne bottle, shape B-9, $55-75; bud vase, B-72, $45-55; and vase, B-73, $28-35. Background: tray, shape B-36, $55-75, hard to find.

Kaolena China. Left to right: large vase, shape B-55, $55-65; blank vase, shape B-55, $28-38.

Kaolena China. Left to right: bottle with lid, shape B-48, $28-35; pitcher, shape B-42, $28-38; and perfume bottle, shape B-29, $28-35.

Kaolena China. Left to right: unusual pieces: leaf dish, shape B-77, $38-45; shoe, shape #unknown, $55-65; and leaf tray, shape B-21, $26-28.

Kaolena China. Left to right: covered box, shape B-24 with lid "A," $22-26; perfume bottle, shape B-47, $32-35; and covered jar, shape B-5, $28-38.

Kaolena China. Left to right: large vase, shape B-37, $55-65; blank vase, shape B-37, $28-38.

Kaolena China. Left to right: ash tray, shape B-13, $12-22; ash tray, shape B-58, $12-22; and small ash tray, shape B-12, $12-22.

Kaolena China. Left to right: large covered candy box, shape B-31 with lid "A," $28-38 and powder box, shape B-8, $22-26.

Kaolena China. Left to right: shell and leaf dishes: tray, shape B-61, $22-26; pear tray, shape B-59, $26-32; and shell tray, shape B-56, $22-28.

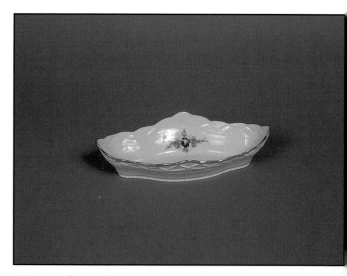

Kaolena China. Basket, shape B-38, $28-36.

Kaolena China. Complete dresser set with ring handles, shape numbers unknown, tray, shape #B-36, $145-165.

Kaolena China. Left to right: covered box, shape B-8, $22-28; perfume bottle, shape B-29, $28-35; and swirl perfume bottle, shape B-10, $30-45.

Kaolena China. Left to right: perfume bottle, shape #unknown, $32-36; perfume bottle, shape B-29, $28-35; swirl perfume bottle, shape B-10, $30-45; and vase, shape B-73, $22-28. In front: Round tray, shape B-68, $22-28.

Kaolena China. Left to right: perfume/cologne bottle, shape B-32, $32-36 and heart covered box, shape B-62, $36-45.

Chapter 10
First Embossed Hand-Painted Table Ware 1940

Gladding, McBean & Co. presented four new lines of art ware: Floral Art Ware, Saguaro Art Ware, Montebello Art Ware, and Reseda.

Tableware introduced was Metropolitan Table Ware and the Victoria Service. Victoria was a 16-piece tea set in an old English pattern. Metropolitan was a complete dinner set, featuring square pieces, the items being nearly square in effect. All hollow pieces are two-toned. Designed by Morris B. Sanders of New York, the Metropolitan shape was made for the Metropolitan Museum of Art's 1940 Exhibition of Contemporary American Industrial Art. This Exhibition included the work of 400 designers and makers. Two designs on the Metropolitan shape were submitted and displayed. Witold Gordon decorated his version with a food decoration. Joan Kahn decorated her version with a male figure. It is not known how many of these decorated versions of Metropolitan were made, however not one has been found today. Gladding, McBean & Co. adapted Morris B. Sanders design for a complete dinnerware service and the name chosen, of course, was Metropolitan.

For the first time ever, Gladding, McBean & Co. introduced a hand-painted *embossed* tableware. Named appropriately, this line was Apple Table Ware. Frederic J. Grant brought the pattern with him from his former employer, Weller Pottery. Weller Pottery had in their line the Zona pattern, which was an embossed apple pattern. Following his divorce from Ethel Weller, Grant asked for and received the right to reproduce Zona tableware as part of his divorce settlement. Mary Grant redesigned and sculpted Zona to become the Franciscan Apple pattern.

In June of 1940, the Parmlee-Dohrman store displayed Franciscan Apple Table Ware and attracted much attention. A table was set up with six place settings and was supplemented by large green leaf plates. (*Ceramic Industry*)

Floral Art Ware with glaze MP-47/42. Left to right: #C-343 narrow bowl, 16", $35-45; back: #C-220 leaf shape bowl, 12" x 10", $35-45; #C-335 flat vase, 6.75", $45-55; and #C-340 bowl, 10", $45-55.

Floral Art Ware with glaze MP-47/42. Leaf dish #C-344, $28-34.

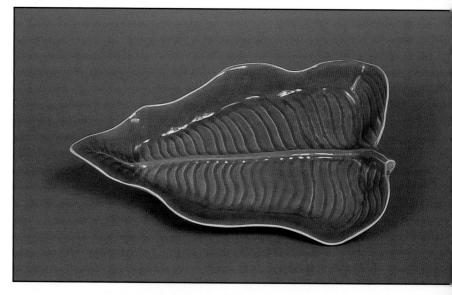

Floral Art Ware

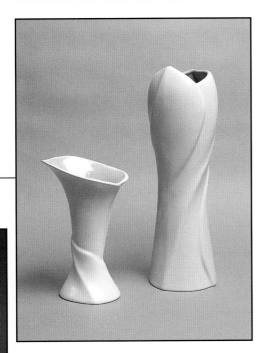

Floral Art Ware. Left to right: #C-333 oatmeal lined with coral vase, $45-65 and #C-338 vase, 11.5" tall narrow, $125-145, in gray lined with satin green.

All shapes are based on floral motifs. The only solid color offered was Matt Ivory (M.P. 5). Otherwise all shapes were two-toned. The two-tone combinations are Matt Green interior with an Silver Gray exterior (M.P. 8/20-Satin Gray), Satin Pink Buff interior with Glacial Blue exterior (M.P. 46/2), Amethyst interior with Dark Green exterior (M.P. 47/42), and Shell Pink Gloss interior with an Oatmeal exterior (M.P. 52/32). Brochures state that the "shapes are specially adapted for Modern Flower Arrangement . . ." referring to low bowl shapes.

These are the shapes that were offered in Floral Art Ware.

C-219	Bowl
C-220	Bowl, Leaf, 12" x 10"
C-225	Bowl, Ivy Leaf, 13" x 12"
C-330	Vase, 6.5"
C-331	Vase, 4"
C-332	Vase, 5" Wide Mouth
C-333	Vase, 7"
C-334	Fancy Bowl, 9"
C-335	Vase, 6.75"
C-336	Candleholder
C-337	Bowl
C-338	Vase, 11.5" Tall Narrow
C-339	Vase, 9.5" Flaring
C-340	Bowl, 10" Low
C-341	Bowl, Curve Top
C-343	Bowl, 16" Narrow
C-344	Bowl, Leaf, 10" x 8"
C-345	Bowl, 13" Long Leaf Shape
C-346	Bowl, Leaf, 11"
C-347	Bowl, Leaf, 13" x 8"
C-348	Bowl, Leaf, 14"
C-349	Bowl, 12.5" Long Narrow
C-349x	Bowl, Leaf, 12" x 11"

Floral Art Ware was discontinued in 1942.

Floral Art Ware. Left to right: #C-346 satin buff pink lined with glacial blue leaf bowl, 11", $35-45; back: #C-220 leaf shape bowl, 12" x 10", $35-45; #C-333 silver gray lined with satin green vase, $45-65; #C-330 satin buff pink lined with glacial blue bud vase, $45-55; and #C-334 silver gray lined with satin green pansy bowl, 9" x 3.75", $45-55.

Saguaro Art Ware

Saguaro Art Ware was based on the shapes of the Saguaro (pronounced "Sawaro") cacti. Except for a solid Matt Ivory (M.P. 5), all shapes were two-toned. They were in the color combinations of Satin Turquoise (M.P. 27-Turquoise Satin) lined with Satin Coral (M.P. 15), Satin Green (M.P. 62) lined with Satin Yellow (M.P. 43-Yellow), Chartreuse (M.P. 45-Satin) lined with Maroon (M.P. 19), and Satin Golden Glow (M.P. 41) lined with Glacial Blue (M.P. 2).

C-250	Candlestick
C-251	Bud Vase, 6.25"
C-252	Vase, 5" Wide Bottom
C-253	Bowl, 6" x 6" Low
C-254	Vase, 6.5"
C-255	Vase, 5" x 6"
C-256	Vase, 5.5"
C-257	Bowl, 8" x 6" x 3.25" Deep Oval
C-258	Bowl, 10" x 6" Low
C-259	Bowl, 8.5" Round
C-260	Bowl, 8" x 4" Deep Round
C-261	Bowl, Triangular
C-262	Bowl, 10.5" Low Round
C-263	Vase, 8.5"
C-264	Vase, 10"
C-265	Bowl, 15" x 8" Oval
C-266	Bowl, 12" Round
C-267	Vase, 12" Large Triangular

Saguaro Art Ware was discontinued in 1942.

Saguaro Art Ware, 1940-42. Left to right: back: #C-253 satin ivory low bowl, 6" x 6", $26; #C-267 satin turquoise lined with satin coral large triangular vase, 12", $85; #C-251 satin ivory bud vase, 6.25", $45; and #C-265 glaze M.P. 41 lined with glacial blue, 14" x 8", $36 (the #M.P. 41 glaze only appears on this line). Left to right: front: #C-250 satin yellow candlestick, $18 and #C-258 satin turquoise lined with satin coral low bowl, 10" x 6", $26.

Montebello Art Ware

Montebello was made with a special glaze treatment with a Catalina Ciel Blue (M.P. 84) interior and a Catalina Persian Blue (M.P. 90) exterior in a pebble-like finish, much like an orange peel. Also found is the Catalina Persian Blue (M.P. 90) exterior in a smooth finish. This may be due to the manufacturing process, however it is not known as a fact thus far.

Shapes found thus far have been the following:

C-275	Vase 5"
C-276	Vase, Handled, 6"
C-277	Vase, 4.5" Low
C-278	Vase, 6"
C-279	Vase, 4.5" Square
C-281	Vase, 6" Footed
C-282	Bowl, 7.5" Low Square
C-283	Bowl, 10" Round
C-284	Vase, 8.25"
C-285	Vase, 9"
C-286	Vase, 11"
C-287	Bowl, 16"

Many other shapes have been found other than those listed. This is one of the most beautiful of all the art ware lines. The glaze is exceptional. Montebello was discontinued in 1942.

Montebello Ware. Left to right: #C-281 footed vase, 6", $125-145; #C-284 vase, 8.25", $145-225; and #C-283 round bowl, 10" diameter, $125-165.

Montebello Ware. Left to right: #132 round vase, 4.5", $65-85; #C-278 vase for Japanese arrangement, 6", $145-225; and #C-276 vase with handles, 6", $145-225.

Montebello Ware. Left to right: #105 vase, bottle shape, 6", $75-95; #C-282 bowl, 7.5" low square, $75-95; and #294 bulb bowl, $75-95.

Reseda

Reseda was a very forward-thinking, modernistic vase ware line. The shapes were designed specifically for this line and not used in any other. The low bowls were great for arranging modernistic floral arrangements. The glazes for Reseda were used only for this line. It was an entirely new series of glazes and colors.

The colors and glazes developed were Verde Green (M.P. 68), Agate (M.P. 69), Gold (M.P. 70), and Matrix Blue (M.P. 72). Shapes introduced were the following:

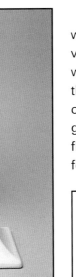

Reseda Ware. Foreground: #402 square candlesticks, 4" in agate, $32-45 with #C-464 tall footed vase, 12" in gold, $85-125, in the background.

C-402	Candlestick, 4"	C-459	Round Vase, 8" x 6.5"
C-449	Bud Vase, 6"	C-460	Vase with Square Top, 10"
C-450	Pansy Bowl, 3" x 10"	C-461	Low Round Bowl, 12"
C-451	Low Wide Vase, 5"	C-462	Square Bowl, 10" x 10" x 3.5"
C-452	Oval Crimped Bowl, 9.5"	C-463	Low Rectangular Bowl, 13.25" x 9.5"
C-453	Flat Footed Vase, 8"		
C-454	Vase with Crimped Top, 8"	C-464	Tall Footed Vase, 12"
C-455	Round Bowl, 8" x 4.5"	C-465	Tall Vase, 12"
C-456	Footed Vase Crimped Top, 9"	C-466	Large Round Bowl, 14"
C-457	Square Bowl, 7.5" x 7.5" x 3.5"		
C-458	Low Flat Bowl, 7.5" x 11"		

Reseda was discontinued in 1942.

Reseda Ware. Left to right: #C-252 matrix blue oval crimped bowl, 9.5" length, $45; upper vase #C-450 matrix blue pansy bowl, 3" x 10", $36; lower vase #C-458 gold low flat bowl, $36; and #C-451 gold low wide vase, 5" high, $45.

Metropolitan Table Ware

Designed by Morris Sanders of New York, Gladding, McBean & Co. produced Metropolitan Table Ware as a complete tableware service. Even though the Exhibition pieces for the Metropolitan Museum were decal decorated, Gladding, McBean & Co. only used solid colors. Metropolitan was two-toned and was offered in the color combinations of Matt Ivory on the interior of the hollowware and the backside of the flatware pieces either Coral Satin (M.P. 15), Turquoise (M.P. 2), Gray Satin (M.P. 76), Mauve (M.P. 67), or Satin Yellow (M.P. 43). In addition there is the solid color version of Matt Ivory (M.P. 5). Very rare is the solid color Shell Pink Buff (56).

Metropolitan Table Ware was produced in the following shapes.

Cup and Saucer
Demitasse Cup and Saucer
Plate, Bread & Butter, 6.5"
Plate, Salad, 8.5"
Plate, Dinner, 10.5"
Bowl, Fruit
Creamer
Sugar with Lid
Coffee Server
Tea Pot
Plate, Chop, 13"
Gravy or Sauce Boat
Salad Bowl
Vegetable Dish
Rectangle Baker [note: also found marked "Catalina Pottery."]

The Metropolitan Table Ware was discontinued in 1942.

Metropolitan Table Ware. Left to right: coral satin sugar, $22-28; satin yellow teapot, $65-85; mauve coffee pot, $65-85; and gray satin creamer, $18-24.

Metropolitan Table Ware. Left to right: turquoise vegetable, $22-28; solid matt ivory chop plate, 13", $35-45; and gray satin salad bowl, $35-45.

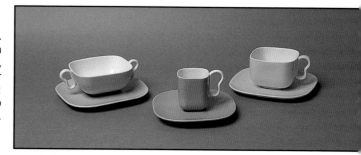

Metropolitan Table Ware. Left to right: gray satin cream soup and saucer, $32-38; mauve after dinner cup and saucer, $32-38; and satin yellow teacup and saucer, $14-16.

Metropolitan Table Ware. Front to back: coral satin fruit bowl, $12-15; solid ivory bread & butter, 6.5", $6-8; gray satin salad plate, 8.5", $14-16; and satin yellow dinner plate, 10.5", $15-18.

Victoria Service

Referred to in advertisements as just Victoria, this was a very short set designed in an old English pattern. It was a Victorian pattern, hence its name Victoria. In 1940, there was a nostalgia for the past. Colonial and Victorian styles were being redesigned and introduced to the buying public. It was offered in solid colors that included Celadon (M.P. 24), Pastel Pink (M.P. 53-Shell Pink Gloss), and Old Ivory (M.P. 7-Transparent Gloss).

Included in the Victoria Service were the following:
Cup and Saucer
Cream Soup and Saucer
Plate, Bread and Butter, 6.5"
Plate, Dessert, 9.5"
Creamer
Sugar
Teapot

Although, never seen, there is some indication that a demitasse cup and saucer were made. Victoria Service was discontinued in 1941.

Victoria Service in the old ivory glaze. Left to right: dinner, 8.5", $22-32; teacup and saucer, $22-32; teapot, $95-145; and sugar, $45-65.

Apple Table Ware

Being one of the most successful patterns in United States manufacturing history, the Apple Table Ware is a classic today.

Here is a listing of all the pieces available up to and including 1942.

After the introduction of Apple Table Ware in 1940, it was not until February 1, 1941 that Gladding, McBean & Co. added the salt and pepper set, cigarette box, ashtray, jam jar, baked apple dish, 14" chop, and gravy boat. And it was not until 1942 that the pieces listed above were all available.

In 1942, a new marketing plan was introduced, whereby in a special box set you could order a Beverage Set consisting of the #752 pitcher, and six #730 tumblers. Also introduced was the 25-piece set including four place settings plus a creamer, sugar, large vegetable dish, and 8.25" and 14" long oval platters. These items were in addition to the already offered starter set of 16 pieces.

Apple Table Ware would continue to be a best seller for the Franciscan Ware Division up until the Glendale plant closed in 1984. Many new shapes were added over the years that are not on the list above. After 1984, Wedgwood's Johnson Brother's Division, under the trademark Franciscan, has manufactured Apple in England.

Basic Items

706	Plate, Bread & Butter, 6.5"
708	Plate, Salad, 8"
710	Plate, Dinner, 9.5"
711	Plate, Large Dinner, 10.5"
712	Plate, Chop or Cake, 12.5"
720-721	Cup and Saucer
701	Fruit
702	Cereal
760	Vegetable Dish, small size, 7.5"

Accessory Items

703	Soup with Rim
792	Salt & Pepper, per pair
796	Baked Apple Dish
740	Creamer
741	Sugar with Lid
754	Syrup Pitcher, 12 ounce
793	Cigarette Box
761	Vegetable Dish, large, 8.25"
732	Individual Handled Casserole and Lid
795	Jam Jar and Lid [large apple knob]
786	Waffle Batter Pitcher, 1.75 quart
770	Oval Platter, 14" long
750	Teapot, 6-cup
755	Coffee Pot, 8-cup
780	Salad Bowl, 10" diameter
794	Ash Tray [shaped like an apple]
752	Water Pitcher, 2.5 quart
782	Covered Vegetable Dish
797	Relish Dish
790	Gravy Boat, Fast Stand
730	Tumbler
714	Large Chop Plate, 14" Diameter
771	Oval Platter, large size, 17"

In the Apple Table Ware line, but also sold in the Catalina Art Ware line under Miscellaneous, were the #793 cigarette box, $125-145 and the #794 ashtray, $26-28.

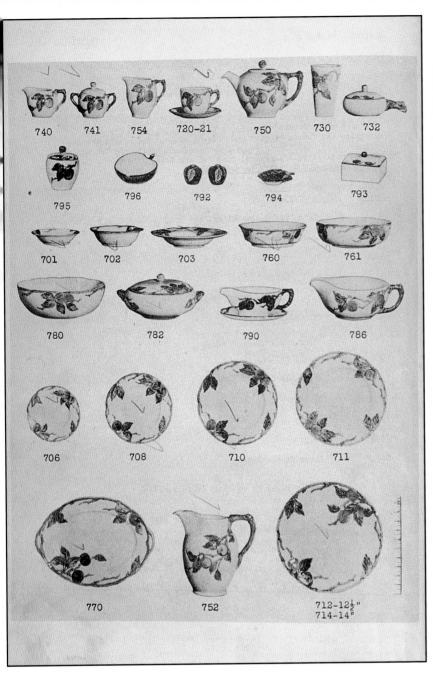

From the January 1, 1942 Franciscan Ware price list and general sales instructions, Apple as we know it was introduced as "The Apple Pattern." These were the very first shapes that were made in The Apple Pattern. See Appendix V, Apple and Desert Rose Price List.

Apple Table Ware. The #720 cup and #721 saucer ($10-12 set) in Apple would become a standard shape for future lines in hand-painted tableware. The #792 salt & pepper set are unique only to Apple, as they are shaped like apples, $22-28 pair.

Apple Table Ware. This is the #796 baked apple dish, $225-245.

Apple Table Ware. #732 individual handled casserole and lid, $45-65.

Apple Table Ware. #786 waffle batter pitcher, 1.75 quart, $245-275.

Apple Table Ware. Left to right: the redesigned #751 syrup jug, $75-85, which was introduced in the 1950s and the original #754 syrup pitcher or jug, 12 ounce, $145-155. The #754 syrup pitcher was discontinued in the mid-1940s.

Apple Table Ware. Left to right: #752 water pitcher, 2.5 quart, $125-165 and the #753 milk pitcher, one quart, $75-95. The milk pitcher was introduced after 1950.

Apple Table Ware. Left to right: redesigned cream pitcher, $28-35 and the original #740 cream pitcher, $26-32. The redesigned cream pitcher was introduced in the early 1970s and the #740 cream pitcher was discontinued. The sugar bowl also was redesigned and discontinued at the same time.

Chapter 11
Desert Rose 1941

Wishmaker, mauve and blue. Front to back: #1340 creamer, $38-45; #1341 sugar with lid, $45-55; #1352 coffee pot, $125-145; and #1314 chop plate, 14", $55-75.

By February 1st, 1941, Gladding, McBean & Co. segregated the entire line of tableware under the general name of Franciscan Ware and all art pottery under the name of Catalina Ware. Only three tableware designs were introduced in 1941, Wishmaker Table Ware, Tiger Flower, and Desert Rose Table Ware. New to the Pottery Department was Mary Jane Winans, who designed and sculpted the Desert Rose Table Ware. Although many designers can be established for certain patterns, Gladding, McBean & Co. had a very strict policy that all designs were from the artists and designers of the Company, not just one particular designer. Most, if not all, designs were created by the staff with the assistance of outside help. Gladding, McBean & Co. would not promote any one particular designer, with the exception of once in the 1950s and that would be George James, designer of the Franciscan Contours line.

Gladding, McBean & Co. did not add any art ware designs or lines in 1941. Although for the first time, tablecloths and napkins were manufactured by other companies to compliment the Franciscan tableware designs and were sold under the trade name of Franciscan.

Through cooperation with one of LA's leading handkerchief and tablecloth manufacturers, Gladding, McBean & Co. salesmen are now presenting with their pottery a line of breakfast, luncheon and dinner cloths designed to supplement the pottery manufactured by this company. The cloths are sold under the trade name of Franciscan, which is the trade name of one of the Gladding, McBean & Co.'s dinnerware lines. The cloths come in organdy and in linen with napkins to match. All complementary colors are available in all-over shades and in matching borders and designs.

The idea behind this move, insofar as Gladding, McBean & Co. is concerned, is better display of the pottery in stores before it is sold and in homes after it is sold. All such cloth designs and patterns are worked out with the manufacturers through the personal cooperation of a Gladding, McBean & Co. artist and table-setting expert. Frank McNiff, advertising manager, believes this is a valuable merchandising idea on the part of both the cloth manufacturer, and the

Wishmaker. Front: #1310 dinner plate, 10.5" in federal gold, $26-32; #1308 salad plate, 7.5" in Copley coral, $16-18; and #1306 bread & butter plate, 6.5" in mauve, $12-16. Left: #1310 dinner plate, 10.5" in blue, $26-32. Right: #1310 dinner plate, 10.5" in Phyfe green, $26-32.

Wishmaker, Copley coral and blue. Left to right: #1320/21 cup and saucer, $18-28; #1322/23 after dinner cup and saucer, $22-28; #1350 teapot, $125-145; and #1332 individual casserole with lid, $32-45.

pottery manufacturer as well as an aid to merchants." – "Linens Designed to Complement Pottery" *Ceramic Industry*, January 1, 1941

Gladding, McBean & Co. continued in 1941 to have success with their tile products. One of the largest installations was for the construction of Radio City, home of the National Broadcasting Company's KPO in San Francisco. Radio City was dedicated the week of April 26, 1942. Albert F. Roller was the Architect and worked with the artists and designers at Gladding, McBean & Co. An 80-foot tower rose above the entrance, and the most dramatic feature was a great wall mural panel, 14 x 40 feet. The mural symbolized the vast extent of radio and the unlimited service it gave to all the lands and all the people of the earth. The building is now KBHK TV-44 in San Francisco, where the mural panel can be viewed today.

Wishmaker Table Ware

Wishmaker Table Ware was again appealing to customers who were decorating in the Colonial Style. By 1941, Americans were fascinated with their early colonial days. Spinning wheels, cobbler benches, bentwood back chairs, and of course the American eagle decorated the interiors of the patriotic and nostalgic homemakers. Colors that were popular included the colors that Wishmaker Table Ware introduced: Revere Red (M.P. 61), Phyfe Green (M.P. 62), Copley Coral (M.P. 63), Blue (M.P. 65), Federal Gold (M.P. 66), and Mauve (M.P. 67). Even the names were reminiscent of America's past decorating history, Revere for Paul Revere, and Phyfe for Duncan Phyfe furniture. This is a two-tone tableware service. The flatware is solid color, and the hollowware is in two-tone with the interior being a different color than the exterior. Wishmaker was referred to in advertisements only as "Wishmaker."

Although styled with the same swirls as Franciscan's Coronado, the swirls are less defined and appear only on part of the hollowware shapes. Some may confuse Wishmaker with Coronado, but they are not the same at all. Wishmaker was only offered in 1941, being discontinued that same year.

The following is a list of shapes that were produced.

Wishmaker. Left to right: Phyfe green lined with federal gold #1340 sauceboat or small pitcher, $85-125 and Copley coral and blue #1360 covered casserole, $145-165.

1320/21	Cup and Saucer	1340	Creamer
1322/23	After Dinner Cup and Saucer	1350	Teapot
		1352	Coffee Pot
1306	Plate, Bread & Butter, 6.5"	1355	Sauce Boat, Gravy Boat or – Small Pitcher
1308	Plate, Salad, 8.5"		
1310	Plate, Dinner, 10.5"	1360	Casserole, Covered
1314	Plate, Chop, 14"	1375	Ash Tray
1332	Bouillon and Lid	1376	Cigarette Box with Lid
1341	Sugar with Lid		

Tiger Flower

Tiger Flower is a very unusual pattern. The pattern is an over glaze enameled design on Celadon (M.P. 24) and on Coral (M.P. 15). You can feel the design outlines with your fingers as they brush across the plate. It is much like an embossed business card; however, it is the application of the enameled pattern over the glaze.

Tiger Flower used the Montecito shapes. However, Tiger Flower does have a restyled cup, and it is not known if this cup shape was ever made in the Montecito Table Ware line.

Shapes offered in Tiger Flower are the following:
Plate, Bread and Butter, 6.5"
Plate, Dessert and Salad, 7.5"
Plate, Luncheon, 9.5"
Plate, Large Dinner, 10.5"
Plate, Chop, 12-3/8"
Cup and Saucer

Fruit
Cereal, or Soup
Vegetable Dish
Creamer
Sugar, Lidded

Tiger Flower was discontinued in 1942.

Tiger Flower. Left to right: overglaze on coral fruit, $15-22 and overglaze on celadon luncheon plate, 9.5", $22-32.

Tiger Flower, overglaze on coral. Front left: cereal or soup, $26-30; front right: vegetable dish, $45-65; and back: chop plate, 12-3/8", $65-85.

Tiger Flower overglaze on celadon cream, $32-42.

Tiger Flower, overglaze on coral. Left: fruit, $18-22; front: bread & butter plate, 6.5", $10-14; back: luncheon plate, 9.5", $22-32; and right: cup and saucer, $22-28.

Desert Rose. Left to right: #894 ashtray, $22-24; #825 bouillon cup with #826 lid for bouillon cup, $225-265; and #892 salt & pepper, $22-24 pair.

Basic Items

306	Plate, Bread & Butter, 6.5"
308	Plate, Salad, 8"
310	Plate, Dinner, 9.5"
311	Plate, Large Dinner, 10.5"
312	Plate, Chop or Cake, 11.75"
320	Tea Cup
321	Saucer, For Teacup or Bouillon
301	Fruit
302	Cereal
361	Vegetable Dish, 8.25" diameter

With Desert Rose Table Ware, Gladding, McBean & Co. created another classic design after the successful introduction of Apple Table Ware. Desert Rose Table Ware was Gladding, McBean & Co.'s second hand-painted embossed tableware. Desert Rose, as it became known, was designed and sculpted by Mary Jane Winans, a Gladding, McBean & Co. employee who was on the design team of the Franciscan Pottery Division.

Many have credited the success of Desert Rose to Mary Jane Winans for her deep and beautifully articulated sculpting of the design onto all of the shapes produced. A master mold would be created from her careful sculpted originals. Molds used would have to be broken up

and recycled after about 100 uses at the most, as the molds would become less sharp, losing the crispness of detail in the shape. The ware was expertly cleaned up with a stylus and sponge. Then the hand-painter would use brushes to put on the glaze paints before the final dipping into transparent glaze. Early, before 1945, painters would scratch their painter marks on the green ware base of the shape prior to glazing. In these very early pieces, you can see these marks along with the ink mark of Franciscan Ware. These marks can also be found on Apple Table Ware, and Wildflower Table Ware.

The following shapes were introduced prior to the end of 1942.

844	Individual Sugar for Tray Service
826	Lid for Bouillon Cup
825	Bouillon Cup, can use #821 Saucer
833	Egg Cup
843	Individual Creamer for Tray Service
869	Toast Cover
822	After Dinner Cup
823	After Dinner Cup Saucer
892	Salt and Pepper, per pair
803	Rim Soup
893	Cigarette Box
896	Relish Dish
840	Creamers
841	Sugar with Lid
895	Jam Jar with Lid
856	Individual Coffee Pot, 18 ounces
870	Oval Platter, 14" long
850	Teapot, 6-cup
880	Salad Bowl
894	Ash Tray
882	Covered Vegetable Dish
852	Water Pitcher
830	Tumbler
890	Gravy Boat, fast stand
855	Coffee Pot, 40 ounces
814	Large Chop Plate, 14"

Besides offering the starter set of 16 pieces and the 25-piece set, as in Apple Table Ware, Gladding, McBean & Co. introduced the Breakfast Set and the Beverage Set.

The Breakfast Set was packed individually. There were twelve pieces which included two #808 (Plate, Salad, 8"), with one each 806 (Plate, Bread & Butter, 6.5"), 820 (Tea Cup), 821 (Saucer), 869 (Toast Cover), 802 (Cereal), 856 (Individual Coffee Pot, 18 ounces), 843 (Individual Creamer), 844 (Individual Sugar), and 833 (Egg Cup).

The Beverage set consisted of the #852 Pitcher and six #830 Tumblers.

Introduced in 1942 was the 12-piece breakfast set. Included in the set were the #820-821 tea cup & saucer; two #808 salad plates, 8"; #806 bread & butter plate, 6.5"; #869 toast cover; #856 individual coffee pot, 18 ounces; #844 individual sugar for tray service; #843 individual creamer for tray service; #802 cereal; and the #833 egg cup. A special price was offered when one would purchase the breakfast set, which was less than what the individual piece prices would be. Two salad plates were included, one for the muffin cover and one for use.

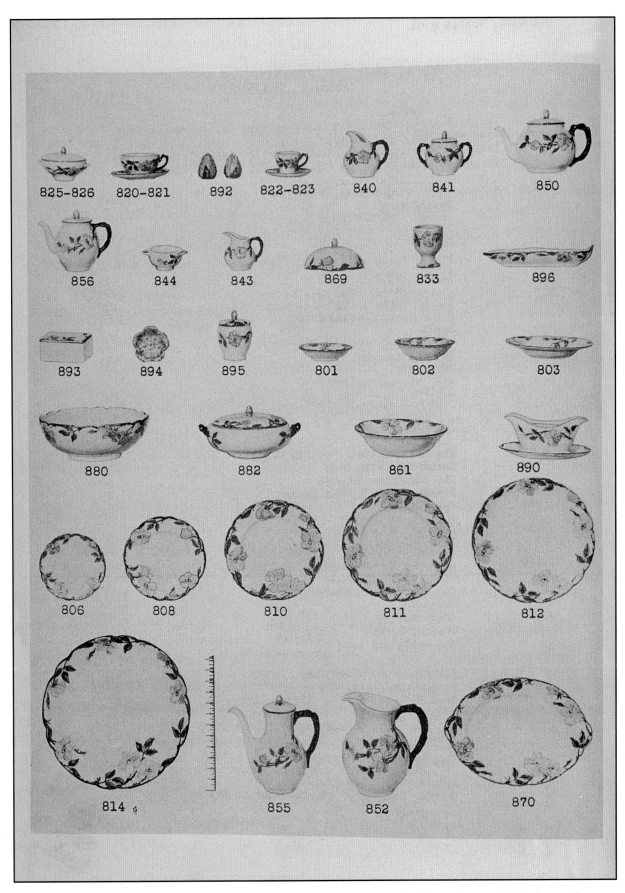

825-826   820-821   892   822-823   840   841   850

856   844   843   869   833   896

893   894   895   801   802   803

880   882   861   890

806   808   810   811   812

814   855   852   870

This is a catalog page from the January 1, 1942 Franciscan Ware price list and general sales instructions. Desert Rose was originally named "The Desert Rose." Pictured are the items that were first introduced for The Desert Rose.

Chapter 12
After Pearl Harbor, December 7, 1941 and through 1942

After Pearl Harbor on December 7, 1941, companies all across the United States were under special provisions handed down by the Government to insure victory in the war with Germany and Japan. Gladding, McBean & Co. was not alone in retooling their plants for the war effort. Supplies were rationed. Some items were even removed from general use and were only available to companies manufacturing goods for the war effort. Many glazes contained minerals that would soon be banned for civilian use. Cobalt and any uranium-based glaze would soon disappear, leaving either dull glazes or no glazes at all for the bright colors of blue or orange. The War Production Board, that required all companies to file an application for a project rating, governed all this. Based on this rating, a company could be denied the materials necessary for their project. When war was declared, all companies could produce only what was in production at the time. This essentially froze a company. Companies without a defense contract could not build, enlarge, or make any unnecessary repairs to their factory holdings. Any controlled material that the company used in their production, if deemed necessary only for the war effort, would no longer be available for their use. Many companies had to cease production of ware, due to the materials being controlled.

Gladding, McBean & Co. was affected by these new orders and regulations by the War Production Board. New tableware or art ware lines could not be introduced. Lines already in production could not have any additional items added. Tile production would continue along with terra cotta wares such as sewer pipe and roof tiles as well as brick for building and refractories. Factories would have to be built for War production, and the plants of Gladding, McBean & Co. were operating under full capacity. Terra cotta garden ware, although not produced in great quantities prior to the War would end completely. However, on one note, cigarette urns would continue to be made for commercial use. The Glendale plant was called upon in a special way. The research department geared up and soon developed materials for use in the War. The Franciscan Ware plant, instead of being devoted to art ware and tableware, would produce cones for bombs. Women of the Gladding, McBean & Co. would take over many jobs formerly occupied only by men.

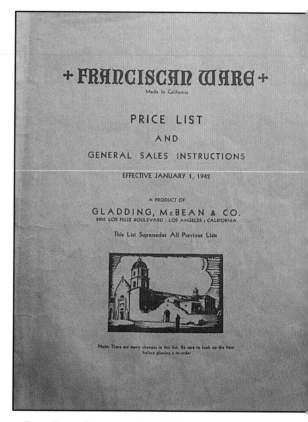

Franciscan Ware catalog 1942, $125-145.

The Home of
FRANCISCAN WARE and *Catalina Art Pottery*
REG. U.S. PAT. OFF.
Made in California

View of Gladding, McBean & Co. Franciscan Ware plant located at
2901 Los Feliz Blvd., Glendale, California, 1942.

January 1, 1942 was the last time Gladding, McBean & Co. introduced any new patterns and these would be the last for the duration of the war. Only one earthenware tableware pattern was introduced. The pattern, which today is the most sought after, was Wild Flower Table Ware. "Wild Flowers," as it was marketed, was an embossed hand-painted tableware.

Gladding, McBean & Co. adapted the shapes of the Encanto Art Ware line to the new Polynesia Ware. Polynesia is the only art ware line ever produced by Gladding, McBean & Co. that was embossed and hand-painted. Angeleno Art Ware was introduced, again adapting shapes from various lines. The Catalina Art Pottery Price List and General Sales Instructions included Reseda Ware (19 shapes), Polynesia Ware (16 shapes), Angeleno Ware (18 shapes), Saguaro Art Ware (15 shapes), Floral Art Ware (18 shapes), Ox-Blood (17 shapes), Catalina Art Pottery (13 shapes), Avalon Art Ware (13 shapes), Capistrano Ware (20 shapes), Coronado Art Pottery (7 shapes), and Miscellaneous Items (14 shapes from various lines).

The year 1942 also saw the introduction of Gladding, McBean & Co.'s first fine china line called Franciscan Fine China.

Not long ago *China and Glass* announced that truly fine glassware is being made in California. Marking another creative milestone, it may now be reported that

truly fine chinaware is emanating from this center, the result of three years work at the plant of Gladding, McBean & Co. under the direction of Frederic J. Grant, vice president in charge of china and pottery.

Mr. Grant admits a longtime ambition to make fine china and Gladding, McBean & Co. has been preparing the way for its production over an even longer period than the three years of development work. The whole thing, though, started from scratch. Employees working with china were all trained within the plant itself; none had previously had china experience. Most of the processes now in use were likewise developed by Gladding, McBean & Co. So, too, was the body, which differs somewhat from other china bodies in actual content. While Mary Kay Grant was responsible for shapes and styling, the actual artwork was done by a number of different artists, and throughout the plant suggestions and ideas were invited from workers and received in abundance.

Known as "Franciscan China," the new line has a highly translucent cream-colored body which takes glaze and decoration extremely well and which is quite sturdy. Decoration is applied by a new process developed by Gladding, McBean & Co. working in conjunction with another

Wild Flowers. Left to right: #902 cereal or soup, $65-75; #901 fruit, $45-55; #906 bread & butter, 6.5", $38-45; #908 salad plate, 8", $65-85; #910 dinner plate, 9.5", $95-125; #911 large dinner plate, 10.5", $95-125; and #920 cup, $75-85 with #921 saucer, $12-22 or $85-125 for a set.

Los Angeles firm, which has done a specialized job of printing on plastics. Decorative motifs are bolder than have been used heretofore, breaking away from conventional types and making considerable use of raised enamels.

For some time Franciscan China has had a limited public sale, permitting accurate testing of the market and of consumer acceptance, which has been highly favorable, according to all reports. A medium to high-priced line, Franciscan fills a little gap in price structure of the American china field. Outlets for the new china are expected to be those stores already handling fine china.

At present Franciscan [China] is being released as a short line, but other pieces will be added to make it a fully rounded dinnerware line. Thus far 14 patterns are active. They are: Fremont, a formal pattern; Cherokee Rose, Mountain Laurel, Woodside, the most popular pattern thus far released; Crinoline, Arcadia, which has three different color treatments; Arden,

Northridge and Laguna, formal patterns combining bands of maroon and gold on white; Shasta, a Norwegian peasant pattern; Westwood, which has the feeling of Swedish Modern; Del Monte and Beverly which are gold patterns and white undecorated. - "Franciscan China, Gladding, McBean's New China Line Goes on General Market After Limited Sale Testing Consumer Acceptance," by H. L. Mitchell, *China and Glass*, date unknown.

At the end of 1942, all Catalina Art Ware and all tableware lines except El Patio, Coronado, Apple, and Desert Rose were discontinued for the duration of the war. Unfortunately, Gladding, McBean & Co. would let the Catalina Pottery trademark and use expire and would never again produce Catalina Art Ware. When the War ended, the time had passed for the tableware lines introduced prior to 1942 to be in fashion. El Patio, and Coronado remained in production into the 1950s. Apple and Desert Rose would continue on and become two of the most popular patterns in the world.

Wild Flower Table Ware

The embossed hand-painted line whose official name was "Wild Flowers" was, "A new, embossed Franciscan pattern which takes its place alongside the famous "Apple" and "Desert Rose". The motifs are the Mariposa Lily, California

Poppy, Shooting Star, and the Desert Lupin, and the colors are the natural yellow-orange, rust red, and blue. Ready for delivery in early April." – Franciscan Ware Price List and General Sales Instructions, January 1, 1942.

The following shapes were introduced in April 1942 in Wild Flowers.

906	Plate, Bread & Butter, 6.5"
908	Plate, Salad, 8"
910	Plate, Dinner, 9.5"
911	Plate, Large Dinner, 10.5"
912	Plate, Chop or Cake, 12.5"
920	Cup
921	Saucer
901	Fruit
902	Cereal or Soup
961	Vegetable Dish
940	Creamer
941	Sugar
950	Teapot
914	Large Chop, 14"

After July 1942, other items were added and are the following. "Wild Flowers" was discontinued in 1942.
Salt & Pepper

Platter, Oval, 14"
Coffee Pot
Covered Vegetable
After Dinner Cup and Saucer
Jumbo Cup and Saucer
Sherbet
Pitcher
Oval Relish
Tumbler
Ashtray, Mariposa
Ashtray, Poppy

The salt and pepper shape was adapted from the Desert Rose Table Ware line. The color of the yellow matches the color of the poppy exactly. Do not be confused with salt & peppers from the Meadow Rose tableware line introduced in 1977.

Wild Flowers. Left to right: number unknown celery, introduced after 1942, $165-185; number unknown oval platter, 14", $165-225; and #961 vegetable dish, $125-155.

Wild Flowers. Left to right: #941 sugar, $125-165; #950 teapot, $350-425; and #940 creamer, $125-165. Not pictured, number unknown coffee pot, $350-425.

Wild Flowers. Left to right: #unknown oval 14" platter, $350-450; and #912 chop or cake plate, 12.5", $245-275.

Wild Flowers. Left to right: number unknown tumbler, $125-145 and number unknown pitcher, $350-425. Not pictured, covered vegetable, $450-550.

Wild Flowers. Left to right: number unknown California poppy ashtray, $85-95; number unknown sherbet, $125-145; number unknown salt & pepper, $125-145; and number unknown mariposa lily ashtray, $85-95.

Wild Flowers. Left to right: #920 cup, $75-85 with #921 saucer, $12-22 or $85-125 for a set; number unknown after dinner cup and saucer, $145-225 set. Not pictured, number unknown jumbo cup and saucer: $175-245 set.

Angeleno Art Ware

Angeleno Art Ware was offered in graceful Chinese shapes in the solid colors of Periwinkle Blue (M.P. 53), Light Bronze (M.P. 71), and Ivory (M.P. 5-Matt Ivory). All of the shapes are from previously issued lines and adapted with the new Periwinkle Blue and Light Bronze glazes.

Angeleno Ware #123 large vase, 11" x 9.75" diameter in periwinkle, $255-345.

41	Flat Bowl, 16"
105	Vase, Small Bottle Shape
115	Vase, 10.5"
116	Vase, 9.5" Bottle Shape
122	Vase, 9.5" Ball Shape
123	Vase, 11" Large
C-276	Vase, Handled, 6"
C-278	Vase, 6"
C-279	Vase, 4.5" Square
C-283	Bowl, 10" Round
C-284	Vase, 8.25"
C-287	Bowl, 16"
C-289	Vase, 9" Wide Mouth
C-290	Vase, 11"
C-291	Bowl, Low, Round, 14"
C-292	Bowl, Round
C-293	Vase, 5.5" (Rose Bowl)
C-300	Vase, 5" Small

Angeleno Art Ware was discontinued in 1942.

Angeleno Ware. Left to Right: Bronze #C-279 low square vase, 4.25", $85-125; Periwinkle #116 bottle shape vase, 9.5", $125-225; and Matt Ivory #C-276 handled vase, 6", $75-95. Angeleno Ware is known by its glazes – Matt Ivory, Bronze, and Periwinkle.

Polynesia Ware. Bottom: #388 round bowl, 14", $225. Left to right: #383 vase, 6" x 5" diameter, $245; #387 cylinder vase, 9", $225; and #380 vase, 4.75", $145.

Polynesia Ware. Left to right: #376 ball vase, 3.5", $145; #377 small pot, 3.5", $145; #378 footed vase, 4.75", $145; and #381 ball vase, 3.5", $145.

Polynesia Ware. Front: #375 cigarette box, $125-175; note that the ashtray #894 (not pictured) is the same as the Desert Rose individual ashtray. Left to right back: #385 round vase, 6.75", $225-245; #379 vase, 5", $145; and #382 oval vase, 5" x 4", $145.

Polynesia Art Ware

Being the only hand-painted, embossed art ware line produced by Gladding, McBean & Co., Polynesia was decorated in what was referred to as South Sea floral motifs. In the same multi-color combinations as the Desert Rose Table Ware, Polynesia is one of the most sought after art ware lines today. All shapes were adapted from the Encanto Art Ware line. Polynesia was discontinued in 1942.

Polynesia was offered in the following shapes:

374	Candleholder
375	Cigarette Box
376	Ball Vase, 3.5"
377	Small Pot, 3.5"
378	Footed Vase, 4.75"
379	Vase, 5"
380	Vase, 4.75"
381	Ball Vase, 3.5"
382	Oval Vase, 5" x 4"
383	Vase, 6" x 5" diameter
384	Oval Bowl, 8" x 4"
385	Round Vase, 6.75"
386	Oval Bowl, 10" x 5"
387	Cylinder Vase, 9"
388	Round Bowl, 14"
894	Ash Tray, Desert Rose Design, also for Polynesia

Many shapes were used in different glazes and were offered in different lines through the years. This is an example of the #387 cylinder vase 9" shape, which was offered in the Encanto Art Ware (not pictured here), Ox-blood, Terra Cotta Specialties, and Polynesia Ware lines. Pictured left to right is the #387 cylinder vase in the Terra Cotta Specialties line with a maroon glaze on a terra cotta base, Polynesia Ware line, which is hand-painted, and the Ox-blood Art Ware line in the ox-blood glaze.

Franciscan China, the first fine china in quantity ever to be manufactured in Los Angeles, went into full-scale production upon its introduction to the market in August 1942. Franciscan Fine China was introduced in two shapes, Merced and Redondo. A Belleek-type of china, it has high translucency and special strength of body. From the *Ceramic Industry* September 1, 1942 issue, in an article titled "Success of Chicago and Forecasts a Busy Season," the reporter stated: "Gladding, McBean & Co. found buyer

acceptance of their Franciscan china very good. The dinnerware comes in 17 patterns and two shapes, Ovide and Footed. The patterns include Swedish modern, traditional, formal china with three gold treatments, center decoration, two full shoulder decorations, the laurel type and inevitably a pink rose."

The first lines introduced in Franciscan Fine China were the following. Included in this list are the pattern name, dates of manufacture, and the shape it is on.

From the 1951 Franciscan Fine China catalog and price list of shapes and patterns are the shapes of the first fine china introduced in 1942. The names of the shapes were Merced and Redondo. All shapes were available for the patterns introduced in 1942.

This is the first nameplate used to identify Franciscan China. Nameplates were used in department and fine jewelry stores to identify Franciscan China. This nameplate was used from 1942 to 1947. A cast triangular tube, closed at each end, this nameplate had a hole in the center on the side that was not glazed. Included with the Franciscan China decal was a decal including the name of the pattern. The plaque was 4.25" long, 1.5" wide, and 1" high. This nameplate was also used in the office with the name of the employee instead of the Franciscan China decal.

Arcadia Blue	1942-1952	Merced
Arcadia Green	1942-1962	Merced
Arcadia Maroon	1942-1952	Merced
Arden	1942-1952	Merced
Beverly	1942-1952	Merced
Cherokee Rose (Gold)	1942-1952	Merced
Crinoline	1942-1951	Merced
Del Monte	1942-1962	Merced
Fremont	1942-1951	Merced
Gold Band 301	1942-1977	Merced
Laguna	1942-1951	Merced
Mountain Laurel	1942-1951	Merced
Northridge	1942-1949	Merced
Shasta	1942-1952	Redondo
Westwood	1942-1961	Redondo
Woodside	1942-1962	Merced

In July and December of 1942, Gladding, McBean & Co. introduced the following patterns:

Arcadia Cobalt	1943-1943	Merced
Arcadia Gold	1942-1977	Merced
Balboa	1942-1951	Merced
Carmel (Turquoise)	1942	Merced (Samples Only)
Cherokee Rose Green	1941-1955	Merced
Cherokee Rose Palomino	1941-1949	Merced
Desert Blossom	1942-1942	Ovide (Samples Only)
Gold Band 101	1942-1954	Ovide
Gold Band 101	1942-1942	Merced
Gold Band 201	1942-1954	Ovide
Gold Band 202	1942-1951	Merced
Gold Band 302	1942-1951	Merced
Gold Band 302	1942-1951	Ovide
Larchmont	1942-1942	Merced
Wilshire (El Camino China)	1942-1951	Merced

Franciscan China, Westwood pattern. Westwood was on the Redondo shape. Left to right: #6640 creamer, $22-28; #6655 coffee pot, $85-95; #6513 chop, 14", $55-65; #6641 sugar with lid, $22-28; and #6650 teapot, $85-95.

The trademark Franciscan Fine China would change to the trademark Franciscan Masterpiece China in 1958. Cherokee Rose Gold was first introduced as Dainty Bess. Arcadia Cobalt, Beverly Cobalt, Monterey Cobalt were only made as service plates.

Wilshire was renamed El Camino China and sold in the Franciscan Shop (Factory Seconds Store) at the Glendale plant. Gladding, McBean & Co. would continue to introduce fine china patterns until 1977, when all fine china patterns were discontinued.

This is a liner used in packing Franciscan China to protect plates. No price determined.

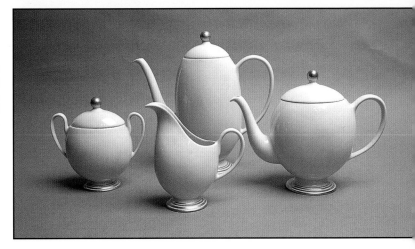

Franciscan China, Merced Shape. This pattern is a variation of Gold Band. Left to right: #6541 sugar with lid, $28-36; #6540 creamer, $28-32; #6555 coffee pot, $95-125; and #6550 teapot, $95-125.

Franciscan China. Left to right: Arcadia Green #6510 dinner plate, $22-28; Arcadia Maroon #6522 after dinner cup and #6523 after dinner saucer, $22-36 set; Arcadia Maroon #6510 dinner plate, $22-28; and Arcadia Gold #6592 salt & pepper set, $22-26.

Franciscan China. Left: Gold Band #6510 dinner plate, $22-28; back: Del Monte 14" chop plate #6513, $35-45; front: Fremont #6509 salad plate, $16-18; and right: Woodside #6510 dinner plate, $22-28.

Franciscan China. Shasta tall oval shaped vase, $75-125. Shasta is the only pattern found thus far on this shape.

Franciscan China. Fremont cigarette boxes, $45-55 and ashtray, $18-22. This is the only Franciscan China pattern that has been found on these shapes.

Afterword

2901 Los Feliz Blvd, Glendale, California, 1991.

New Gladding, McBean & Co. terra cotta ware from the Lincoln, California, plant. This piece was never made prior to 1990. Designed in 1990, this form was produced for only a very short time. It is cast rather than hand-formed. $145-165.

Gladding, McBean & Co. would prosper after World War II. New dinnerware lines would be added every year. All art ware lines made prior to 1942 were discontinued permanently. Gladding, McBean & Co. returned the use of the trademark "Catalina Pottery" to the Santa Catalina Island Company in 1947. The molds would later be sold to Weil of California. Gladding, McBean & Co. would not produce any other art ware lines until the introduction of the fine china Contours line in 1954, which was designed by George T. James. Contours would be the last art ware line produced by Gladding, McBean & Co.

Max Weil came to the United States after World War II, bringing with him molds for figurines and soon opened his own pottery: Weil of California. Weil of California produced figurines, art ware, and dinnerware. Weil Ware was the trade name of products produced by Weil of California. In late 1952, Frederic Grant resigned as Corporate Vice President from Gladding, McBean & Co. and Mary Grant resigned as the head of the Design Department. Prior to 1954, Frederic Grant purchased the controlling interest of Weil Ware. Weil of California acquired the molds of the former Catalina art ware lines from Gladding, McBean & Co. You will find the Polynesia and Encanto shapes marked "Weil Ware" as well as the Nautical line shells and other art ware previously manufactured by Gladding, McBean & Co.

The burro, not a donkey, on the back stamp of Weil of California is an interesting story in itself. The factory had a pet burro that roamed freely at the Weil Ware plant. His name was Dopey. Beloved as he was by the employees and Max Weil, he became the symbol of Weil Ware and appears as the factory's mark. After Max Weil passed away in 1954, Weil of California was soon in financial trouble. Renamed The Grant Ceramic Co., Weil Ware was still produced and other lines were added including a line called Granoby "Lanai Ware" designed by Mary Grant. By the end of the next two years however, the company was forced into liquidation.

At present, Desert Rose and Apple are enjoying a renaissance. Wedgwood's Johnson Brothers division is adding new pieces to the lines every year. Desert Rose and Apple tableware is still preferred by collectors when made in the USA, prior to the Glendale plant closure in 1984. However, that is what makes made in USA Desert Rose and Apple tableware so collectible today. Both in all probability will never be manufactured in the United States again.

The Pacific Coast Building Products Gladding, McBean & Co. division still produces terra cotta tile, sewer pipe, and other building products in Lincoln, California. In 1990, the company reintroduced the garden ware line. Truly a tradition of hand-made terra cotta ware, the garden ware is a very special product of Gladding, McBean & Co.

The tradition of Franciscan dinnerware and Gladding, McBean & Co. lives on.

Appendix I

Experimental Art Ware and Tableware

Through the course of designing, and manufacturing, Gladding, McBean & Co. would use existing shapes to experiment with different glazes and designs. Some of these examples can be excellent in execution, while others are just what they are: experiments. The Company would use cups without handles to test glazes as well. In the manufacturing process, the initial glaze batch would be run through the kiln to see if the proper color and quality was obtained. These cups are usually marked with the M.P. glaze code and sometimes a date. Small vases would also be used.

As with all companies, employees would run pieces through the kiln for their own use. Usually these pieces are marked with an employee's initials so that the piece would be returned to them. Ox-blood was a favorite glaze used by employees. Over the years many pieces have shown up; however, the quality varies greatly among them.

When buying or selling an experimental piece, keep in mind whether or not the piece is a quality piece or one that was just run through the kiln for testing. Pricing varies, and should be considered when purchasing a piece.

These #118 vases are glazed in a drip glaze of turquoise and celestial white. Both are unmarked. No price determined.

This #C-801 bust of peasant girl was made by a gentleman when he worked at the Franciscan plant in Glendale. The glaze is in a dark green gloss over the stained Malinite body. Many employees were able to dip various pieces in different glazes to be fired. Usually workers marked such pieces with their initials so that the items would be returned to them. This piece is unmarked. No price determined.

Another two great examples of experimental art ware include this #C-289 vase, wide mouth, 9" and this spotted #C-284 vase, 8.25". No prices determined.

This #122 vase, ball shape, 8.25" x 9.5", has a flambé exterior with a celestial white interior. Though this could be in the Cielito Art Ware line, it is marked with large numbers scratched in the body indicating the glaze colors. No price determined.

This #C-284 vase, 8.25" tall, has been glazed with a redwood exterior and a turquoise interior. It is marked with numbers scratched in the bottom indicating the glaze colors. Scratching the glaze number into the bottom marked many experimental art ware pieces. Whenever a glaze was tried out, the appropriate shape would be chosen to best see the glaze coverage on the shape. With experimental pieces, you will find a piece that is clearly beautiful, but many times it is after all just an experiment and experiments can be not very desirable. Pricing should be based on whether the experimental piece in itself is both well done and nicely executed. There should be a minimum of obvious flaws for the piece to have a value above what the piece would be in a production glaze.

One of the most wonderful experimental pieces is known as the "Cyclops" vase as it seems to be looking back at you. This is shape #C-390. No price determined.

Various experimental glazes on shapes. Left to right: #105; #C-304; and #150. The various marks used are pictured as well. No prices determined.

Bowls were used quite frequently for quality control and experimentation. No prices determined.

Left: This is an El Patio dinner plate with an experimental design. Never put into production. No price determined.

Right: Another El Patio shape, large dinner plate with experimental design. Other pieces have been found and this may be a pattern that was produced in a short line. No price determined.

Left: Montecito dinner plate shape. Many patterns were created and were taken to local stores to see whether or not the public liked it. Company employees would take a number of experimental patterns, set up a booth, and ask customers which patterns they liked and why. If a pattern proved to be popular, the company would consider its production. This would be a practice followed through the years. No price determined.

Right: Large 14" chop plate in a plaid design. No price determined.

Left to right: El Patio shape dinner plate in plaid. Plaids have been found on the El Patio shape, including cups and saucers. This again may have been produced as a short line. In front is a decorated custard cup in the Cocinero pattern. The base is marked with the initials F.G. – maybe Frederic Grant? Employees would mark their initials on ware to be returned to them. Many employees made their own sets for their personal use. The glazed chair cane plate has been found in other colors and may have been a short line. The salad bowl is of the same design but a different color way. No prices determined.

Large 14" chop plate, decorated. The back is marked with initials and could have been produced by an employee for personal use. The back also has the red and gold Franciscan Ware sticker. Employees would use these stickers on items produced for their own use. However, if just a sticker is used, be aware that it may have been placed there by someone else and may not be a Gladding, McBean & Co. product. No price determined.

Large 14" chop with a lighting bolt pattern. This could have been either an experimental piece or made by an employee for their own use. No price determined.

Apple items produced in Coronado Table Ware colors. Whether an experiment, a trial run, or an employee's favorite, various pieces have surfaced. No price determined.

Various test satin glazes on the Metropolitan cup shape. Each are numbered differently. To be sure the glaze batch would fire correctly, cup shapes would be run through the kiln. No prices determined.

This set of El Patio Table Ware cream and sugar are hand-painted and the handles and lid knob are in gold. The bottom of the sugar is signed in a black signature, but it is illegible. Both are marked with the GMcB small oval stamp. A small vase in the Cielito Art Ware line also has been found with the same decoration and signature. No price determined.

225

More test glazes on the Coronado cup shape. No prices determined.

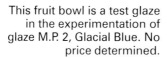

This fruit bowl is a test glaze in the experimentation of glaze M.P. 2, Glacial Blue. No price determined.

Metropolitan Table Ware 8" salad plate with hand-painted decoration with gold. This piece is very similar to the hand painting found on Max Schonfeld's Kaolena line. This piece is marked with the round Franciscan Ware stamp. No price determined.

Copies. Left to right: unmarked shell, Nautical Art Ware shape, glazes are incorrect and piece is light and not made of Malinite. Small cactus pot, unmarked, again, wrong glaze. Shell shaped bowl, Kaolena shape, unmarked, wrong colors and not china. Candlestick, Gladding, McBean & Co. art ware shape, however this one is marked "Made in Japan."

Copies. Frederic Grant and his wife Mary would eventually acquire the Max Weil of California company early in the 1950s. Frederic Grant acquired the Catalina Pottery molds from Gladding, McBean & Co. and used them to produce ware for the Weil Ware company. Hence, this is the reason why so many Catalina Pottery shapes appear with the Weil Ware mark. Left to right: Weil Ware vase compared to Gladding, McBean & Co.'s Polynesia #381. An unmarked copy compared to the Floral Art Ware shape #C-330. Many molds made it into use by amateur ceramists; however, most are shapes that were made by making a mold over an existing piece and will be smaller.

Appendix II
Art Ware Shapes and Lines

This complete listing of all shape numbers will enable you to identify which line an art ware shape belongs in and what other lines a shape can be found in. Not all pieces are marked on the bottom, but many do have the number embossed or ink backstamped. Gladding, McBean & Co. kept a running list of numbers to all shapes produced. As you will notice, some numbers are reused, while there are duplicate numbers for others.

Shape #	Item	Line(s)
3	Vase or Wine Cup	Tropico Ware, Garden Ware
16	Bowl small	Ox-blood
22	Vase or Wine Cup	Tropico Ware, Garden Ware
41	Flat Bowl, 16"	Angeleno Art Ware
44	Flower Pot, 4"	Tropico Ware, Garden Ware
44a	Saucer	Tropico
45	Flower Pot, 5"	Tropico Ware, Garden Ware
45a	Saucer	Tropico
46	Flower Pot, 6"	Tropico Ware, Garden Ware
46a	Saucer	Tropico
47	Flower Pot, 7"	Tropico Ware, Garden Ware
47a	Saucer	Tropico
48	Flower Pot, 8"	Tropico Ware, Garden Ware
48a	Saucer	Tropico
50	Flower Pot, 10"	Tropico Ware, Garden Ware
50a	Saucer	Tropico
51	Flower Pot, Chinese Design, 9.5" Diameter	Tropico Ware, Garden Ware
52	Flower Bowl	Tropico Ware, Garden Ware (old 105)
53	Flower Bowl (special)	Tropico Ware, Garden Ware (old 55)
54	Wall Pot, small	Tropico
54-T	Large Vase, terra cotta (old 303)	Garden Ware
55	Wall Pot, medium	Tropico
55-T	Large Vase, terra cotta (old 305)	Garden Ware
56	Wall Pot, large	Tropico
56-T	Large Vase, terra cotta (old 301)	Garden Ware
57	Small Frog	Tropico Ware, Garden Ware
58	Large Frog	Tropico Ware, Garden Ware
59	Sitting Girl (special)	Tropico Ware, Garden Ware (old 99)
60-T	Sitting Boy (old 1107)	Garden Ware
61-T	Standing Boy (old 1108)	Garden Ware
62	Small Handmade Basket (special)	Tropico Ware, Garden Ware (old 66)
63	Large Handmade Basket (special)	Tropico Ware, Garden Ware (old 53)
64-T	Porch Jar or Palm Pot, 12" (old 225)	Garden Ware
65-T	Umbrella Stand or Vase (old 11)	Garden Ware
66-T	Large Flaring Vase (old 14)	Garden Ware
67-T	Small Oil Jar, 21" (old 45A)	Garden Ware
68-T	Medium Oil Jar, 26" (old 45)	Garden Ware
69-T	Large Oil Jar, 33" (old 88)	Garden Ware
70-T	Pedestal, 27" (old 4)	Garden Ware
71	Flower Bowl	Tropico Ware, Garden Ware
72	Cigarette Box	Miscellaneous Items
72-T	Sand Jar (old 143)	Garden Ware
73-T	Sand Jar (old 126)	Garden Ware
74 to 79	Flower Pots	Garden Ware
79	Bowl round	Ox-blood

80	Flower Pot, 10" rolled edge	Tropico Ware, Garden Ware
81	Opium Bowl	Tropico Ware, Garden Ware
81a	Opium Bowl Stand	Tropico Ware, Garden Ware
82-T	Saucer for Bird Bath or large Pots, 16"-20"-27" (old 240)	Garden Ware
83	Pedestal Bowl, 8.5"(old 174), 11" (old 173)	Garden Ware
83-8	Petal Bowl, 8.5"	Tropico
83-11	Petal Bowl, 11"	Tropico
84-T	Boy on Turtle (old 145)	Garden Ware
85	Pet Feeding Bowl	Garden Ware
86	Goose on Pedestal base	Capistrano
86-T	Bird Bath & Pedestal (old 1098)	Garden Ware
87	Sun Bonnet Vase	Capistrano
87-T	Porch Jardinière (old 132)	Garden Ware
88-T	Jardinière (old 167)	Garden Ware
88-8	Jardinière, 8"	Tropico
88-10	Jardinière, 10"	Tropico
89	Handled Vase Grecian, 6"	Tropico Ware, Garden Ware
90-T	Sand Jar deep (old 410-G)	Garden Ware
90A-T	Sand Jar shallow (old 410-G)	Garden Ware
91	Ash Tray	Tropico Ware, Garden Ware, Miscellaneous Items
92	Jardinière with ribs	Tropico Ware, Garden Ware, Florist Special
93	Utility Flower Vase, 9.5"	Tropico Ware, Garden Ware, Florist Special
94	Flower Bowl square	Tropico Ware, Garden Ware
95	Small Cactus Pot	Florist Special
96	Candlestick	Tropico Ware, Garden Ware (old 40)
100	Ash Tray	Cielito Ware, Tropico Ware, Garden Ware, Miscellaneous Items
101	Ash Tray	Cielito Ware, Miscellaneous Items
102	Vase	Cielito Ware
103	Vase (or small lamp base)	Cielito Ware
104	Ball Shape Vase	Cielito Ware, Tropico Ware, Ox-blood
105	Vase Small Bottle Shape	Cielito Ware, Ox-blood, Angeleno Art Ware
106	Candlestick	Cielito Ware
107	Footed Vase	Cielito Ware, Tropico
108	Bowl, Petal Shape, 8.5"	Cielito Ware
109	Vase	Cielito Ware
110	Vase	Cielito Ware
111	Lidded Box	Cielito Ware,
112	Wide Mouth Vase	Cielito Ware, Tropico
113	Beaker Vase	Cielito Ware, Tropico
114	Vase, 2.75" Flaring	Cielito Ware, Ox-Blood
115	Vase, 10.5"	Cielito Ware, Ox-Blood, Angeleno Art Ware
116	Vase, 9.5" Bottle Shape	Cielito Ware, Ox-Blood, Angeleno Art Ware
117	Vase	Cielito Ware
118	Vase	Cielito Ware
119	Footed Comport	Cielito Ware
120	Bowl, Square Shape	Cielito Ware
121	Bowl, Petal Shape, 11"	Cielito Ware
122	Vase, 9.5" Ball Shape	Cielito Ware, Ox-Blood, Angeleno Art Ware
123	Vase, 11" Large	Cielito Ware, Ox-Blood, Angeleno Art Ware
124	Opium Bowl	Cielito Ware
125	Flower Bowl with metal stand	Cielito
126	Flower Bowl, oval	Cielito
130	Cactus Bowl	Cielito
131	Low Bowl Vase	Tropico
132	Vase, round	Cielito
133	Candlestick	Miscellaneous Items, Cielito, Capistrano, El Patio
134	Candlestick, match #126	Cielito
135	Vase, low bottle shape	Cielito
136	Vase, slender neck	Cielito
137	Vase, round	Cielito, Avalon Art Ware
138	Low Vase	Tropico, Cielito
139	Large Flaring Vase	Tropico, Cielito
140	Cigarette Box & Lid	Cielito (# reused later)
140	Vase, Low	Ox-Blood
141	Vase, 7.25" Beaker Shape	Ox-Blood
142	Bowl, Rectangular, 6" x 9"	Capistrano Ware
143	Bowl, Rectangular, 7.5" x 10.25"	Capistrano Ware
144	Bowl, Rectangular, 9" x 11.75"	Capistrano Ware
145	Bowl, Oval, 10.5" x 15.25"	Capistrano Ware
L-145	Bird Bath & Pedestal, 22"	Garden Ware
146	Bowl, Leaf Shape, 9.75" x 14"	Capistrano Ware
147	Bowl, oval 6" x 10"	Capistrano Ware
150	Ball Vase, 4.5" x 3"	Coronado Art Pottery
151	Vase, 6.5"	Coronado Art Pottery
152	Footed Vase, 5.5"	Coronado Art Pottery

153	Low Candlestick	Coronado Art Pottery
154	Vase, 9.5"	Coronado Art Pottery
155	Vase, Lancastrian Style, 5" x 8"	Coronado Art Pottery
156	Vase, 7.5"	Coronado Art Pottery
157	Vase, Unique Design, 5.5"	Coronado Art Pottery
158	Cornucopia, Footed, 6.75"	Coronado Art Pottery
159	Lidded Box, 4.5"	Coronado Art Pottery
160	Vase, 9"	Coronado Art Pottery
161	Vase, 10.5"	Coronado Art Pottery
163	Low Bowl, 13" Diameter	Coronado Art Pottery
164	Deep Bowl, 11.5"	Coronado Art Pottery
165	Flat Bowl or Deep Plate, 13" Diameter	
166	Footed Compote, 5" x 10.25"	Coronado Art Pottery
167	Vase, 10"	Coronado Art Pottery
168	Low Bowl, 9" Diameter	Coronado Art Pottery
169	Oval Bowl, 9" x 13"	Coronado Art Pottery
170	Compote 1-3/8"	Coronado Art Pottery
171	Bud Vase 6-1/8"	Coronado Art Pottery
172	Low Bowl 2-5/8"	Coronado Art Pottery
173	Vase 5.5"	Coronado Art Pottery
174	Vase Footed 6"	Coronado Art Pottery
175	Vase Footed 6-5/8"	Coronado Art Pottery
176	Vase 5-5/8"	Coronado Art Pottery
198	Ashtray, Individual	Coronado Art Pottery
200	Chop Plate for Flowers	Coronado Art Pottery
C-202	Bowl, Oval, 15"	Avalon Art Ware, Aurora Art Ware, Catalina Art Ware
C-204	Bowl, Oval, 18"	Avalon Art Ware, Aurora Art Ware, Catalina Art Ware
214	Relish Dish 9.5"	Coronado Art Pottery
C-216	Bowl	Aurora Art Ware
C-217	Bowl	Aurora Art Ware
C-218	Bowl	Aurora Art Ware
C-219	Bowl	Aurora Art Ware, Catalina Art Ware, Terra cotta, Floral Art Ware
C-220	Bowl Leaf, 12" x 10"	Floral Art Ware
222	Cigarette Box	Coronado Art Pottery
C-225	Bowl, Ivy Leaf, 13" x 12"	Floral Art Ware
231	Small Bird Bath (old 76)	Tropico
C-231	Plate	Aurora Art Ware, Catalina Art Ware
C-232	Plate	Aurora Art Ware
C-233	Plate	Aurora Art Ware
C-234	Bowl Flat, 13.5"	Avalon Art Ware, Aurora Art Ware, Catalina Art Ware
C-235	Bowl	Aurora Art Ware, Catalina Art Ware
C-236	Bowl, Giant Clam Shell, 16"	Catalina Art Ware, Nautical Art Ware
C-237	Bowl, Clam Shell med, 11"	Catalina Art Ware, Nautical Art Ware
C-238	Bowl, Clam Shell small	Catalina Art Ware, Nautical Art Ware
C-240	Bowl, Footed	Aurora Art Ware
C-241	Bowl, Footed	Aurora Art Ware
242	Bowl, Rectangular, very low, footed, 4.5" x 6.5"	Capistrano Ware
C-242	Bowl, Footed	Aurora Art Ware
C-250	Candlestick	Saguaro Art Ware
C-251	Bud Vase, 6.25"	Saguaro Art Ware
C-252	Vase, 5" Wide Bottom	Saguaro Art Ware
C-253	Bowl, 6" x 6" Low	Saguaro Art Ware
C-254	Vase, 6.5"	Saguaro Art Ware
C-255	Vase, 5" x 6"	Saguaro Art Ware
C-256	Vase, 5.5"	Saguaro Art Ware
C-257	Bowl, 8" x 6" x 3.25" Deep Oval	Saguaro Art Ware
C-258	Bowl, 10" x 6" Low	Saguaro Art Ware
C-259	Bowl, 8.5" Round	Saguaro Art Ware
C-260	Bowl, 8" x 4" Deep Round	Saguaro Art Ware
C-261	Bowl, Triangular	Saguaro Art Ware
C-262	Bowl, 10.5" Low Round	Saguaro Art Ware
C-263	Vase, 8.5"	Saguaro Art Ware
C-264	Vase, 10"	Saguaro Art Ware
C-265	Bowl, 15" x 8" Oval	Saguaro Art Ware
C-266	Bowl, 12" Round	Saguaro Art Ware
C-267	Vase, 12" Large Triangular	Saguaro Art Ware
271	Small Vase, Leaf Design 5.25"	Florist Special
272	Large Vase, Leaf Design 12"	Florist Special
273	Wall Pocket, Leaf Design	Florist Special
275	Jardinière, Leaf Design	Florist Special
C-275	Vase, 5"	Montebello
276	Jardinière, Leaf Design	Florist Special
C-276	Vase, Handled, 6"	Angeleno Art Ware, Montebello
277	Jardinière, Leaf Design	Florist Special
C-277	Vase, 4.5" Low	Ox-Blood, Montebello

278	Jardinière, Leaf Design	Florist Special
C-278	Vase, 6"	Ox-Blood, Angeleno Art Ware, Montebello
C-279	Vase, 4.5" Square	Ox-Blood, Angeleno Art Ware, Montebello
C-281	Vase, 6" Footed	Ox-Blood, Montebello
C-282	Bowl, 7.5" Low Square	Ox-Blood, Montebello
283	Cactus Pot	Tropico, Florist Special
C-283	Bowl, 10" Round	Ox-Blood, Angeleno Art Ware, Montebello
284	Cactus Pot	Tropico, Florist Special
C-284	Vase, 8.25"	Ox-Blood, Angeleno Art Ware, Montebello
285	Azalea Pot	Tropico, Florist Special
C-285	Vase, 9"	Ox-Blood, Montebello
286	Azalea Pot	Tropico, Florist Special
C-286	Vase, 11"	Ox-Blood, Montebello
287	Jardinière	Tropico, Florist Special
C-287	Bowl, 16"	Ox-Blood, Angeleno Art Ware, Montebello
288	Jardinière	Tropico, Florist Special
C-288	Vase	Ox-Blood
289	Jardinière	Tropico, Florist Special
C-289	Vase, 9" Wide Mouth	Ox-Blood, Angeleno Art Ware
290	Jardinière	Tropico, Florist Special
C-290	Vase, 11"	Ox-Blood, Angeleno Art Ware
291	Jardinière	Tropico, Florist Special
C-291	Bowl, Low, Round, 14"	Angeleno Art Ware
292	Jardinière	Tropico, Florist Special
C-292	Bowl, Round	Angeleno Art Ware
293	Florist Stock Vase, 12"	Tropico, Florist Special
C-293	Vase, 5.5" (Rose Bowl)	Ox-Blood, Angeleno Art Ware
294	Bulb Bowl	Tropico, Florist Special
295	Florist Stock Vase	Tropico, Florist Special
296	Jardinière square	Tropico, Florist Special, Capistrano Ware (number changed to #429)
C-300	Vase, 5" Small	Ox-Blood, Angeleno Art Ware
C-304	Vase, 6.5"	Avalon Art Ware, Aurora Art Ware, Catalina Art Ware
C-305	Vase, 8"	Avalon Art Ware, Aurora Art Ware, Catalina Art Ware
C-306	Vase, Footed	Aurora Art Ware
C-307	Vase, 12"	Avalon Art Ware, Aurora Art Ware, Aurora Art Ware, Catalina Art Ware
C-308	Vase, Footed	Aurora Art Ware
C-310	Vase, Flat Fan Shape, 7.5"	Avalon Art Ware, Catalina Art Ware
C-311	Vase, Fluted, 8"	Avalon Art Ware, Catalina Art Ware
C-312	Vase, Bulge Foot, 7.75"	Avalon Art Ware, Catalina Art Ware
C-314	Candleholder	Avalon Art Ware, Catalina Art Ware
C-317	Bowl, 10" Deep	Catalina Art Ware
C-322	Vase, Footed	Aurora Art Ware
C-323	Vase, Footed	Aurora Art Ware
C-324	Vase, Footed	Aurora Art Ware
C-326	Vase, Shell	Catalina Art Ware, Nautical Art Ware
C-330	Vase, 6.5"	Catalina Art Ware, Floral Art Ware
C-331	Vase, 4"	Catalina Art Ware, Floral Art Ware
C-332	Vase, 5" Wide Mouth	Catalina Art Ware, Floral Art Ware
C-333	Vase, 7"	Catalina Art Ware, Floral Art Ware
C-334	Fancy Bowl, 9"	Catalina Art Ware, Floral Art Ware
C-335	Vase, 6.75"	Catalina Art Ware, Floral Art Ware
C-336	Candleholder	Catalina Art Ware, Floral Art Ware
C-337	Bowl	Catalina Art Ware, Floral Art Ware
C-338	Vase, 11.5" Tall Narrow	Catalina Art Ware, Floral Art Ware
C-339	Vase, 9.5" Flaring	Catalina Art Ware, Floral Art Ware
C-340	Bowl, 10" Low	Catalina Art Ware, Floral Art Ware
C-341	Bowl, Curve Top	Catalina Art Ware, Floral Art Ware
C-342	Vase, 7.5" Oval	Catalina Art Ware
C-343	Bowl, 16" Narrow	Floral Art Ware
C-344	Bowl, Leaf, 10" x 8"	Floral Art Ware
C-345	Bowl, 13" Long Leaf Shape	Floral Art Ware
C-346	Bowl, Leaf, 11"	Floral Art Ware
C-347	Bowl, Leaf, 13" x 8"	Floral Art Ware
C-348	Bowl, Leaf, 14"	Floral Art Ware
C-349	Bowl, 12" Long Narrow	Catalina Art Ware, Floral Art Ware
C-349x	Bowl, Leaf, 12" x 11"	Floral Art Ware
C-350	Sea Shell Cornucopia	Catalina Art Ware, Nautical Art Ware
C-351	Sea Shell Vase	Catalina Art Ware, Nautical Art Ware
C-352	Double Clam Shell Vase	Catalina Art Ware, Nautical Art Ware
C-353	Shell Vase	Catalina Art Ware, Nautical Art Ware
C-354	Shell Vase	Catalina Art Ware, Nautical Art Ware
C-355	Shell Vase	Nautical Art Ware
C-356	Shell Bowl, 15"	Nautical Art Ware
C-357	Shell Bowl, 9.5"	Nautical Art Ware
C-358	Shell Vase, Murex Design	Nautical Art Ware

C-359	Shell Vase, Strombus	Nautical Art Ware
C-360	Oval Bowl, Fish Pattern	Catalina Art Ware, Nautical Art Ware
C-361	Small Fish Vase	Catalina Art Ware, Nautical Art Ware
C-362	Fan Vase, Fish Pattern	Catalina Art Ware, Nautical Art Ware
C-363	Large Vase, Fish Pattern	Catalina Art Ware, Nautical Art Ware
C-364	Large Bowl, Fish Deco	Nautical Art Ware
C-370	Shell Vase, Conch Design	Nautical Art Ware
C-371	Shell Ash Tray	Nautical Art Ware
C-372	Shell Ash Tray	Nautical Art Ware
C-373	Clam Shell, Large Double	Nautical Art Ware
C-374	Shell Compote, Double	Nautical Art Ware
374	Candleholder	Polynesia Ware
C-375	Shell Bowl, Low Round	Nautical Art Ware
375	Cigarette Box	Polynesia Ware
376	Ball Vase, 3.5"	Polynesia Ware
377	Small Pot, 3.5"	Polynesia Ware
378	Footed Vase, 4.75"	Polynesia Ware
379	Vase, 5"	Polynesia Ware
380	Vase, 4.75"	Polynesia Ware
381	Ball Vase, 3.5"	Polynesia Ware
C-381	Candleholder	Aurora Art Ware
382	Oval Vase, 5" x 4"	Polynesia Ware
C-382	Candelabra, 3-branch strait base	Avalon Art Ware, Catalina Art Ware
383	Vase, 6" x 5" diameter	Polynesia Ware
384	Oval Bowl, 8" x 4"	Polynesia Ware
385	Round Vase, 6.75"	Polynesia Ware
386	Oval Bowl, 10" x 5"	Polynesia Ware
387	Cylinder Vase, 9"	Polynesia Ware
388	Round Bowl, 14"	Polynesia Ware
400	Candlestick with flutings	Capistrano Ware
401	Square Dish or Ash Tray	Capistrano Ware
402	Candlestick, 4"	Reseda Art Ware, Capistrano Ware
403	Round Vase	Capistrano Ware
404	Lid for #403	Capistrano Ware
405	Vase, Ball & Cylinder	Capistrano Ware
406	Square Vase, 4.5" x 3.25"	Capistrano Ware
407	Centerpiece, semi-circular	Capistrano Ware
408	Square Bowl	Capistrano Ware
409	Round Vase	Capistrano Ware
410	Vase or Bowl, low round	Capistrano Ware
411	Square Jar or Flower Pot, 6.25" x 4.25"	Capistrano Ware
412	Rectangular Bowl, 8.25" x 4.5" x 3.25"	Capistrano Ware
413	Round Vase, flared	Capistrano Ware
414	Low Square Bowl, 8.5" x 2.5"	Capistrano Ware
415	Long Rectangular Pansy Jar, 10" x 3.75" x 3.25"	Capistrano Ware
416	Bowl Fluted	Capistrano Ware
417	Jar round flaring	Capistrano Ware
418	Hexagonal Bowl, 8-5/8" x 10" x 5-1/8"	Capistrano Ware
419	Large Oval Bowl, 15.75" x 7.75" x 3.5"	Capistrano Ware
420	Fruit Bowl, flaring	Capistrano Ware
421	Bowl, large rectangular	Capistrano Ware
422	Square Bowl, 9.75" x 4"	Capistrano Ware
423	Bowl with six grooves	Capistrano Ware
424	Bowl with grooves, large	Capistrano Ware
425	Vase, tall cylinder & ball	Capistrano Ware
426	Vase, tall cylinder & ball	Capistrano Ware
428	Tall Square Vase, 10"	Capistrano Ware
429	Jardinière (old #296)	Capistrano Ware
430	Bowl, round flaring 8"	Capistrano Ware
431	Bowl, oval	Capistrano Ware
440	Bowl, rectangular 3.5" x 7"	Capistrano Ware
441	Low Rectangular Flower Bowl, 5" x 9"	Capistrano Ware
442	Low Rectangular Flower Bowl, 7" x 12"	Capistrano Ware
443	Low Rectangular Flower Bowl, 10" x 15"	Capistrano Ware
444	Tall Footed Vase, 12"	Capistrano Ware
C-449	Bud Vase, 6"	Reseda Art Ware
C-450	Pansy Bowl, 3" x 10"	Reseda Art Ware
C-451	Low Wide Vase, 5"	Reseda Art Ware
C-452	Oval Crimped Bowl, 9.5"	Reseda Art Ware
C-453	Flat Footed Vase, 8"	Reseda Art Ware
C-454	Vase with Crimped Top, 8"	Reseda Art Ware
C-455	Round Bowl, 8" x 4.5"	Reseda Art Ware
C-456	Footed Crimped Top, 9"	Reseda Art Ware
C-457	Square Bowl, 7.5" x 7.5" x 3.5"	Reseda Art Ware
C-458	Low Flat Bowl, 7.5" x 11"	Reseda Art Ware

C-459	Round Vase, 8" x 6.5"	Reseda Art Ware
C-460	Vase with Square Top, 10"	Reseda Art Ware
C-461	Low Round Bowl, 12"	Reseda Art Ware
C-462	Square Bowl, 10" x 10" x 3.5"	Reseda Art Ware
C-463	Low Rectangular Bowl, 13.25" x 9.5"	Reseda Art Ware
C-464	Tall Footed Vase, 12"	Reseda Art Ware
C-465	Tall Vase, 12"	Reseda Art Ware
C-466	Large Round Bowl, 14"	Reseda Art Ware
C-506	Mexican Hat	Catalina Art Ware
600	Candleholder (same as 374)	Encanto Ware
C-600	Vase Oval	Catalina Art Ware
601	Bud Vase	Encanto Ware
C-601	Vase Oval	Catalina Art Ware
602	Bud Vase	Encanto Ware
603	Ball Vase, 3.5"	(same as 376) Encanto Ware
C-603	Vase Round, Scroll Foot, 5"	Avalon Art Ware, Catalina Art Ware
604	Small Pot, 3.5" (same as 377)	Encanto Ware
C-604	Vase Round, Scroll Foot, 6.5"	Avalon Art Ware, Catalina Art Ware
605	Footed Vase, 4.75" (same as 378)	Encanto Ware
606	Vase, 5" (same as 379)	Encanto Ware
607	Vase, 4.75" (same as 380)	Encanto Ware
C-607	Candelabra, 3-branch curved base	Avalon Art Ware, Catalina Art Ware
608	Ball Vase, 3.5" (same as 381)	Encanto Ware
C-608	Candelabra	Avalon Art Ware, Catalina Art Ware
609	Oval Vase	Encanto Ware
C-609	Ribbed Vase, 5.75"	Catalina Art Ware
610	Cigarette Box (same as 375)	Encanto Ware
C-610	Ribbed Vase, 7.75"	Catalina Art Ware
611	Flat Oval Vase with Fish	Encanto Ware
C-611	Ribbed Vase, 10.5"	Catalina Art Ware
612	Oval Vase, 5" x 4" (same as 382)	Encanto Ware
613	Round Footed Vase with Fish	Encanto Ware
614	Vase, 6" x 5" diameter (same as 383)	Encanto Ware
C-614	Bud Vase	Catalina Art Ware
615	Cylinder Vase, Small	Encanto Ware
C-615	Vase, 4.75" Star Design	Catalina Art Ware
616	Oval Bowl, 8" x 4" (same as 384)	Encanto Ware
C-616	Vase	Catalina Art Ware
617	Round Vase with Fish	Encanto Ware
618	Round Vase, 6.75" (same as 385)	Encanto Ware
619	Cylinder Vase, 9" Medium (same as 387)	Encanto Ware
C-619	Vase, 7.5" Octagonal	Catalina Art Ware
620	Vase, 7.75"	Encanto Ware
621	Oval Bowl, 10" x 5" (same as 386)	Encanto Ware
C-621	Vase, 7" Flat	Catalina Art Ware
622	Cylinder Vase, Large	Encanto Ware
623	Vase Large (1934 Museum Expo Piece)	Encanto Ware
624	Round Bowl, 14" (same as 388)	Encanto Ware
C-627	Vase, 7.5" Fluted Neck	Catalina Art Ware
C-630	Vase, 8" Round	Catalina Art Ware
C-633	Vase, 8.5" Round	Catalina Art Ware
C-636	Vase, 7" Flat Offset	Catalina Art Ware
C-641	Dolphin Table piece	Catalina Art Ware, Nautical Art Ware
C-703	Bowl, Flat Oval, 14.75"	Avalon Art Ware, Catalina Art Ware, Terra cotta
C-709	Bowl, Star Shape, 9.5"	Avalon Art Ware
C-724	Compote, 8"	Avalon Art Ware, Catalina Art Ware
C-725	Compote, 13"	Avalon Art Ware, Catalina Art Ware
793	Cigarette Box, Apple Design	Hand Decorated
794	Ash Tray, Apple Design	Hand Decorated
C-801	Bust of Peasant Girl	Catalina Art Ware, Terra cotta
C-802	Bird	Catalina Art Ware, Terra cotta
C-803	Girl With Fan	Catalina Art Ware, Terra cotta
C-804	Large Girls Head	Catalina Art Ware, Terra cotta
C-805	Lady With Hat	Catalina Art Ware, Terra cotta
C-806	Bird on Base	Ox-Blood
C-807	Samoan Mother & Child	Catalina Art Ware, Terra cotta
C-808	Reclining Samoan Girl	Catalina Art Ware, Terra cotta
C-809	Turbaned Head of Malayan Woman	Terra Cotta, Catalina Art Ware
C-810	Grape Table Ornament	Catalina Art Ware
C-812	Fruit & Nut Table Ornament	Catalina Art Ware
C-813	Mermaid	Catalina Art Ware
C-814	Bust of Lady with Corsage	Catalina Art Ware
C-835	Ash Tray	Catalina Art Ware
893	Cigarette Box, Desert Rose Design	Hand Decorated
894	Ash Tray, Desert Rose Design, also for Polynesia	Hand Decorated

Appendix III

Glaze Colors: Numbers and Names

Glaze Number	Color Name
M.P. 1	White
M.P. 2	Glacial Blue/Turquoise
M.P. 3	Light Yellow (Gloss)
M.P. 4	Dark Green Gloss
M.P. 5	Matt Ivory
M.P. 6	Celestial White
M.P. 7	Transparent Gloss
M.P. 8	Matt Green
M.P. 9	Matt Blue
M.P. 10	Dark Green Matt
M.P. 11	Golden Glow
M.P. 12	Redwood
M.P. 13	Flame Orange
M.P. 14	Mexican Blue
M.P. 15	Coral Satin
M.P. 16	Chinese Yellow
M.P. 17	Tangerine
M.P. 18	Apple Green
M.P. 19	Maroon
M.P. 20	Gray (Satin)
M.P. 21	Coral Gloss
M.P. 22	Oxblood Red
M.P. 23	Deep Yellow
M.P. 24	Celadon (Gloss)
M.P. 25	Light Blue
M.P. 26	Flamingo
M.P. 27	Turquoise Satin
M.P. 28	Royal Blue
M.P. 29	Eggplant (Gloss)
M.P. 30	Sequoia Green
M.P. 31	Blue
M.P. 32	Oatmeal
M.P. 33	Yellow Gloss (Dark Yellow)
M.P. 34	Saddle Tan
M.P. 35	Shell Pink (Gloss)
M.P. 36	Light Blue (Gloss)
M.P. 37	Old Rose (Satin)
M.P. 38	Chartreuse
M.P. 39	Flambé
M.P. 40	Oxblood (over glaze)
M.P. 41	Golden Glow (Satin)
M.P. 42	Dark Green (Satin)
M.P. 43	Yellow Satin
M.P. 44	Lilac (Satin)
M.P. 45	Chartreuse (Satin)
M.P. 46	Buff Pink (Satin)
M.P. 47	Amethyst
M.P. 48	Old Ivory
M.P. 49	Cerise
M.P. 50	Gunmetal (Satin) (81a)
M.P. 51	Gunmetal (Satin)
M.P. 52	Shell Pink Gloss
M.P. 53	Periwinkle Blue
M.P. 54	Chocolate Brown
M.P. 55	Matt Over Glaze (WF)
M.P. 56	Light Gray/Stone (Gloss)
M.P. 57	Transparent for China
M.P. 58	Insulator Green
M.P. 59	Ruby (Periodic)
M.P. 60	Chocolate
M.P. 61	Revere Red (Satin)
M.P. 62	Phyfe Green (Satin)
M.P. 63	Copley Coral (Satin)
M.P. 64	Dark Green/Leaf (Gloss)
M.P. 65	Blue (Satin)
M.P. 66	Federal Gold (Satin)
M.P. 67	Mauve
M.P. 68	Verde Green
M.P. 69	Agate
M.P. 70	Gold
M.P. 71	Light Bronze
M.P. 72	Matrix Blue
M.P. 73	Catalina Red
M.P. 74	Tulip Green
M.P. 75	Chartreuse
M.P. 76	Satin Gray
M.P. 77	Catalina Turquoise
M.P. 78	Bright Green
M.P. 79	Catalina Dark Blue (Satin)
M.P. 80	Catalina Light Blue (Satin)
M.P. 81	Catalina Sand (Satin)
M.P. 83	Catalina Red Brown
M.P. 84	Catalina Ciel Blue (Satin)
M.P. 85	Light Green/Sprout (Gloss)
M.P. 86	Mustard
M.P. 87	Wild Flower Clear Glaze
M.P. 88	Catalina Green
M.P. 89	Grape
M.P. 90	Catalina Persian Blue (Satin)
M.P. 91	Hotel Ware — Coral
M.P. 92	Hotel Ware — Turquoise
M.P. 93	Hotel — Dark Yellow
M.P. 94	Copper
M.P. 95	Hotel Ware — Pastel Pink
M.P. 96	Peppermint Stick
M.P. 97	Pebble
M.P. 98	Hotel Ware — Green
M.P. 99	Transparent (Schonfeld)

Garden Ware, Standard Pottery

Glaze Number	Color Name
1	Italian Finish
2	Turquoise
3	Warm Grey
4	Pulsichrome
5	Green
6	Blue (dark)

Garden Ware, Semi-Porcelain

Glaze Number	Color Name
1	Neptune
2	Yellow
3	Tiber
4	Orange
5	Black
6	Titian

Appendix IV

Marks

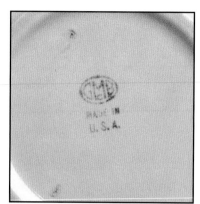

These underglaze ink stamps were on ware manufactured by Gladding, McBean & Co. since 1934. Two sizes are used with or without the "Made in USA." The paste on Franciscan Ware sticker in red and gold was used on ware from 1937-41.

Catalina Pottery mark with "Reg. U.S. Pat. Off." in two sizes in brown ink, used from 1937-42. The mark on the right was used with or without the "Reg. U.S. Pat. Off."

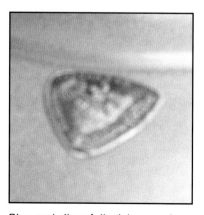

Catalina Pottery mark with "Made in USA" used from 1937-42 in blue ink. This mark was used with or without the "Made in USA."

Blue and silver foil sticker used on Catalina Art Pottery. This sticker is sometimes found on Catalina Island ware as Gladding, McBean & Co. purchased all ware that had been manufactured by the Catalina Island Pottery.

This is the "Made in USA" ink mark, which was made in two sizes. The smallest was still in use in 1962 in the earthernware department.

  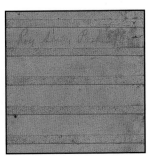

Left to right, top to bottom:

The first ink back stamp to indicate the Franciscan name. Two sizes were used for nine months in 1938.

The ink stamp Franciscan Pottery replaced the big "F" and was later to read as in the above mark "Franciscan Ware." This mark was used in 1939.

Variation of the Franciscan Ware stamp used from 1940-47.

These ink stamps were used on Franciscan Ware from 1940-47.

Two stamps were used in 1939 with acid on second grade ware and sold in the Franciscan Shop that was located at 2901 Los Feliz Avenue, the site of the Glendale plant. Either "2nd" or "RK" were used. "RK" stand for "run of kiln" and replaced "2nd." The acid partly dissolved the glaze and left a colorless imprint. This practice was discontinued after only one or two months, when it was found that acid fumes also left marks on the face of the ware when stacked for storage. After this, ware was scratched with an "X" or with a loopy "X" over the marks. This practice was to discourage the return of second grade ware to department stores or shops for full price or a replacement with first grade ware.

Kaolena mark used on ware from 1939-51. Kaolena was the trade name of products made by Gladding, McBean & Co. for the Max Schonfeld Company.

This decal stamp was used for Franciscan China from 1942-47.

Coronado jumbo saucer with gold highlights and marked with the oval GMcB as well as marked in gold ink "Pickard." Pickard used other companies' wares for decoration prior to making china products.

Pueblo Pottery ink stamp used on ware sold as premiums from 1938-39.

Barker Brothers ink stamp used on ware made exclusively for the Barker Brothers in 1939. This is found on two-toned Montecito Ware and on items with special glazes sold at the Golden Gate International Exposition.

Southern Pacific Railroad ink mark used on hotel ware in 1937 for the "Daylite" trains between San Francisco and Los Angeles.

Tropico tile mark used on Gladding, McBean & Co. tile products manufactured at the Glendale plant from 1923-37.

Nasco ink stamps used on ware for National Silver Co. from 1934.

Appendix V

Apple and Desert Rose Table Ware Price List

Shapes included in this price list are only for those shapes introduced prior to 1942. After 1942, many new shapes were added to Apple and Desert Rose Table Ware. The prices for Apple and Desert Rose tableware are based on early marks prior to the 1950s. Prices for shapes with marks after 1950 are slightly lower.

Apple Table Ware

Basic Items

706	Plate, Bread & Butter, 6.5"	$5-8
708	Plate, Salad, 8"	$12-15
710	Plate, Dinner, 9.5"	$22-26
711	Plate, Large Dinner, 10.5"	$22-28
712	Plate, Chop or Cake, 12.5"	$45-55
720-721	Cup and Saucer	$12-15
701	Fruit	$8-10
702	Cereal	$12-18
760	Vegetable Dish, small size, 7.5"	$28-36

Accessory Items

703	Soup with Rim	$26-32
792	Salt & Pepper, per pair	$22-28
796	Baked Apple Dish	$145-185+
740	Creamer	$18-22
741	Sugar with Lid	$18-26
754	Syrup Pitcher, 12 ounce	$145-165+
793	Cigarette Box	$125-145
761	Vegetable Dish, large, 8.25"	$28-38
732	Individual Handled Casserole and Lid	$55-75
795	Jam Jar and Lid [large apple knob]	$125-145
786	Waffle Batter Pitcher, 1.75 quart	$265-285+
770	Oval Platter, 14" long	$36-48
750	Teapot, 6-cup	$145-165
755	Coffee Pot, 8-cup	$125-165
780	Salad Bowl, 10" diameter	$85-95
794	Ash Tray [shaped like an apple]	$26-28
752	Water Pitcher, 2.5 quart	$145-165
782	Covered Vegetable Dish	$125-155
797	Relish Dish	$45-55
790	Gravy Boat, Fast Stand	$32-45
730	Tumbler	$28-35
714	Large Chop Plate, 14" diameter	$75-85
771	Oval Platter, large size, 17"	$195-245
	Linens — Tablecloths or Napkins	No Price Determined

Desert Rose Table Ware

Basic Items

806	Plate, Bread & Butter, 6.5"	$5-8
808	Plate, Salad, 8"	$12-16
810	Plate, Dinner, 9.5"	$29-32
811	Plate, Large Dinner, 10.5"	$29-32
812	Plate, Chop or Cake, 11.75"	$65-75
820	Teacup	$8-12
821	Saucer, For Teacup or Bouillon	$2-3
801	Fruit	$8-12
802	Cereal	$12-18
861	Vegetable Dish, 8.25" diameter	$28-36

Accessory Items

844	Individual Sugar for Tray Service	$75-95
826	Lid for Bouillon Cup	$95-125
825	Bouillon Cup, can use #821 Saucer	$95-145
833	Egg Cup	$32-36
843	Individual Creamer for Tray Service	$75-95
869	Toast Cover	$145-225
822	After Dinner Cup	$32-42
823	After Dinner Cup Saucer	$18-28
892	Salt and Pepper, per pair	$22-28
803	Rim Soup	$32-36
893	Cigarette Box	$145-195
896	Relish Dish	$45-55
840	Creamer	$29-35
841	Sugar and Lid	$22-45
895	Jam Jar and Lid	$145-185
856	Individual Coffee Pot, 18 ounces (Green Line on Lid)	$275-350+
870	Oval Platter, 14" long	$45-65
850	Teapot, 6-cup (Green Line on Lid)	$95-145+
880	Salad Bowl	$95-125
894	Ash Tray	$22-28
882	Covered Vegetable Dish	$95-138
852	Water Pitcher	$125-145
830	Tumbler	$28-34
890	Gravy Boat, fast stand	$28-45
855	Coffee Pot, 40 ounces (Green Line on Lid)	$125-165+
814	Large Chop Plate, 14"	$125-145
	Linens — Tablecloths or Napkins	No Price Determined

Gladding, McBean & Co. discontinued lining the lids for the sugar, teapot, coffee pot, and individual coffee pot for Desert Rose Table Ware in 1947. Prices are higher for these shapes when the lid is green lined. For a non-lined lid, use the lower price, the higher price is for items with a lid that is green lined.

Glossary

Biscuit: Fired, unglazed ware.

Bisque: Same as biscuit.

Body: The substance of a piece of ware, its physical composition as opposed to glaze or decoration.

Casting: The process of forming wares, in which liquid clay, called slip, is poured into a plaster of Paris mold, which shapes it. The plaster absorbs water from the slip adjacent to the mold walls, causing a thin layer of clay to be deposited on the plaster. The layer thickens, according to the amount of water in the slip and the time allowed; the excess slip is poured off and a clay form is left in the mold, shaped exactly to it.

Ceramics: Products made of earth materials, processed by baking or firing. Includes pottery, earthenware, china, glass, porcelain, glaze, porcelain enamel, structural clay products, refractories, insulating porcelain, and abrasives. Silica is an important basic ingredient. Also, ceramics is the art of forming these products.

China: A non-porous, non-absorbent type of ware made of a special white clay, kaolin and feldspar, that is fired twice – once at high temperature, then at a lower temperature. Strong, highly glazed wares, resonant when struck, usually thinly potted and translucent where thin enough.

Clay: A common earth material, frequently found as a type of soil, or in surface deposits all over the world. Produced in nature by the weathering of rocks of different mineral constitution, clays have different qualities and properties, different colors, resistance to fire, etc.

Coupe Shape: Plate shape, flat across the diameter of the plate, except for the rim, which rolls up slightly. An ancient Chinese plate shape, adopted for tableware.

Crazing: A defect in ware glazes, caused by different rates of expansion between the body and glaze, resulting in a network of fine, irregular cracks in the surface of the glaze. Sometimes this effect is produced purposefully, and carefully controlled, resulting in a texture called crackle.

Decalcomania: A design transfer used in decorating tableware. A design printed on a duplex paper backing in ceramic colors is transferred to the ware surface by rubbing the design against the ware made tacky by size, removing the paper backing, then firing the paint on.

Decorations: Various types of surface patterns applied to wares and glass by any one of a number of processes.

Earthenware: A type of tableware, made of white or cream-burning clay, fired at a rather low temperature. Rather porous ware, with no vitrification, fairly heavy, not very strong, opaque, and lacking in resonance.

Embossing: Raised or molded decorations. May be molded with the ware or made separately and applied in the green state.

Enamel: A type of opaque ceramic paint used to decorate ware.

Firing: Baking. Clay objects are put into an oven or kiln and baked, to strengthen or fuse pieces together.

Flatware: Any flat clay item, such as a plate or saucer.

Glaze: A glossy finish or coating on ware, designed to protect the porous surface of the clay from wear and moisture. A glassy substance, fired to the clay, forming a fused on surface. White or colored, the reflecting surface of the glaze adds beauty and utility to the ware.

Gloss Glaze: A shiny, reflective surface glaze.

Green Ware: Ware in the unfired state, after forming. Green ware is dry, leather-hard, holds its shape, but has little or no mechanical strength.

Ground-Lay: A type of under-glaze decoration for which a coat of oil is painted on where the design is to be, color then being dusted over it, after which the ware is glazed and fired. The color is permanent under the glaze. Used for wide borders of dark colors such as cobalt and maroon.

Hollowware or Hollow Ware: Hollow pieces of ware, such as cups, bowls, pitchers, casseroles, etc.

Intaglio: A type of decoration in which the design is sunk in relief into the surface of the ware. Reverse of embossing.

Jigger: The adaptation of the potter's wheel, used in forming tableware. Consists of a turning platform that holds the ware, and a swinging arm, holding a profiled shaping blade that can be brought down against the ware as it revolves on the jigger head. The blade of the jigger replaces the potter's fingers in forming ware.

Kaolin: Relatively scarce type of clay, non-plastic and used in making porcelain.

Kiln: The furnace in which ware is fired. Tunnel kilns, built like long tunnels, with the oil or gas-fed flames burning continuously, permit ware to move along on small flatcars past the flames in a continuous operation. Muffle kilns have an intermediate wall of firebrick between the flames and the ware, to keep combustion gases and ash away from the ware.

Kiln Car: Small, flat platforms on wheels, resembling miniature railroad flatcars that move on a track through tunnel kilns, carrying ware through the fire. These cars move very slowly, so slowly that it is hard to see any motion at all. It takes twenty to thirty hours for one car to make the complete journey through the kiln, during which time the ware it carries is heated up to top temperature, fired, and cooled.

Lining: Decoration of tableware, consisting of thin or thick lines of color or gold or silver, running around the ware and parallel to the rim. Any number of lines, of any thickness, may be used. Lining, once done by hand, is now done by machine. Lines may be combined with any other motifs, or ware may have a gold edge line.

Lug Soup: Soup dishes with small extensions of the rim, called lugs, by means of which the plate may be carried.

Matt Glaze: A glaze with a dull surface, without gloss. For all intents and purposes, Gladding, McBean & Company used the spelling of "matt" instead of "mat."

Mold: A form used to give shape to clay. Ware forms are customarily made of plaster of Paris. Clay may be jiggered on a flat mold or cast in a hollow mold, usually made in two, three, or more pieces.

Muffle Kiln: See Kiln.

Open Stock: Method of selling tableware by the individual piece or in dozens as opposed to the method of selling it in sets. Open stock tableware patterns are kept available for a period of five to ten years for breakage replacements.

Over-glaze: Decorations painted on after the ware has been glazed and fired. Most painted and decal decorations are applied over-glaze.

Porcelain: A ware similar in type to china, but made by a slightly different process. Porcelain is fired first to biscuit at a low fire, just sufficient to cause the bisque to hold its shape. The second glaze fire is the high fire, creating complete vitrification and a glassy, somewhat brittle finish.

Pyrometer: A heat-measuring device used in controlling fire in a kiln.

Refractory: Resistant to heat. Refractory clay is clay that can resist a high degree of temperature in firing, permitting use of other materials that will vitrify before the clay reaches a melting temperature. Refractories are clay products made of refractory clay, resistant to high temperature. Industries used refractories in the production of glass, ceramics, and metal products.

Resonance: Quality of giving off a deep, musical tone when struck.

Rim Shape: Plates have a center well and a slanting shoulder at the rim.

Run Of Kiln: R.K. is a grading term used by tableware manufacturers to indicate quality ware that is nevertheless not all completely perfect.

Sagger: A box of refractory clay, used as a container for ware going through the kiln.

Semi-vitreous: A type of tableware made of white clay and some china ingredients; formed by the china process, it is fired at a relatively high temperature, causing partial vitrification. A fine, high-grade type of earthenware made by American potters.

Short Set: A basic tableware service without many accessory pieces.

Satin Glaze: Same as matt glaze.

Semi-matt Glaze: Between satin or matt and gloss glazes, the gloss is slightly dulled. A semi-matt glaze is very hard to distinguish with the naked eye.

Texture Glaze: Colored glaze in which some sort of controlled disturbance, such as spotting, crystallization, crackling, eruption of colors, dripping, running, etc. Very lovely effects are produced by this method.

Under-glaze: Decorating technique whereby the pattern is produced directly on the biscuit, which is then glazed and fired. Since the design is under the glaze coat, it is completely permanent on the ware, or approximately so.

Vitrified: Glass-like. Vitrified ware contains a percentage, as much as twenty-five percent of silica, which fuses through the body of the ware and produces a sort of glass in the pores of the body during firing. Vitrified ware must be fired at a high temperature. It is strong, non-absorbent, and translucent.

Vitrification: The process of being vitrified.

Bibliography

Allied Arts of Seattle, Inc. *Impressions of Imagination: Terra cotta Seattle*. Seattle, Washington, Allied Arts of Seattle, 1986.

"Building Products Firm Buys Inventory." Sacramento, California: *The Sacramento Bee,* August 13, 1997.

"Capital's Best Kept Secret." Sacramento, California: *The Sacramento Bee,* October 9, 1989.

"City Oasis for Country Residents." Sacramento, California: *The Sacramento Bee*, February 28, 1985.

Duke, Harvey. *Official Price Guide to Pottery And Porcelain*. Eighth Edition. New York, New York: House of Collectibles, 1995

Enge, Delleen. *Franciscan Ware. An Illustrated Price Guide*. Paducah, Kentucky: Collector Books, 1981.

_____. *Catalina Art Pottery*. (Reprint) Ojai, California: Delleen Enge, 1982.

_____. *Franciscan Lamps 1937/1951 By GMcB*. Ojai, California: Delleen Enge, 1997.

_____. *Franciscan Plain & Fancy*. Ojai, California: Delleen Enge, 1996.

_____. *Franciscan Embossed Hand Painted*. Made in California Only. Ojai, California: Delleen Enge,1992.

Elliot, James (ed.). *Franciscan Newsletter*. Volumes I, II, III, & VI. Seattle, Washington: Franciscan Collectors Club, 1994-present.

Ferriday, Virginia Guest. *Last of the Handmade Buildings. Glazed Terra cotta in Downtown Portland*. Portland, Oregon: Mark Publishing Company, 1984.

"Fired Up Over Terra cotta Public Buildings Around With Choice Decorations; Many Locally Designed, Made." Sacramento, California: *The Sacramento Bee,* September 14, 1985.

"Fred Anderson, Tycoon and Sports Booster, Dies at 72." Sacramento, California: *The Sacramento Bee,* March 25, 1997.

Gladding, McBean & Co. *Shapes of Clay*. San Francisco, California: Gladding, McBean & Co., various issues, 1923-37.

_____. *1975*. Lincoln, California: News Messenger, 1975.

_____. *Gladding, McBean & Co. Clay Products Price List No. 50*. San Francisco, California: Taylor & Taylor, c. 1923.

_____. *Gladding, McBean & Co. Illustrated Catalog and Price List*. San Francisco, California: Gladding, McBean & Co., date unknown.

_____. *Gladding, McBean & Co. Clay Products Price List No. 50*. San Francisco, California: Taylor & Taylor, c. 1923.

_____. *Gladding, McBean & Co. Catalog No. 22*. San Francisco, California: Gladding, McBean & Co., date unknown.

_____. *Latin Tiles.* San Francisco, California: Taylor & Taylor, c. 1919.

_____. *Latin Tiles*. San Francisco, California: Taylor & Taylor, c. 1923.

_____. *Serving the World From Lincoln, Calif., Since 1875*. Lincoln, California: Gladding, McBean & Co., 1986.

_____. *Tile. Tropico Faience Decorative Floor*. San Francisco, California: Gladding, McBean & Co., c. 1925.

_____. Unprocessed papers. California State Library.

_____. Unprocessed photograph collection. California State Library.

Howser, Huell. *California's Gold. Gladding McBean*. Los Angeles, California: KCET-TV, Huell Howser Productions, California State Library Foundation, distributor. (Video)

Kreisman, Lawrence. *The Stimson Legacy. Architecture in the Urban West*. Seattle, Washington: Willow Press, 1992.

Kurutz, Gary F. *Architectural Terra cotta of Gladding, McBean*. Sausalito, California: Windgate Press, 1989.

Lardner W.B and M.J. Brook. *History of Placer and Nevada Counties*. Los Angeles, California: Historic Record Company, 1924.

McBean Corporation. *McBean Japan*. Fukuoka, Japan: McBean Corporation, c. 1913.

"Overlooked Splendor Art of 1920s Abounds in State Library." Sacramento, California: *The Sacramento Bee,* June 15, 1985.

Pacific Coast Building Products. *Terra cotta, A Product of all Ages*. Sacramento, California: Pacific Coast Building Products, Promotional and Advertising Department, Rase Video Productions, 1988. (Video)

Page, Bob and Dale Fredericksen. *Franciscan. An American Dinnerware Tradition.* Greensboro, North Carolina: Page/Frederiksen Publications, 1999.

Snyder, Jeffrey B. *Franciscan Dining Services. A Comprehensive Guide with Values*. Atglen, Pennsylvania: Schiffer Publishing, Ltd., 1996.

Taylor, Sally. *Ceramics for the Table*. New York, N.Y.: Fairchild Publications, Inc., 1950.

"Top of the Heap, The Late Fred Anderson's Pacific Coast Building Products Has Achieved Powerhouse Status in the Construction Trade." Sacramento, California: *The Sacramento Bee,* June 1, 1997.

Unknown. *1875 - Gladding, McBean – Interpace 1975. 1875 Lincoln Plant Centennial*

Quick Index to Lines & Patterns